ABOUT THE AUTHORS

Billy Hayes was born in New York City and
grew up on Long Island, where he worked as a
lifeguard during the summer. He went to
Marquette University, dropped out before
graduation – and the following few years of his
life are those recounted in this book! He is
now completing his interrupted studies at
Fordham.

William Hoffer is co-author of *Caught in the
Act* and has written for numerous magazines.
He is a director of the American Society of
Journalists and Authors and lives with his wife
and two daughters in Maryland.

Midnight Express

BILLY HAYES and WILLIAM HOFFER

SPHERE BOOKS LIMITED
30/32 Gray's Inn Road, London WC1X 8JL

First published in Great Britain by André Deutsch Ltd 1977
Copyright © Billy Hayes 1977
First Sphere Books Edition 1978
Reprinted 1978 (three times), 1979 (five times),
1980

The people in this book are real. However, in some cases names and
other identifying characteristics have been changed.

TRADE
MARK

This book is sold subject to the condition that
it shall not, by way of trade or otherwise, be lent,
re-sold, hired out or otherwise circulated without
the publisher's prior consent in any form of
binding or cover other than that in which it is
published and without a similar condition
including this condition being imposed on the
subsequent purchaser

Set in VIP Baskerville

Printed in Great Britain by
William Collins Sons & Co Ltd
Glasgow

This book is dedicated to my father

ACKNOWLEDGMENTS

I want to thank my family and relatives, old friends, new friends, and friends I've never met. Names that come most readily to mind are: James and Rita Archambault, Barbara Belmont, Senator James Buckley, Mark Derish, Bulent Ecevit, Bob Greene, Michael Griffith, Harriet James, Howard Mace, William Macomber, Nick Mann, Robert Mcbee, Irene Moore, Dr Bernard Schwartz, Norman Shaw, John Sutter, and Gene Zajac. Special thanks to Dr Ronald Rosen.

CHAPTER ONE

Some twelve miles west of Istanbul, beyond the outskirts of the city in the flat farm country near the coast, is Yesilkoy International Airport. Every day at noon Pan American Flight No. 1 arrives from Teheran. It sorts out its incoming and outgoing passengers, then takes off again at one to continue its journey to Frankfurt, London, and New York. On 6 October 1970, feeling like an Ian Fleming character, with dark aviator sunglasses over my eyes and my trenchcoat collar pulled up to my ears, I watched Flight No. 1, a Boeing 707, land on the concrete runway. I pulled the brim of my lucky hat low over my eyes and eased up against the wall near the passenger check-in counter.

A short pudgy man in his mid-thirties pushed past me and heaved his suitcase onto the scale. A good-looking dark-haired girl behind the counter tagged his bag, stamped his ticket, and waved him through to the security checkpoint. From where I stood I could see the balding spot on his head flush with effort as he walked down the long corridor. There, at the end, a bored Turkish officer in a rumpled uniform halfheartedly looked into the carry-on bag and glanced at the man's passport. Coughing on his cigarette, the guard waved the passenger on his way. I watched the pudgy man disappear into the Pan Am passenger lounge.

'Yes, yes,' I assured myself. 'That's the way. It looks easy. . . .'

I stepped up to the counter and with the last of my money bought a ticket to New York for the following day.

I'd planned to watch the flight actually depart, but what more was there to see? Did I really need to be that thorough? Security here seemed to be a joke, almost an afterthought. If I hurried into a cab I could make it back to the Pudding Shoppe in time for my date with that English girl I'd met at breakfast. She said she was in Istanbul studying belly dancing. I really didn't care if her story was true; all I wanted was some company before my adventure. That afternoon, that

7

night, tomorrow, all seemed like scenes from a movie. And I – a little jittery but trying my best to stay calm – was the leading man.

I scrapped the last half hour of my careful plans and jumped into a cab. Pan Am Flight No. 1 could see itself off that day.

The Pudding Shoppe had almost become my home during those ten days in Istanbul. I'd heard about it all over Europe, this wild Turkish hangout where hippie travellers gathered. I wouldn't have called myself a hippie and my short hair wasn't exactly in style there, but the Pudding Shoppe seemed like a place where I could mix in quietly with the other foreigners.

At a small outdoor table I sipped sweet Turkish tea and waited for the girl. Everywhere around me people talked and laughed and shouted. Hawkers and beggars and street pedlars weaved their way through the brightly dressed crowds. Street vendors cooked shish kebab. The aroma of the meat mingled with the smell of horse manure in the gutter. A small gipsy-eyed boy came around the corner, leading a huge muzzled bear on a leash. And there I sat. Anxious but excited, I awaited tomorrow's danger.

The belly-dancing English girl never showed. Perhaps I should have taken it as an omen.

I was early. I went into the airport restroom, locked myself into a stall. I lifted my bulky turtleneck sweater. Everything was in place. I tucked the sweater back underneath my corduroy sports jacket, then looked at my watch. The moment was approaching.

It was time now. It would be easy. I'd checked it all out yesterday.

I closed my eyes and relaxed. Then I drew a deep breath. The tightness of the tape around my chest made me wince. Trying to look casual, I walked out of the bathroom. There was no turning back now.

The same smiling dark-haired girl was at the ticket counter. 'Good afternoon, Mr Hayes,' she said in accented English as she looked at my ticket. 'Have a nice trip. This way, please.'

She pointed down the same corridor I had watched yesterday. The bored, olive-skinned guard waited at his checkpoint. I tried not to stare at the gun in his holster as I approached.

'Passport,' he demanded.

I pulled it from my jacket pocket and handed it over. He glanced at it for a moment and shoved it back into my hands.

'Bag,' he said.

I opened my shoulder bag for him to see. He pushed aside the books and grabbed a white plastic dish. *'Nebu?'* he said, using a Turkish expression I'd heard before. It meant, 'What's this?'

'It's a frisbee.'

'Nebu?'

'A frisbee. A frisbee. You throw it and catch it. It's a game.'

'Aaaah!' He shoved the frisbee back into the bag and picked up a small yellow ball.

'Juggling ball,' I explained.

He scowled. Then he took a puff on his cigarette, coughed and narrowed his eyes for an instant.

'Aaaaah!' He waved me through.

I continued along the corridor to a stairway leading down to the lower level passenger lounge.

Passenger lounge! I made it through customs. No problems at all.

A hostess asked if I'd like a drink and I accepted a coke. I chose a corner of the lounge where my back would be against the wall. For perhaps twenty minutes I sat there, pretending to read the *International Herald-Tribune*. It looked as if my plan was working perfectly.

Loudspeakers interrupted my thoughts. A woman's voice announced in Turkish and then English that the plane was ready for boarding. Passengers rose to file out of the lounge. I walked into the bright sunshine, flowing along with the crowd towards a battered olive drab bus waiting to take us out to the airplane. I took an aisle seat in the middle of the bus.

'I've been visiting my son,' said a voice next to me. I nodded politely and the grey-haired woman took it as a

9

friendly response. She was from Chicago, she said. Her son was a jet mechanic. He did very well in the Air Force, travelling all over the world. He'd just been promoted to technical-something-or-other. I smiled. She reminded me a little of my mother. I closed my eyes and concentrated on thoughts of a girl named Sharon; I'd left her in Amsterdam and planned to meet her again back in America. I was feeling good.

The bus slowed to a halt and the passengers reached around for their possessions. The driver pushed a lever that swung the front door open and a Turkish policeman hopped on. He said in English, 'Attention, please. Women and children remain on the bus. All men exit by the rear door, please.'

I glanced out the dirty windows of the bus. Oh, no! the bus and plane were circled with wooden barricades lashed together by ropes. Twenty or thirty Turkish soldiers, with rifles at the ready, ringed the area. And a long wooden table blocked the way to the boarding ramp. Men in business suits waited quietly next to the table.

For several seconds I stared out the window in disbelief. I told myself to stay calm. Panic wouldn't help. I needed to think of a plan.

The bus hummed with mild concern and annoyance. Dutifully, the other male passengers began to file out of the back door. I dropped to my knees in the aisle and tried to crawl under my seat. Think! Think!

'What's the matter?' the grey-haired lady asked me. 'Are you ill?'

'I . . . I can't find my passport.'

'Why, there it is,' she said, beaming, pointing to the top pocket of my jacket.

And there it was, indeed, snuggled up against the trouble I'd been heading towards during the past few aimless years. I couldn't quite believe that my careful plans were falling apart. I thought I'd figured all the angles. I thought I was too clever to be caught. I'd passed through customs all over Europe without ever running up against anything like this. I fought desperately to keep what was left of my self-control.

I took a few deep, painful breaths. There was one last

10

chance. Hoping that my voice didn't tremble, I thanked the lady from Chicago and stepped slowly out of the bus onto the tarmac.

I found myself at the tail end of a group of male passengers who were funnelling into two lines that passed on either side of the inspection table. I looked around at the vast open expanse of the airport. There was no place to go, no hole to dive into. I would need a lot of luck.

Two plainclothes officers were on each side of the table, searching the men alternately. The passengers milled around, jostling one another. I pulled some books from my shoulder bag and waited until the first officer on the left began to pat down a passenger. I just glided past him on the outside of the line. The second officer was still busy with another passenger. I replaced the books in my bag as though I'd already been searched and was on my way to take my seat on the airplane. I floated past the second officer and approached the boarding ramp. I raised one foot off Turkish soil.

A hand touched me lightly on the elbow

The hand grasped me by the arm.

I turned and casually, I hoped, gestured towards the first officer. At that very same moment the first officer happened to glance up.

'*Nebu?*' said the man holding me.

The first officer answered him in Turkish and the grip on my arm suddenly tightened.

He pulled me over to the table. He was young and inexperienced. He hesitated for a moment. Then his dark brown eyes narrowed as he realized that I'd just lied to him.

He grunted a command and gestured for me to spread my arms out. Then he began patting my body carefully, moving down the outside of my arms. As his hands passed my armpits they brushed against something hard. Incredibly, he didn't seem to notice. He worked his way down over my hips and legs.

Then he paused.

I found myself praying. 'Please, God, let the search be over. Don't let him come back up my body again.'

Slowly, his hands moved back up, on the inside of my legs

11

and then onto my belly. The fingers touched the hard bulge below my navel. I almost winced. But once again, unbelievably, he didn't notice.

The probing fingers continued to move up and there was no way to stop them. Helplessly I stood there as his hands settled firmly upon the packets taped under my arms.

For an instant our eyes met.

Suddenly he jumped back and grabbed a pistol from inside his coat. He crouched on one knee and aimed the gun barrel at my belly, his hands shaking. All around me I could hear screams and the sounds of other passengers scrambling for cover. My arms flew straight up and my eyes clamped shut. I tried not to breathe.

Deathlike quiet settled over Yesilkoy International Airport. Five seconds passed, maybe ten. It seemed like for ever to me.

Then I felt a hand tug at the bottom of my sweater. The barrel of a gun jammed into my belly. I opened an eye to see the shiny black hair of the young officer as he leaned forward to look under my sweater. He moved slowly, not knowing what to expect. Behind him I could see the soldiers on the tarmac all pointing their rifles at my head. The officer's hand trembled as he brought the sweater up over the edge of one of the packages. He paused for a moment, then drew the sweater even higher.

His face relaxed. I could feel the tension drain out of him. There was no bomb, no hand grenades or dynamite taped to my body. He dropped the sweater and yelled something out in Turkish. I understood only one word . . . 'hashish'.

Pan Am's Flight No. 1 rose into the clear blue sky. As I watched it go I was suddenly very lonely for New York. I wondered how long it would be before I saw the city again.

CHAPTER TWO

The customs officers drove me back to the terminal on the same olive drab bus. They pushed me into a small room near the passenger lounge. I sat quietly in a chair while several officers took seats in a row arranged in a neat line near a desk. All immediately lit cigarettes and began chattering among themselves. The chief sat behind the desk and made a few phone calls. It was strange. They hardly seemed to notice me.

What was happening? This wasn't the way I planned it at all. I was supposed to be on that plane to New York. Could I really have been caught? And would I have to go to prison? Prison! No, not me.

The Turks were so slow and disorganized that I actually became impatient for something to happen, even though I knew I probably wasn't going to like it when it did. Finally the chief got off the phone and motioned me over to the desk. He studied my face, opened his mouth to say something and seemed to search with difficulty for the right word.

'. . . Name?'

'William Hayes.'

'Vil . . . Vilyum . . . Vilyum . . .'

'Hayes.'

'Hi-yes.' He wrote it on an official form. ' 'merican?'

I nodded. 'New York.'

He looked puzzled.

'New York, New York,' I repeated.

He pondered this for a moment. 'Ahhh . . . New York.' He wrote that down. He grinned and offered me a cigarette.

I wasn't a smoker but I wanted to co-operate with every suggestion, so I took the cigarette from him. It was a Turkish brand. When the chief lit it for me I inhaled strong, harsh smoke, far worse than any American cigarette I had ever tasted. I coughed. Then I doubled over in pain from the pressure in my chest. I would have to try hard not to cough again.

The chief motioned for me to stand up. Two of the other officers came over and stripped off my jacket, sweater, and T-shirt to reveal the bulging packs fastened with adhesive tape under my armpits. They cut through the tape and ripped the packages from my skin. I jumped in pain. The hashish, pressed into thin, hard plaques, clattered onto the stone floor.

Again the chief searched for a word. 'More?'

I nodded, and unzipped my pants to reveal a few more plaques taped below my navel. One of the policemen eagerly reached in to help but I stopped him self-consciously and cut the tape myself.

The forty or so plaques made a little pile on the floor. As far as smugglers go, they could see I was small-time. Hashish in Istanbul had been cheaper than I'd expected. The two kilos (about four pounds) had cost me only two hundred dollars. Sold on the streets of New York City it would bring, I supposed, about five thousand dollars. But I had no intention of selling it on the streets. I planned to smoke some of it myself and sell the rest to my friends. Most of my friends smoked marijuana and hashish. But now my clever adventure had turned into a disaster. Stacked up on the floor of the airport security office, the little pile of hashish looked like a lot of trouble.

The door flew open and another policeman walked in. He was paunchy and had a thin clipped moustache. The room suddenly grew silent and the man who'd been questioning me quickly jumped up from the desk and gave a little bow. The new chief acknowledged this and took the vacated chair. The ex-chief moved to the second chair in line, pushing the occupant of that chair further down. He, in turn, shoved the next man over. The last man in line now stood up against the wall.

'Name?' the new chief asked.

'William Hayes.'

'Vil . . . Vilyum . . .'

'Hayes,' I repeated. We went through exactly the same routine. As the new officer was inspecting the hashish, still another rushed in. He also was apparently a man of authority. Again each man was shoved over one chair until another man at the end was forced to stand. This new chief asked me my name. I pointed to the sheet of paper already on the desk but he looked annoyed.

'William Hayes,' I told him. 'New York.'

By the time the fourth and fifth chiefs arrived I began to see the importance of hierarchy in the Turkish system of things. Each officer had to establish his position. And this was an eventful day – some dumb kid from New York got caught with two kilos. The official game made me smile in spite of myself.

The door opened once again and two men rushed in, one with a huge camera. They spoke excitedly with the most recently arrived chief. He grabbed his first assistant from the line of chairs and motioned for me to pick up the hashish. I gathered up the plaques and held them awkwardly in front of me. The two senior officers flanked me and put their arms around my shoulders, ready for a big-game-hunter picture. The room was filled with Turkish officers and smoke and photographers, and there I was, standing in the middle of it all, with my arms full of drugs. The two officers – who had nothing to do with the actual arrest – had their arms around me and they were grinning into the camera. Maybe it was a nervous reaction but I couldn't quite believe the seriousness of it all. I grinned.

The chief on my left hit me a quick backhanded fist to the groin. The plaques dropped to the floor and I sank to my knees, gasping for breath.

'Gel! Gel!' one of the policemen growled, grabbing my arm. He motioned for me to pick up the hashish again. With shaking hands I gathered it up and he pulled me to my feet. The two men put their arms around my shoulders again. This time my face displayed the proper pained submissive expression for the photographers.

The policemen made me drop the hashish back onto the floor and shoved me into a chair. I felt woozy and nearly sick to my stomach, and I panted for breath.

I was sitting there resting, waiting for the next shift in seating arrangements, when an uncomfortable thought struck me. I was carrying more hashish. I'd slipped two plaques into each boot and completely forgotten about them

15

Sooner or later I knew the Turks would search me thoroughly and find them, so it seemed best to volunteer the information.

I sat there until my body stopped throbbing. Then I raised my hand for permission to speak. The chief nodded and all the others turned to look at me. Moving slowly, partly out of caution and partly out of pain, I pulled off one of my boots, banged it on the heel and two plaques clattered to the floor. Their mouths all dropped open. They watched me repeat the process with the other boot.

There was a moment of awkward silence. I'd been in custody several hours and supposedly had been thoroughly searched; there'd been several changes in the chief seat up front; the photographers had been in to take pictures – so what was I doing still shaking hashish out of my boots?

The policeman in charge turned upon the man in the second position. His voice rose in anger and he yelled and screamed. The second in command wheeled around and vented his anger on the third man down the line. He passed it on further until it finally reached the last chair. The final officer was enraged. He yelled something at two of the policemen now standing against the wall at attention. They raced over and lifted me off my chair, then stripped the clothes from my body, ignoring my assurances that there was nothing more to find. The two of them searched me while others went through my clothing. When they finished I stood there stark naked and extremely uncomfortable. Since I'd been in Turkey I'd come to think that many Turkish men tend towards bisexuality. Every cab driver, every waiter, every bazaar vendor had seemed to leer at me. Now standing naked in front of the customs officers I felt the same hungry stares. They made no effort to conceal their interest. I grabbed for my clothes and quickly put them back on.

More talk, more phone calls, more cigarettes. Hot, sticky, reeking air. I knew I'd get sick soon if I didn't get out of the room.

The door opened again and in stepped a tall, lanky, blond-haired man in a business suit. He was definitely American. He walked over to me without saying a word to the Turks. He

16

thrust his big jaw at me and in a perfect Texas drawl said, 'Howdy.'

I said hello.

'How ya doin'? You OK?'

I nodded.

He went up to the desk, spoke to the current chief in Turkish, and signed some papers.

'OK, follow me,' he said, and we walked together out the door, followed by a couple of the Turkish officers. The air was fresh and clean and somewhat revived my spirits. He sat me in the front seat of his car and walked around to the driver's side. For a few moments he stood outside the car talking with the Turks.

I was saved! The Texan was on my side. Maybe he'd take me to the American consulate.

Suddenly I realized how close I was to freedom. No one had bothered to handcuff me. I was alone in the front seat and it seemed like it would be so easy to roll out of the car after we got going and race off down some alley. I'd keep my eyes open during the ride to . . . wherever we were going.

Tex got into the car and started the engine. I wondered how closely he would watch me. I turned to look at him, but my head was stopped by the pressure of something metal pushed up against my temple. It was the second time in my life, and the second time that day, that a gun had been shoved up against me.

'I feel real sorry for you, William,' he drawled, '. . . and you seem like a nice enough kid. But if you try to escape from this car I'll blow your fucking brains out.'

'Where are we going?' I asked, as the car began to move.

'To the Sirkeci police station. It's in the harbour section of Istanbul.'

'What's going to happen there?'

'Well . . . they'll book you . . . ask you some questions. You'll probably go out to the prison tomorrow.'

'Are you with Interpol or something?'

'Or something,' Tex replied. He didn't offer his name.

'Can I call the American consul? Can I make a telephone call? Can I get a lawyer?'

'All of that later,' Tex drawled. 'They'll let you do all of that, but later.'

I watched the ribbon of highway that led back to Istanbul All thoughts of escape had been squelched by Tex's gun. I was definitely going to jail.

'What . . . then?' I asked uncertainly.

Tex considered the question before slowly answering. 'It's hard to say. You could get a couple of years. You could get twenty.'

'Twenty years!'

'It's a very serious crime, William. Especially in Turkey.'

Twenty years!! 'It's just hash,' I said. 'It's not heroin or opium. It's just pot . . . marijuana . . . hashish . . . all the same.'

'Well, William, I'm not really up on all that. A drug's a drug, seems to me. But what I do know is that you're in trouble.'

I closed my eyes against the sudden pounding in my head. Twenty years! That just couldn't be. I tried to tell him that hashish is the oil of the marijuana plant – not addictive, not dangerous unless, like anything, you abuse it. But he wasn't listening.

We both grew silent, and for the first time it all began to grow real. I was in trouble. This was going to be a very bad experience, and not just for me. It would be so hard on my folks. When I dropped out of Marquette in my senior year, my father warned me that I was making a big mistake that I'd be sorry for later. He had worked hard all his life, building a solid, respectable career as a personnel manager for Metropolitan Life Insurance Company. He'd never gone to college himself. And one of his greatest hopes was to see all three of his children graduate. I was to be the first. I came close, but somehow I couldn't get excited about a diploma. I really didn't know what I'd do with it. I wanted to travel the world, experience all sorts of situations.

Travel was fine, Dad said. Experiences are fine. But he advised me to finish school first. I wouldn't listen.

That was strike one. Strike two came a few months later when the Army called me in for a pre-induction physical. Dad saw me starve myself for two days before the physical,

18

and he knew I acted crazy in front of the army doctors. They rated me psychologically unfit to serve. Dad was furious. How could I refuse to serve my country? To him, service in the United States Army was an honour. We argued violently that evening. Mom, with a worried look on her face, rushed off to church to play bingo. Dad's face grew red under his snowy white hair and his Irish temper flashed. Words flew. It was clear that neither of us could understand the other's viewpoint. Finally Dad levelled a finger at me. 'OK,' he said. 'You drop out of college. You get a psychiatric report on your records. Go bum around the world. Go ahead. But I'm telling you now – you're going to wind up in trouble.'

Dad, you were so right.

Was this strike three, I wondered? Would my father wash his hands of me? I really didn't know. Dad and I had never discussed drugs. I'm sure that he thought hashish and heroin were pretty much the same. If I'd been caught smuggling *heroin* he'd be justified in leaving me here to rot . . . but did he understand the difference? And Mom and Rob and Peggy – how much pain it would cause them. Would I ever see them again?

'I've got to contact the consul!' I blurted out to Tex.

'You'll have time for that later. You can talk with them after.'

'After . . . what?'

Tex watched me out of the corner of his eye. Maybe he had a kid brother about my age. Maybe it was just my curly hair or my Irish blue eyes. I was a slim, clean-shaven American college dropout. I didn't look like a smuggler and the relatively small amount of hashish I was carrying proved that I wasn't in the big leagues. I knew he thought I'd done something dirty, but I began to sense that he felt sorry for me anyway.

'Got a family back in New York?' he said.

I nodded. 'Long Island.'

'. . . be tough on them.'

'Yes.' Oh, God!

'OK, get out,' Tex said. We had stopped in a narrow cobble-stone street. Dingy, ugly old buildings crowded above us. He gently pushed me into one of them. There was noise and confusion everywhere. Just inside the doors was a raggedy line of peasant women dressed in black, holding crying children by the hands. They moaned and whispered among themselves, waiting there for some reason or other. They looked at me with narrow guarded eyes.

The filthy room stank of stale sweat and tobacco. Turkish police dragged prisoners back and forth. Most of the men had chains dangling from their wrists.

Tex took me over to a desk where he spoke in Turkish to a couple of policemen. Then he turned to me. 'OK. They'll take care of you here.'

I didn't want him to go. I didn't even know his name. I didn't know if he was from the consulate, Interpol, the CIA – or what. But he was American. He spoke English. 'Can you call the American consul for me?' I asked.

'It's not necessary. You'll be able to contact them. They'll let you make a phone call or something.'

'Could you do it? Please.'

Tex paused. 'OK.' He nodded to the policemen and was gone.

The two Turks glared at me, then pushed me towards some stairs. I hesitated. They growled out some command and shoved me forward. On the first landing a prisoner with a bloody mouth was backed into a corner, pleading with his tormentors. He screamed as they closed in and beat him again.

I was taken to a small foyer off the main room upstairs. I could still hear the screams of what now sounded like several men. My eyes moved quickly around the room, afraid that I might become the next screaming prisoner.

I was seated across a desk from a Turkish detective who spoke passable English. Next to him was a big, dark, swarthy-looking man in a business suit. He had no moustache, which is unusual for a Turk. In contrast to the others in the building, police as well as prisoners, he was clean. He grinned silently.

'Where did you get the hashish?' the detective asked slowly.

I remembered the cab driver who had sold me the hashish.

20

Maybe he'd tipped off the police, but I didn't think so. He seemed genuinely friendly and even introduced me to his family. I didn't want him to be brought here, maybe beaten, but I didn't want to get myself into any further trouble either. Suddenly, inspiration hit. I made up a story about two young hippie Turks and their older friend whom I had met in the bazaar. I gave the detective descriptions of them. 'They sold me the stuff,' I said.

'Would you recognize them again?'

'I'm . . . I'm not sure. I think so.'

The big man sitting next to the detective spoke in Turkish.

'He's asking if you're afraid,' the policeman translated.

'I'm not afraid,' I lied.

They looked at each other and grinned.

'Well, maybe a little,' I admitted.

'He says, "Don't be," ' the policeman said.

'Who is he?'

The detective pointed towards some large, round, brass-coloured cans sitting on his desk. The top was pried open on one. He reached in and pulled out a bag of hashish in powdered form, not yet pressed into plaques like mine. I peered inside the can. It was jammed with the drug. There must have been five or six kilos in it. The detective pointed to eight or ten similar cans sitting off to one side of the room. 'They're his,' he indicated, pointing to the grinning Turk. 'He gets arrested also, but with sixty kilos. Is much, no?'

'Yes, it's much,' I said.

I accepted a cigarette from the detective in order to be friendly. But I inhaled it carefully. Then the detective proposed a deal. If I would go with the police back to Sultan Ahmet, the section where I had supposedly bought the drugs, and point out the sellers, I would be on a plane for New York tomorrow. I suspected that the man was lying, but I had nothing to lose. At least I'd have a few more hours outside. And maybe, who knows, even a chance to escape.

So I found myself walking back towards the Pudding Shoppe that evening, flanked by a team of four detectives. They were trying very hard to make themselves inconspicuous. I saw hippies clear the sidewalk one hundred yards away as our little squad made its way around the area. The

Pudding Shoppe emptied of customers the moment we walked in. I sat down at a table. I'd had no food since morning and was suddenly very, very hungry. I got up my courage and to the anger of the policemen I ordered scrambled eggs and tea. I savoured each bite, lingering until the detectives became impatient enough to blow their cover, pull me up from the table, and drive me back to the station.

Down, down the dark slimy stairs to the basement of the station. Night now, the walls and the darkness closing in on me. The game was over. Now I was scared, really scared.

In a tiny anteroom the detectives signed me over to a crusty old jailer. He squinted at the official papers in the dim light of a single bare bulb that dangled from the high cobwebbed ceiling. I heard grunts, and turned to see a huge barred door. From the darkness behind it, blackened, bearded faces peered out at me. The stench of human waste was overwhelming. I wanted desperately not to vomit in front of these men. I had to look tough. I was more conscious than ever of my blond hair and my slim build. Slim, but wiry, I reminded myself. I was tough and in good condition from wrestling and all those summers of life-guarding on Long Island. But why had I stopped the karate lessons?

The jailer grabbed his keys. *'Git!'* he yelled at the prisoners, who backed away from the barred door. He turned an over-sized iron key in the lock, tugged open the heavy door, pushed me inside and slammed the bars behind me. The *clang* echoed inside my pounding head.

My back was to the door. Six or seven curious Turks gathered around me in a half circle. They were dressed poorly, all of them dirty. One of them scratched his bearded face and flashed a toothy grin. Another burped. The room was dark, almost black. The stench was sickening.

What were they going to do? Anything could happen in here. The police were all upstairs and didn't seem to care. There was a big man looming off to the right. I wondered if I should smash him in the throat as hard as I could. Maybe the others would get the message and leave me alone. If there was going to be a fight, I wanted to at least throw the first punch

The man with the toothy grin reached over and lightly touched my hair. *'Nebu?'* he said and the men roared with laughter.

Suddenly, 'Rrragghh!' from the back of the room.

The men scattered away. Out of the darkness came a gruff but soothing voice. 'Hey! Hey, Joe. *Gel. Gel.*'

I looked in the direction of the voice but could see nothing. *'Gel. Gel.'*

I stepped over a few snoring bodies and moved towards the voice. It seemed to be carrying me away from the worst part of the stench. As my eyes adjusted to the light I blinked. I couldn't believe what I saw.

There, on the dirty floor, amidst this filth, someone had laid out a clean blanket. On the blanket was spread a feast of roast chicken, oranges, grapes, and bread. Sitting like a king upon the blanket, surrounded by a half-dozen smiling friends, was the big Turk I had met earlier, upstairs in the detective's office.

He grinned and held out a drumstick. 'Sit,' he said, gesturing.

I removed my boots and slowly settled onto the blanket. Before I even reached the ground someone handed me a huge lighted cigarette.

I smelled the unmistakable odour of hashish.

CHAPTER THREE

'Smoke. Smoke,' the Turk said.

I glanced towards the door in fear. The men sitting around the blanket laughed. I stared at the cigarette a moment, bewildered. Earlier in the day I'd been arrested for hashish. Because of that I was thrown into a dungeon where the first thing I encountered was more hashish. It didn't make sense at all.

But there it was in my hand and it didn't seem like the right time to upset my host. To the encouragement of the others I puffed on the cigarette and choked back a cough. I was used to smoking tiny bits of hashish in a pipe, but the Turks mixed the drug with their rough tobacco and rolled it up in a big brown paper. It looked like a Havana cigar. I took several cautious puffs. Then I passed it to the man next to me.

They talked loudly, animatedly, as they ate. Their hands flew about in exuberant gestures. They seemed unconcerned about where they were. One of the men barked out an order to a shabby prisoner lurking near by. Instantly the prisoner poured a cup of water from a plastic pitcher. He seemed like an alert servant, eager to please his master.

I sat there trying to make sense of it all. Who were these men who feasted and smoked hashish in the police lockup? I wondered how they got away with it, and why the other prisoners respected them.

Sharp, hungry eyes peered at me from the surrounding gloom. But the other prisoners seemed afraid to come close as long as I shared the hospitality of my hosts.

The well-dressed Turk pointed at me and grinned. He held up two fingers. 'Two kilos,' he told his friends. He pointed towards his own chest, then raised both hands, opening and closing them six times. He had sixty kilos. All his friends burst into laughter.

They ate and smoked and talked and laughed for hours. I wasn't in the mood for a party, but I wasn't going to leave the safety of this circle. Their laughs were infectious. In spite of myself I joined in. The smoke burned my eyes but at least it masked the barnyard odours coming from the other end of the room.

We finished the meal. The men rose, burping and farting as though it were the height of good taste. My host grunted. The servant quickly brushed the garbage off the blanket. Immediately a fight broke out over chicken bones and orange peels, but none of the men in the élite group seemed concerned. They moved, instead, to a corner of the room where a rotting wooden platform was bolted to the stone wall, braced up underneath by thick wooden pillars. A short ladder led up to a shelf. Men dressed in rags slept huddled together for warmth. My friends climbed up and casually rolled the sleepers off the shelf down onto the hard stone. '*Allah!*' the sleepers screamed as they tumbled to the floor. But when they saw who had dispossessed them, they scurried away meekly.

The servant carried the blanket over and spread it on the planks. The big Turk sat down. The others in the group produced newspapers from somewhere and laid them down. They motioned for me to accept an honoured position on the newspaper. The big Turk grunted and waved at me to join him on the blanket. I smiled graciously, shook my head, and pointed to a spot at the edge of their territory. I didn't want to sleep with these powerful men, just be close to them.

I sat on the narrow wooden shelf, my back pressed against the cold stone wall. My friends stretched, yawned, grunted, and dropped quickly to sleep. Their contented snores indicated that they were used to all this.

I certainly wasn't. My head whirled, partly from the buzz of hashish, but more from the throb of reality. For the first time all day I was alone with my thoughts. They weren't pleasant. Tex said maybe twenty years. No! Twenty days would drive me crazy.

'Hey. Hey. Joe,' someone whispered. I glanced over to see a young, slick-haired Turk in a double-breasted suit several sizes too big for him. 'Come over here, man,' he said knowingly. '*Fik fik. Fik fik.* Come on. Come over here.'

I turned my head away. He kept whispering, but I ignored him. Neither he nor the other Turks seemed willing to come too close. Even in their sleep my protectors held a powerful influence.

My bladder was bursting. The smell from the other side of the room – too far away – told me where the toilet was. I just gritted my teeth. I would hold on till morning.

My body ached from the damp cold and hard wood. I needed sleep. But my throbbing head wouldn't allow it.

This was so hard to believe. Could I cope with it? I didn't have any choice. I got myself into this mess; now I'd just have to see it through. But could I? Would I be tough enough to survive a Turkish prison? Thick, choking darkness settled around me. I wanted to cry out. God, I had to get out of there!

Eventually I dropped off to sleep. Deep in the night I was startled awake by the touch of light fingers on my thigh. A small dark figure scurried away. He leaped down from the bench onto the floor amid shouts and moans as he stumbled over the sleepers. One of my friends woke.

'*Noldu?*' he asked sleepily.

I forced a smile and shrugged. He went back to sleep immediately. Somehow I wasn't sleepy any more.

Far off, a dog grieved in the dark.

I was sweating, in spite of the cold. A mosquito touched down lightly on my neck. I didn't move. There were so many it was useless to swat them. My eyes were closed. Time passed. My thoughts drifted to a morning long ago.

I sat in our kitchen. Yellow sunlight flooded in through the windows, and the white lace curtains glowed. My mother sang softly to herself as she cooked breakfast, and her happiness filled the room. Her face was so young. Her eyes shone as she turned to look at me. 'Billy, I just don't know what to do about you. You've finished that whole glass of milk already. No wonder your hair's so blond. I'm going to have to get a cow, just to keep you in milk.'

'Can we keep her in the backyard, Mom?'

'Sure. And you and Bobby can ride around on her.'

'Oh, great! Let's get her today!'

She laughed and hugged me up against her apron. 'I think maybe we should talk to your father first about this idea.'

'Naw. Let's just buy one and surprise him.'

' "Naw," ' she imitated. 'Let's just finish our breakfast and go out to play. Your father doesn't need that kind of surprise.'

'OK,' I said, running out the door to find my friends Lillian and Patrick. 'But I'll talk to you about it later when I come home. . . .'

When I come home. . .

When I come home. . . .

The mosquito finished feeding on me. It lifted off my neck. I was awake again. I opened my eyes and stared at the wall.

Until now things had always gone easily for me. Mom and Dad had provided a comfortable existence. The house in North Babylon, New York, was modest but warm. From my earliest days the course of my life had seemed settled. I would go to good Catholic schools, get good grades, go to a good college, marry a nice girl, find a good job, and live a good life.

Good. I didn't question it.

At school, the sisters praised my efforts, but there was little, if any, effort involved. In sports, I was always a starter on the school teams, and always without exerting myself.

Then came college. Dad wanted me to go to Marquette, a Jesuit university in Milwaukee. No question there; he was paying the bills. My freshman year in 1964 was the first time I'd lived away from home. Suddenly I found myself among people who asked questions. I began to question too. Did my life have to run along a track? Life seemed so full of possibilities beyond what my family considered to be normal.

Surfing, for example. After my freshman year I decided to take a long vacation to sort out my troubled thoughts. I thumbed my way to Mexico, to the Pacific Coast, where I picked up various odd jobs to survive. I spent lazy hours surfing on the coast. I stayed there for what would have been the first semester of my sophomore year. Mom and Dad were upset. It was the first time I had openly rebelled against their wishes.

But the war in Southeast Asia crowded me. I was forced to return to Marquette or lose my student deferment from the draft. When I went back to Milwaukee my friends introduced me to something new. It had replaced beer drinking as

27

the campus pastime. I smoked my first marijuana cigarette Then hashish.

The next years were even more unsettling. I stayed in school to stay out of the army. But my heart wasn't in it. My grades, which had been good, became average. I spent a lot of time bumming around Milwaukee when I should have been in class. For a while I seriously tried to write short stories. The wall of my room was soon plastered with rejection slips. I gave it up.

Back home, my folks were puzzled over the steady decline in my grades. They couldn't seem to understand when I said that I didn't know what I would do with a college education – so how could I work hard at it? Mom and Dad grew up in an age when a college education was a privilege. But for me, in the sixties, it seemed commonplace. We drifted farther apart.

Encouraged by friends, I joined a few protest marches against the war. But I never thought deeply about the issues. I enjoyed the party atmosphere of the protests. The life I remembered had been one big party.

My eyes were still open when the first pale rays of the morning sun sliced down through small barred windows high up on the black wall. The yellow beams filtered sluggishly through the thick smoky air. I stared at the sunlight. I was glad the night had ended. But I was afraid of what the day might bring.

The man next to me stretched and yawned, letting loose a long, drawn-out 'AAAaaaallah!' at the end. Then he belched, farted, and scratched at his crotch. He hacked and coughed and spat stale juices out onto the floor. Then he lit a Turkish cigarette and flung what had to be a stream of curses out to greet the morning. All over the room the same ritual took place. The noise level rose to a roar as the hundred or so men in the lockup joined together in one hacking chorus.

The man next to me eased down off the bench. He shuffled across to the far side of the room. I could see several holes cut into the floor. My neighbour stopped in front of one hole, dropped his pants and squatted. A couple of men gathered in front of him to stare. He didn't seem to care.

*　　*　　*

28

He grunted an answer to nature's call. He missed the hole.

'*Turist*. Vilyum. Vilyum. Vilyum Hi-yes.'

I bolted for the door. A policeman led me upstairs to a small quiet room, bare except for a low table and two chairs. I waited alone for a moment. A thin, dapper Turk walked in, dressed in a business suit.

'My name is Erdogan,' he said in precise English, pumping my hand. 'Call me Erdu. I work for the American consulate.'

Relief! Help at last.

'I am very sorry for you, William. I will try to help you all I can.'

'What's going to happen to me?'

Erdu shuffled nervously through a sheaf of papers. 'We really don't know. You will need a lawyer. In Turkey this is a very serious crime.'

He pulled out a list of Turkish names. They were lawyers, arranged alphabetically, with a list of credentials after them

'Which one?' I asked.

Erdu shrugged. 'I cannot make a recommendation. You just pick one.'

'Do they speak English?'

'Yes. Several of them.'

I glanced over the list until my eyes settled upon the name Yesil. He'd graduated from the University of Maryland. He'd lectured at the University of Michigan.

'I'll take Yesil. Do you know him?'

Erdu nodded. 'I'll contact him. He will see you in a few days. This afternoon the soldiers will take you to Sagmalcilar prison. It's on the other side of the city. Yesil will see you there. The consul will also come out to visit you there in a few days.'

Then the question I feared. 'Do you want us to contact your parents?'

'No. I'd like to write them a letter first.'

Erdu gave me a pen and some blank paper. Then he left me alone in the room.

8 October, 1970
Mom and Dad,

This letter will be hard for you to read. It's hard for me to write. I'm aching inside because I know the pain it will bring you.

I'm in some trouble. Maybe big trouble. At the moment I'm all right. I'm sitting here writing in a small locked room in jail in Istanbul. This is such a crazy place to be. I won't try to explain it all now. Just that I was arrested at the airport yesterday, attempting to board an airplane with a small amount of hashish. I've just spoken with an official of the American consulate. They're contacting a lawyer for me. There's some chance that I could go free but maybe I could receive a few years in prison, I can't really tell what's going to happen now. I might be here for a while.

I wish I didn't have to write and tell you all this. I know the sorrow and confusion it will cause. And the disappointment. I know you love me. But I know you're not proud of me.

I really thought I knew what I was doing with my life. I'm not so sure now. I'd hoped to somehow get out of this quickly so that you'd never know about it. That just isn't possible.

So now I'm in jail in Turkey, around on the other side of the world. The other side of a lot of worlds. And what can I say to you? Will 'I'm sorry' make any difference now? Will it ease the pain, the shame, you must be feeling? I feel like such a fool for letting my life slip away like this. I cry to think how I'm hurting you. Forgive me.

I'll write soon,

>   *Love,*
>   *Billy*

Soldiers came early in the afternoon and called out about fifteen of us. They lined us up in twos and chained us together at the wrists. We marched outside and into the open back door of a red panel truck. We clambered inside and sat on wooden plank benches. They drove us somewhere across town and unloaded us in back of a large stone building. We shuffled downstairs into a long, low rectangular room. Like the lockup, this place was filthy. The dingy whitewashed walls glowed pale green in the light of one bare bulb. When the chains were removed the other prisoners formed a line. I slid down to a place at the far end.

The other prisoners stood with slightly bowed heads.

Their arms hung limply at their sides. The burly sergeant in charge barked a question at the first prisoner in line. The man answered meekly but the sergeant cuffed him back-handed across the mouth. Another question. Another humble answer. Another, more vicious, slap. The man's mouth trickled blood. He whimpered. The sergeant spat harsh words at him and moved on to the second prisoner.

More questions. More slaps. The second man tried to raise his arm to block the blows, but this enraged the sergeant further. He hit harder.

Down the line he moved, yelling at each prisoner and beating him in turn. He seemed to get angrier the further he went. And I was at the end. I tried desperately to copy the Turks' humble stance.

The sergeant had almost reached the centre of the line when one prisoner seemed to respond with a particularly unfavourable answer. He was smashed in the face and knocked back against the wall. He clutched at his bloody nose. The sergeant roared at the squirming man. He punched him in the belly. The prisoner doubled up and sank to the floor. Then the sergeant grabbed him by the hair and dragged him to the centre of the room.

The poor man tried to crawl away but the other soldiers joined in. He screamed and pleaded and begged for mercy as the soldiers systematically beat his ribs, kidneys, and legs with black rubber truncheons. He scuttled around on the ground, trying desperately to cover himself up. One soldier jabbed him viciously in the groin whenever he could. The man wailed in pain and fear.

The rest of us stood silently in line, waiting. A cold sweat broke out all over my body. What's going to happen when they reach the end of the line and find a stupid *turist* standing there?

The soldiers finally dragged the bloody man to a corner, where he collapsed, whimpering. Then the soldiers fanned out down the line, slapping and beating the other prisoners. Curses and screams echoed through the small room. Soon it would be my turn.

A big, sallow-complexioned soldier came near me. He leaned over and looked into my shoulder bag.

'*Nebu?*' he grunted, holding up two small yellow balls. '*Nebu? Nebu?*'

I motioned for the balls. Slowly, trying not to alarm him, I reached into my bag for the third one.

'*Nebu? Nebu?*' the soldier demanded.

Stop shaking, hands! I began to juggle.

'*Nebu? Nebu?*' said another soldier, hurrying over to look.

I stopped.

'*Yap! Yap!*' He motioned for me to continue.

I juggled again, spinning the coloured balls up in front of me.

Soon other soldiers gathered around, fascinated, as people always are, with the motion and the dexterity. The sergeant charged over and shouted at me. I dropped a ball. He reached out and caught it on one bounce. He thrust it at me. '*Yap!*'

I juggled. What else could I do? As long as the soldiers were watching me they weren't beating anyone. Especially not me. So I went into the routine that had entertained friends so often in New York and Milwaukee. A simple three-ball weave. Two in one hand, one in the other. A quick middle pass. Throw one catch two, throw two catch one. A little overhand shuffle.

Then I stopped.

'*Yap! Yap!*' from all over the room.

I *yapped*.

I juggled for fifteen minutes or more. My arms tired. I dropped a ball again. The sergeant grabbed it, but instead of returning it to me, he held out his hand for the other two.

I gave them to him. He tossed one in the air, then the other two. All three bounced away into the crowd. The sergeant growled an order and immediately had them in his hands again. He held them for a moment. Then he sheepishly gestured for me to show him. We went off into a corner where I tried to teach him. His co-ordination was good but there was no way for me to explain that it took lots of practice. He couldn't get it right. He grew edgy. So did I. I didn't want him to return to what he was good at.

Politely I gestured for the balls. I held up my hand. Suspiciously, the soldiers watched. Moving slowly, I pulled a chair beneath the room's light bulb. I held the three balls close to the light for a few minutes. Then I climbed down and motioned for the sergeant to turn out the light. His eyes narrowed. But then he barked something at the soldiers. Two of them stationed themselves at each door. Another flicked off the light switch.

I juggled some more. The yellow balls now glowed pale green and blue as they whirled through the dark in neon patterns. Several times I climbed back up to recharge the balls. Everyone in the room watched spellbound.

Finally, I heard a truck pull up outside. The sergeant yelled another order. The prisoners formed a line, some helping the others to stand. I put the balls away. I was chained to a grizzled old man who seemed to have escaped the beatings too. Perhaps it was his age. Aside from the two of us, everyone else in the room was bruised and bleeding.

A strange, almost light-hearted mood fell upon me as we drove out to the prison. I'd been lucky. I hoped my luck would hold.

The first sight of the great grey prison walls brought me back to reality. The truck pulled into an underpass and braked to a halt. Soldiers got out, unlocked the van and marched us into a receiving room. Everything was cement or steel, all covered with a flaky whitewash. The chains were removed. The soldiers turned us over to prison guards in rumpled blue uniforms. They all had cigarettes dangling from their lips. A surly little guard sauntered over to me and asked something in Turkish. I shrugged. Quickly his eyes narrowed and he drew back a fist . . .

Suddenly a door shot open and two men walked in. They wore the same uniforms as the other guards, but theirs were neat and clean. Four stripes on their sleeves seemed to indicate some sort of seniority. The other prisoners quickly went into their POW stance.

The larger, younger of the two guards, walked down the line of prisoners. He moved his huge bulk easily in a slow insolent swagger. He stopped in front of one prisoner whom he seemed to recognize. Slowly he drew a huge hammy hand across his body, as if he were cocking a gun.

Wham! He backhanded the prisoner across the face, sending him sprawling into the wall. Quietly he moved down the line.

The second guard was older, with short salt-and-pepper hair. He had a long, thin, hawk face and hard brown eyes. He stood with his back ramrod straight. He seemed like the kind of Turk I used to read about in history books, one of those who had driven the Greeks into the sea at Smyrna.

He stopped in front of me. He looked coldly at my hair. Then he stared into my eyes.

I met his gaze, then realized that perhaps this wasn t how a prisoner should react. My eyes flicked away. Then back again. A thin smile creased his leathery face. I smiled back.

'Gower!' he exploded, spraying my face. My grin was gone now.

I looked down at the stone floor. I tried not to breathe He called out something to the old records-keeper and I heard, 'Vilyum Hi-yes.'

'Vilyum Hi-yes,' the hawk-faced guard repeated. 'Vilyum Hi-yes.' He moved on down the line.

Our heads were shaved. We were photographed and fingerprinted. Then I was separated from the others and led down a long narrow concrete hallway to a steel-barred door. A guard unlocked it, shoved me inside and slammed it shut.

I was in my new home.

CHAPTER FOUR

It was all cold stone and grey steel. A narrow length of corridor stretched in front of me. On the left side was a line of barred windows that looked out onto darkness. On the right ran a row of ten or twelve small cells. A set of stone steps led up to what looked like another tier above.

It was rather quiet. At the moment the corridor was deserted. I could hear music playing somewhere but it was muffled. Voices echoed softly against the stone.

Someone stepped out of a cell halfway down the corridor and stood there looking at me. A head popped out from another cell. It snapped a glance at me, then popped back in. The sound of the door must have alerted the inmates. Others appeared, gazing curiously.

I took a few steps away from the door and came abreast of the first cell. It was a small cubicle of a room, a little cement box about six feet by eight feet. The end facing the corridor was open except for a set of grey metal bars that stretched from ceiling to floor. The door was a section of bars on rollers that slid back and forth. I looked in at three prisoners sitting together, eating what looked like some kind of soup from tin cups.

'Hey, man, look at this!' shouted a tough-looking prisoner who sat at the end of the bed. His thick hairy arms were covered with tattoos. 'How you doing, man?' He rose and reached over to slide open the door. 'Where you from? What they bust you for? What's your name?'

He spoke fluid, nonstop English with a heavy accent I couldn't place. His dark eyes were bright. He grinned at me and babbled on.

'Hey, guys, look at this, a new *macum*. What's your name, man?' he asked again, pumping my hand.

'William . . .' I began, but he cut me off.

'William. Crazy! My name is Popeye and this is Charles and Arne.' He indicated the others – one black, one white – who quietly ate their food. 'Why don't you sit down here,

35

William?' Popeye said, as he reached under the bed for something.

I moved to sit on the end of the bed but Popeye quickly grabbed my arm. Arne looked alarmed.

'NO! Over here, man,' Popeye said, hastily setting up a large metal can on the floor. The bed looked more comfortable but I got the message. I sat on the can. Popeye hopped onto the bed.

'So, where you from, William?'

'New York.' I gazed around in amazement. The cell was almost beautiful. A delicate Japanese silkscreen of a mountain scene was taped to the wall above a desk. There were soap carvings and intricate paper cut-outs of birds and animals scattered all around the room. A bedsheet had been elaborately painted with astrological symbols. It covered the wall behind the bed. After the events of the past two days the room seemed warm and cosy.

'Hey, Charles, we got another American,' Popeye shouted.

Charles just nodded.

'Charles's from Chicago. He's the Windy City spade. Oh yeah! Now we got the black American and the white American. All we need is the . . .' and Popeye started singing. It was a rock song, a record by a group called The Guess Who. *'American woman . . . da da da da dee-eee. . . .'*

I had to grin at Popeye.

Then I looked at Charles. 'Hi, how're you doing?'

'OK,' he admitted, reluctantly shaking my offered hand and dropping it quickly.

'Hello, Willie,' Arne said in a soft quiet voice. 'Welcome to my cell.' He looked Scandinavian – tall, thin, and pale, with piercingly calm blue eyes.

I was thrilled to find myself among three English-speaking men about my own age. And one of them was even an American.

'Hey, it's pretty nice here,' I said.

Charles scowled and shook his head.

Popeye began laughing. 'Oooohh, the new American guy You're too much, William. "Nice place here," he says Hoooo!' And off he went, laughing into his tin cup.

Arne merely smiled politely. He handed me a cup of lentil soup, and watched as I drained it ravenously.

'William?' a quiet voice interrupted my dinner.

I looked up to see two men standing at the door of Arne's cell, where we were eating our dinner. One of them was middle-aged and stout with thin strands of black hair slicked back over his round bald head. He squinted at me through murky brown eyes. The other was slightly built and gangly. He wore thick brown-rimmed glasses. He was the one who spoke to me in English. 'This is Emin,' he said, pointing to the older man. 'My name is Walter. Emin is our *memisir*. He's the prisoner in charge of the foreigners' cellblock, the *kogus*. Come. Emin will show you to your cell.'

'You can finish your food later,' Arne reassured me.

I dutifully followed behind Walter and Emin. They led me to an empty cell near the end of the corridor. Emin muttered a few things in Turkish, slobbering a bit as he spoke. He pointed inside. I nodded. Emin seemed satisfied and walked away.

The cell was the same as Arne's except bare. It was cold. Dust covered everything. A small grey metal bunk was bolted to the stone floor. It held a lumpy mattress that looked as if it had been there for a long time. Stuffing fell out of one end. Dark stains covered the middle. A battered wooden table and bench folded up into the wall. At the rear of the tiny room was a waist-high partition and behind it a toilet hole cut into the stone floor. It reeked of urine. A metal locker filled the small space between the bars and the foot of the bed.

It wasn't the sort of place I'd want to spend much time in. But certainly I wouldn't be there long. Twenty years? That was just a scare tactic. No one would give me twenty years for two kilos. I knew I wouldn't have to bother about decorating my cell like Arne's. He had obviously been here a long time. What for, I wondered.

I went back down the hall to finish my soup. Popeye had returned.

'Who are those guys?' I asked.

'Shitheads,' Popeye replied. 'Emin's a Turk. He's been

37

inside for a long time now, so they put him in charge of the *kogus*. Walter's just some little ass-kisser who speaks about six different languages. And all of them behind your back.'

'Oh, yeah?'

'Oh, yeah?' Popeye mimicked. 'Do you think you're at college, William? This is prison, man. Prison. You see your cell yet?'

'Yeah.'

'So, how do you like your new home?'

'It's fine,' I said without much enthusiasm.

'Yeah, well, that's because it's such a really nice place here,' said Charles.

I changed the subject.

'What are you in for?' I asked Arne

'Hash.'

'What'd you get?'

'Twelve and a half years.'

'Wow! How much did you have?'

'A hundred grams '

What! Twelve and a half years for a hundred grams. Impossible. That was only one-tenth of a kilo. I'd had twenty times that much.

'What'd they bust you for, William?' It was Popeye.

There was tension in his voice.

'Hash,' I replied.

'How much?'

'Two kilos.'

'Where?'

'At the airport. Trying to get onto a plane.'

'Oh, wow. Gonna be bad. You go through customs?'

'Uh, yeah, I did. I was busted right at the plane.'

Popeye whistled like Harpo Marx and shook both of his hands in the air. 'Heavy, heavy. Could be ten or fifteen. Maybe even twenty.'

'Twenty *what*?'

'Years, man, years. I say definitely ten at the least '

I couldn't believe it. They had to be kidding

Arne stood up. He looked kind and undisturbed by the depravity around us. He stretched out past me, reaching for something on top of the locker. 'Don't listen to him, Willie,'

38

he said. 'He's just trying to blow your mind. You don t know what sentence you'll get here in Turkey. Anything's possible.' He brought a small wooden bowl down from the top of the locker. There were apples in it. He offered me one and passed the bowl around. I trusted him somehow. There was something reassuring about him. I felt close to him immedi ately.

'Hey, don't play games with him, Arne,' Popeye said. 'He'd better start expecting the worst right now so he'll be prepared for it. I say the guy's looking at ten or fifteen at least.'

'Is this for real?' I asked. 'Twelve and a half or twenty years for hash? You're crazy.'

There was an embarrassed silence.

Charles, who'd been quiet for a while, looked up from his bowl. 'Everybody's crazy in here,' he said.

We all turned back to our food. I hardly tasted mine. I tried to sort out my thoughts. Popeye *had* to be crazy. No country in the world, no matter how mixed up, could possibly give twenty years for two kilos. It wouldn't happen to me. And besides, I was an American. Everyone knew that Americans got special treatment.

'What did you get?' I asked Charles.

He scowled. 'Five. And I've got ten goddamn months to go.'

Five years. An American. Well, that was certainly better than Popeye's prediction. Now I knew Popeye's accent. Israeli. Sure. He had to be pessimistic in a Moslem country. But I was American. And I'd always been lucky. Somehow I'd get off easy.

Arne seemed to read my thoughts. 'You might make bail,' he said quietly.

Popeye scowled and said, 'Bullshit!'

'Bail?'

'Depends . . .' Arne made a serious face, as if he were thinking deeply. Then he looked at me and smiled. 'If you make bail you're free. The Turks know that you'll skip out of the country and never come back. They just keep the bail money. If they give you bail it means they expect you to split '

This sounded interesting. 'But how would I get out of the country?'

'Easy,' Arne said. 'Any halfway crooked Turkish lawyer – and none of them are straight – can get you a false passport. Or else you could just try to sneak across the border into Greece. Greece is the place to go. They hate the Turks so bad there's no way they'd send you back. If the Turks give you bail they know you'll split. And if you get to Greece, you're free.'

'Hey, that sounds great. You think I have a chance for bail?'

'Well,' said Arne, 'it all depends. Yeah, you have a chance if you've got some money and a good lawyer.'

'Well, I'll just get it,' I said. 'I'll have to!'

'Shit!' Popeye snapped. His jovial mood was gone now. 'Why don't you just take a bath and shut up. Get those filthy lice off you.'

'I don't have any lice, Popeye,' I said, surprised at his accusation.

'Where were you last night?' he demanded.

'In the police lockup.'

'Then you've got lice, man. Why do you think we didn't want you to sit on the bed? Take a bath and boil your clothes.'

Arne nodded in agreement.

Actually, a bath sounded terrific but I didn't want Popeye to push me around. 'A shower sounds better,' I said.

Charles let loose a whistle and pushed up from his seat. 'I've had enough of this crap,' he said and stalked out of the room.

Arne drew me aside. 'There are no showers here,' he said. 'You have to wash from a sink in the kitchen.' He led me next door to his own cell and lent me a towel, a plastic pitcher, and a small piece of soap. He explained that the hot water would be turned on shortly for about a half hour. He took me back to the kitchen area beyond the stairs. He showed me how to stop up the sink with a dirty rag. To bathe I would have to lather myself with soap, then pour hot water over my body with the pitcher. But first I decided to wash the sink. It was filthy.

'Don't let Popeye and Charles get to you,' Arne said

gently. 'They've both been in for a long time. New people . .
well . . . they don't really understand what's going on. New
guys get on people's nerves.'

'How did he get the name "Popeye"?'

'He's a sailor. He was busted trying to smuggle forty kilos
onto his ship.'

'How much time did he get?'

'Fifteen years.'

'No wonder he's crazy.'

Arne was quiet for a moment. 'Yeah,' he said finally. 'But
he's a nice guy, really.'

Hot water rattled through the rusty pipes. Arne smiled
and left me alone to bathe. I scrubbed the sink with soap. It
didn't look any cleaner. As the sink filled with steaming
water I stripped off my wrinkled clothes. They did stink.
Standing naked in front of the sink, I lathered my face and
head. It felt strange not to have any hair. The prickly stubble
on my scalp reminded me of the crewcut I wore in my high
school wrestling days. With Arne's old pitcher I scooped
water out of the sink and poured it over myself. It felt good
oozing down over my head and shoulders. I lathered the rest
of my body slowly. Then I remembered what Popeye had
said. I examined my crotch for lice.

Suddenly I realized I wasn't alone. I turned to see a man
who looked like an Arab standing in the doorway. He stared
at my naked body with a grin on his face. He clattered
something excitedly in Turkish. I shrugged my shoulders to
indicate I didn't understand.

The Arab disappeared but returned a moment later with
Arne. I watched in confusion, soap suds dripping onto the
floor.

'You can't wash like that,' Arne warned. 'You can't wash
naked.'

'What? Then how am I supposed to take a bath?'

'You have to keep your underwear on. You can't ever be
naked in the *kogus*.'

'What are you talking about? How can I wash with my
clothes on?'

Arne grew more insistent. 'You can't, man. The Turks are

41

very uptight about anything that looks like, you know, sex among the prisoners.'

'What sex? I'm just taking a bath. Go away and let me finish.'

Arne shrugged. 'OK. But you better hurry. *Sayim*'s coming.'

I didn't care who Sayim was. The water felt too good. Arne left me alone. As I poured another pitcher of hot water over me I remembered the afternoon. How lucky I was to escape the beating.

Keys rattled. The cellblock door opened.

A Turkish voice yelled, '*Sayim. Sayim.*' I could see the edge of the guard's arm as he stood just outside the open door.

Arne came running back. 'I told you to hurry, man. They're having *Sayim.*'

I had no idea what *Sayim* was but I was getting tired of all these orders. I continued soaping my legs.

'Are you crazy?' Arne said in a fierce whisper. 'If they catch you naked they'll beat you.'

This time the words sank in. I remembered the poor Turkish prisoner lying on the floor in his own blood with guards kicking him and beating him with their clubs. Quickly I wrapped the towel around my waist. I ran out of the room, my wet feet slipping and sliding on the stone floor.

I bumped into Emin. He was now wearing a suit and tie. He growled at me but I kept on running.

Charles and Popeye were near the end of the line. They both gawked at me. Popeye reached out and grabbed my arm. He pulled me behind himself and Charles. Charles tore off his white sweater and shoved it at me. I pulled it over my head. They were both tall. They shielded the lower half of my towel-clad body from view.

All the prisoners stood quietly at attention while a guard raced along the line and counted. He shouted something to another guard who checked a clipboard. The count was apparently correct.

'*Allah kutarsink,*' the guard intoned.

'*Sowul,*' the prisoners replied.

'Screw you,' Popeye said under his breath.

Later that evening Arne brought out his guitar. Someone else had a flute, and Charles brought bongo drums. I sat contentedly and listened to the music. The Turks, Arne explained, enjoy music. So they allow the prisoners to keep instruments.

I was strangely happy. The foreigners' *kogus* seemed relatively civilized, certainly a far better place to spend a few days – a few weeks, perhaps – than Sirkeci police station. I floated along with the music and reflected upon the possibility of making bail. Maybe I'd be back home on Long Island in a few weeks.

The music stopped for a while and Charles began scribbling on a note pad. I asked him what he was writing.

'Poem,' he replied quickly.

'You write a lot?'

'Yeah, got to.'

'Why?'

'Because if you've gotta be here, you've gotta do something.'

'Yeah, well, I'm a writer, too. I took journalism at Marquette.'

Charles eyed me knowingly. 'Uh, huh. You ever get anything published?'

'Well, no. But I sent this story to *Esquire*. They just wrote back and said they really liked it and . . .'

'Shit,' Charles said. He gathered up his note pad and bongo drums and stormed out.

About nine o'clock Emin came around with Walter trailing behind him.

'*Saat dokus*,' the younger man called out down the corridor. 'Nine o'clock,' he said to me.

'Lock up time, Willie. Goodnight.'

'Goodnight, Arne,' I said. 'Thanks.'

He smiled.

I walked down to my cell. Behind me Emin and the younger man moved along the corridor locking each prisoner into his cell. I shivered in the evening air. The barred window across from my room had a broken pane. A storm was blowing up outside. Cold air poured through my bare cell.

As Emin approached I asked Walter for sheets and blan kets. He translated but Emin merely shrugged

'I'm cold. I need sheets and blankets.'

'Tomorrow.' Walter translated. 'He says you'll get them tomorrow.'

The barred door slid shut across my face. Emin fumbled with his huge ring of keys. He couldn't seem to find the one for my cell. I could see him merely pretend to lock it.

I walked around the tiny cell, hugging myself for warmth. I listened as Emin locked the cells on the other side of the cell block and walked upstairs to the second tier. I was really cold. I couldn't take a whole night of this. Quietly I slid open my door. Where could I find a blanket?

'Pssssst.' A hand motioned to me from the bars of the cell next to mine. I walked over to see a huge, hulking man, maybe a German or Austrian, with blond hair. He was shirtless, with muscles bulging along his shoulders and arms. He thrust a long stick toward me and I grabbed it. It had a big nail pounded into the end, twisted over to form a hook.

'Down that way,' he whispered. He pointed toward the front of the cell block. 'Two or three cells down.'

Curiously I walked down the corridor. Surprised but quiet men peered at me through their cell doors. I came upon an empty cell, locked, with sheets, blankets, and pillows stacked upon the bunk. Poling through the bars, stretching and straining, I managed to hook a sheet and two blankets. I dragged them into the corridor. I padded softly back to my cell and gave the stick back to its owner. Then I offered him one of the blankets.

'Thanks,' he whispered.

I noticed that the light was out in his cell, while a bare bulb burned in the centre of mine. 'The light,' I said. 'How do I turn it off?'

'You're not supposed to,' he replied. 'But they don't say anything. Just stand on your bunk and stretch. You can twist it off.'

I slipped back into my cell. I could feel exhaustion creep-ing over me. I had gone more than forty hours with hardly any sleep. Now, with a fairly full stomach, a clean body, a private room and a thin but adequate blanket, I felt very tired. I spread the sheet and blanket on the bed. Then I twisted the light off and settled onto my bunk.

I must have fallen asleep immediately. I don't know how much time passed. But suddenly I was jerked awake by a rude pair of hands. Emin glared down at me. He screamed something in Turkish. I jumped up in confusion. Angrily Emin jerked the blanket off my bed. He threw it to the floor Then he grabbed the sheet. Still half asleep, I grabbed back. He yanked on it but I held firm. *'Brack!'* he growled and tugged harder. Mad now, I threw the sheet in his face and he stumbled backwards.

Enraged, he ran up to me and screamed in my face. He jabbed a finger in my chest for emphasis.

I reacted without thinking. Before I knew what I'd done, Emin was sprawled out on the floor. Blood dripped from his nose.

He looked at me for a moment in fear. Then he jumped up and ran down the hall. He screamed like he was dying.

What had I done now? More trouble for sure.

I looked out the door. Emin was at the end of the corridor pounding on the barred door.

'He's crazy, you know.' It was the prisoner in the cell next to mine. 'He's been here nine years now. He murdered his wife with a razor.'

Oh great! A murderer. I glanced around the cell, looking for something to defend myself with. Before I could collect my thoughts I heard a commotion down the hall. Keys rattled. Quickly I jumped into my pants and shoes. I didn't know what to expect but I wanted to be prepared.

Guards barged into the cell, screaming at me. They dragged me down the hallway. Emin chattered angrily. I tried to explain but it was hopeless. The guards couldn't understand me. The blood on Emin's face was clear enough evidence that I had hit the trusty.

They dragged me out of the cell block and downstairs into a basement room. The two chief guards – whom I'd seen earlier – sat on metal folding chairs, smoking cigarettes. They looked up as we entered. The one with salt-and-pepper hair stood up in front of me. He clasped his hands behind his back.

'Vilyum Hi-yes,' he said, staring into my eyes. 'Vilyum Hi-yes.'

Still glaring at me, he asked the guards sharp questions. Slowly he raised his right arm and smashed me across the face with an open palm. I fell back into the grasp of the guards. I opened my mouth to protest.

Wham! A shock wave ran through my left leg. It collapsed beneath me. As I fell to the floor I felt severe pain and heard myself scream. I turned my head to see the big guard. He looked like a grizzly bear standing above me, staring down at me with cold black eyes. In his hand was a thick wooden club about four feet long and two or three inches wide. It looked like a tree branch.

I tried to scramble away. He swung the club again, catching me across the lower back. The blow knocked me back to the floor. The pain was terrible. Another blow landed on my leg and I jerked away. I tried to block the next one and the club struck my thumb. My hand went numb.

The other guards pounced on me. They tore my shoes off. Then my pants. I kicked and screamed. But they held tight. They grabbed a heavy rope and wrapped it around my ankles. Two guards held either end of the rope, pulled it apart, and dragged my bare feet up into the air. I lay on my back on the cold stone floor, terrified. I looked up into the dark eyes of the big guard with the club.

He took his time. Slowly he pulled the club back, cocked it, and then brought it forward with full force against the soles of my bare feet. The blow stunned, then exploded in waves of hot agony up my legs and backbone. I screamed in pain. Again he cocked the stick. I tried to pull my feet away. The club caught me on the ankle-bone. Blinding flashes raced in front of my eyes. I almost fainted. Then I tried to faint. But I couldn't. Slowly, slowly, the beating continued. I writhed and jerked in pain. Each blow seemed worse. I screamed and cried and cursed at them but they wouldn't stop. All I could see were the leering faces of the guards gathered around above me.

The blows kept coming . . . ten, twelve, maybe fifteen in all. I wasn't counting. I twisted around and grabbed at one of

46

the guard's ankles. The big guard jammed the club down between my legs. I doubled up. I vomited all over myself.

'*Yetair,*' the big guard grunted. The others dropped their hold on the rope. My burning feet crashed to the stone floor in one final burst of pain.

Roughly, they untied me. I hardly knew or cared. Pain swirled all around me. Two guards dragged me to my feet, but I crashed back to the floor. Again they picked me up. My feet screamed. I was sick again. The guards yelled at me angrily and dropped my arms. Again I fell to the floor. They left me there for a moment. Then, somehow, they managed to drag me back upstairs and throw me into my cell. I fell onto the bed, where my precious sheets and blankets still sat.

I lay on the bed panting, trying to control my muscles. The sharp knife points of the blows became a pulsing throb. The pain in my groin was excruciating. Oh, God! Let me out of this nightmare.

The cell block was quiet, except for my moans. Each prisoner knew what had happened. They were sorry for me. But glad it hadn't been them.

The burning in my feet wouldn't stop. I couldn't sleep. But I couldn't stand to be awake.

'Psssst,' from the next cell.

Again. 'Psssst. William.'

I raised my head to look up. My neighbour had reached out through the bars and around the wall between our cells. He flicked a burning cigarette into the air and it landed on my bed. I grabbed for it. I sucked a deep lungful of smoke.

'Thanks,' I whispered.

Hashish. The cause of all this trouble. I was grateful for its sedative qualities. I sucked on it and slowly, gradually, felt my body relax. The pain subsided a bit. After a while I fell into a merciful sleep.

CHAPTER FIVE

Patrick lit the fuse and held the cherry bomb loosely in his hand.

'Throw it! Throw it!' I yelled.

He grinned, daring to hold onto it for what seemed like an impossible length of time. In slow motion he heaved it into the dark night air over Loch Ness. What a way to spend Halloween! If that didn't scare up Nessie, nothing would. Patrick had dozens of cherry bombs ready. I sat across from him in the rowboat, floodlights and movie camera ready. The pictures were sure to make us rich and famous.

But something was wrong. The cherry bomb went straight up into the dark air and seemed to float there. Its fuse sputtered out bright red sparks. It hung in space above our heads.

'Oh, no!' It grew larger and larger. It fell right towards me. It kept falling and falling and falling but it never reached the boat. I scrambled to get out of the way. My feet caught under the edge of the seat, spilling me onto the wet bottom of the boat. In panic I dropped the rented movie camera over the side. It slid beneath the black surface of the loch.

And above me, still, the cherry bomb fell. Slowly, slowly it approached, huge now, heading directly for my trapped feet. I couldn't breathe. I couldn't move. I could only watch in horror. The flaming firecracker exploded beneath the soles of my feet.

. . . I woke. My feet were on fire. Throbbing and aching in unbelievable pain, they snapped me out of my dream. Or was this the nightmare? In less than three weeks I was supposed to meet my old friend Patrick in Scotland. We planned to fulfil our boyhood fantasy of searching for the Loch Ness monster on Halloween. That hardly seemed likely now.

My sheet was soaked in perspiration, despite the freezing cold of the morning. I lay on the bed, covered with my own vomit. I listened as the prison woke up around me. Water gurgled through the pipes. I could hear the metal clanging of keys in doors. Just as in the police lockup, coughing and hacking and spitting was the morning hymn. Down at the other end of the cell block someone turned on a radio. Loud music blasted out.

'Turn that thing OFF!' someone yelled.

Someone else yelled a reply in German.

More shouts and yells. There was the sound of a scuffle. Something smashed to the floor. The radio was off.

A horrible smell drifted down from the tier above. It seemed like burning rubber. I wondered what it could possibly be.

The call of nature was worse than the pain of my feet. I forced myself to swing to the edge of the bed. I nearly fell to the ground. By holding onto the wall I managed to hobble over to the hole in the floor that served as a toilet. I tried not to breathe. A rusty tin can sat next to a low dripping spigot. I drew cold water into it and sloshed it onto the stone. It was futile. Ammonia fumes rose up into my nose. I held the wall with one hand for support, leaned back as far as I could and splattered the hole.

I hobbled back to bed and examined my feet. They were bright pink. Twice their normal size. Despite the pain I forced myself to wiggle each toe. Incredibly, no bones seemed to be broken. My ankle was tender. A large purple bruise rose where the club had made contact. My back throbbed. So did my groin. Once during a high school football game I'd been kicked there and thought that no pain could be worse. I'd been wrong. Now I was afraid that something had burst up inside of me.

Arne and Popeye stopped at my cell with hard-boiled eggs and a small glass of tea.

'How you doing, Willie?' Arne asked.

'Well, I'm not dead. Quite.'

'Yeah, they really did a job on you. Think you can eat something?'

'I'll try. Do they give you food like this all the time?'

'Hell no,' Popeye said. 'They never give it to you. Sometimes they come around with a cart to sell it to you. Not too often. But we get by. If you have some money you can get

49

things here. If you have to live on the fasoulia beans they feed you, you're in trouble.'

I ate hungrily. Arne examined my feet. Very carefully he lifted them up in his hands. He gently probed for broken bones.

'You've got to run some water on these,' he ordered.

'No way. They're killing me.'

'You've got to. It's necessary. If you don't, they'll swell up even worse. Otherwise you won't be able to walk for weeks.'

Popeye added his Harpo Marx whistle for emphasis.

They helped me over to the sink. They lifted my feet into a slow stream of cold water. I winced, but after the initial shock it felt good.

'Now you've got to go outside and walk in the yard.'

I looked at Arne in amazement. 'Are you crazy?'

'No. I told you. It's the only way. If you lay around on them they'll swell up real bad and you'll be a mess for weeks. But if you walk on them a little for the next few days they'll start to get better right away.' Again Popeye whistled in agreement.

'OK. OK.'

I rested a bit. Then with my arms around their shoulders I hobbled out of the cell, down the corridor, and into the yard.

It was a small concrete box without a top. Walls loomed fifteen feet high all around. Cigarette butts, orange peels, rumpled newspapers, rocks, sticks, broken glass littered the place. Dirty-looking men paced back and forth. Some marched up and down nervously. Others strolled around in tight little circles, staring at the ground. At the far end two men goose-stepped back and forth in unison.

I was amazed by the children. Screaming little Turkish street urchins played football – soccer – in the yard. They raced around the pacing men as though they were merely obstacles planted to make the game more difficult. Some of the men ignored the kids. Others grew angry at the slightest interruption of their routine.

The soccer ball bounced off Popeye's head. He turned and screamed something in Turkish. The kids ignored him.

'Who are the kids?' I asked Arne.

'They're from that *kogus*,' Arne said, pointing to the other

50

long cell block that fronted on this yard. 'We share the yard with them. That's the kids' *kogus*.'

'But what are they doing here? In prison?'

'Well, the Turks figure that the kids are relatively harmless. They won't stab the foreigners ... at least not very often. And the foreigners have a little bit of money. We help the kids out. They're great beggars. It's better for them and it's better for us like this.'

'Yes ... but what are their crimes?'

'Same as the other Turks,' Popeye said. 'The little bastards are horse thieves. Pickpockets. Rapists. Murderers.'

'What? But they're just kids.'

'They grow up fast here,' Popeye said. 'Hoo, boy, do they ever!'

We walked for a while, then Arne and Popeye left me alone. I slumped into a corner of the yard against the wall. I kept a wary eye on the kids lest they trip over my aching feet. There was something fascinatingly frightening about the kids. They played football with skill and energy. But there was a viciousness to their sport.

Charles came out into the yard. I watched him walk towards me in his old, faded blue jeans and ankle-high sneakers. He was tall and moved loosely, like a basketball player. Thick-rimmed glasses were on his nose. He had a notebook in his hands. He knelt down and examined my feet.

'*Getchmis olsun,*' he said.

'What's that mean?'

'May it pass quickly.'

'Yeah. Thanks, I sure hope it does.'

'I'm sorry you had to get beaten like that, Willie. But I'm glad you stood up to Emin. No American who's ever been in here has been a pussy. I'm glad you didn't break the image.'

'Better the image is broken than my feet.'

'No. It's good you stood up to him. If the Turks think they can push you around, they'll never stop hassling you. Now, at least, most people will leave you alone. They know you're willing to fight. You have to be, in here.'

I was glad he was trying to be friendly. 'Listen, Charles, I'm sorry about the *Esquire* baloney last night.'

'It's all right, man. Don't worry about it. Everyone who

comes in here has something to prove. It takes a while to learn. In a way you're lucky. You learned an important lesson last night. Everybody has to learn the hard way that the Turks can really screw you. And you got off easy, considering.'

'Easy?'

'Did they break any bones?'

'No.

'You got off easy. A couple of months ago they busted up one of the foreigners really bad. Was an Austrian guy name of Pepe. They broke the bones in his foot. He complained to the consul and they raised a stink. So the Turks are careful now. They try not to break up the foreigners too bad.

I guess I was lucky, but I certainly didn't feel it.

Charles said he had some writing to do. I stayed awhile. The cold stone of the yard soothed my feet. I sat against the wall in the brisk October morning air. Suddenly I noticed something unusual about the courtyard. Most of the yard was solid concrete. But a small rectangle in the centre was bare earth, and in the middle of the earth was some sort of drainage grate. I lifted myself up to get a better look at it.

'It's no good,' said a husky voice. I turned to see my next-door neighbour. 'The hole's big enough to squeeze into, but under the ground it narrows. There's no way you could get through.'

'I was just curious.'

'Look,' he lowered his voice. 'I'm sorry about what happened with the blankets. This is just your first day. You already saw what happened your first night. So learn everything you can about this place right away. It's your only chance to survive. Your only chance to get out.'

'I don't know. I have this feeling that somehow I'm going to get off easy, make bail or something.'

'Yeah, well, just in case you don't, you better learn fast.'

His name was Johann Seiber. He was Austrian, sentenced to forty months for car smuggling. In Turkey, he explained, you always got a third off your sentence for good behaviour. So in reality his sentence was twenty-six and two-thirds months. He'd been inside for twenty-one months now and had less than half a year left. In the beginning he thought

52

constantly of escaping, he said. But somehow he never managed to pull it off. Now he was resolved to serve his final six months and go free legally. But he wanted me to go with him to the kitchen. He had something there to show me.

I groaned in pain as he helped me walk back inside the *kogus*. I sank down onto a bench in the small room at the front of the cell block – the same room I'd washed in the night before. There were three burners on a small gas stove. A prisoner worked at them. Water boiled in several pots. Johann walked over, slipped a few coins out of his pocket, and brought back two small glasses filled with hot, weak Turkish tea.

'This is horrible,' I said. 'Tastes awful.'

Johann sampled his own tea. 'It's not bad. Maybe a little better than average. Each month someone else gets to sell the tea. Some of them really make it weak. They get more money that way. You'll learn to like it.'

I wasn't convinced that I'd learn to like anything about this place. I knew now that it wasn't much better than the police lockup. No wonder Charles was upset at me the night before. How would anyone put up with the filth, the noise, the smells, the rotten slop of greasy bean soup I saw them ladling out for lunch?

Johann turned his back to the tea seller and nodded almost imperceptibly towards the back wall. I followed his gaze. There was a door, perhaps three feet square, cut into the wall.

'Dumbwaiter,' Johann whispered. 'They never use it. It's been broken for years. Ever since some revolution they had. The shaft runs between the basement and the second tier of cells.'

'What's in the basement?'

'You saw the room last night, remember?'

'Oh, yeah. How would you get out of there?'

'I don't know. But at least you'd be out of the cell block. Maybe if you bribed a guard or had a gun or something you could do it.'

'It must be risky to bribe a guard.'

'Well, yeah, but everybody does it. You'll learn what you

53

can buy around here with just a good pack of Marlbor s. Those damn Turkish cigarettes are terrible.'

We drank our tea and stared at the dumbwaiter.

'If I was really going to get it on,' Johann said suddenly, 'I think I'd go to Bakirkoy.'

'What's that?'

'Bakirkoy. It's the mental hospital. Turks escape from there all the time. Security must be real loose. Everybody says Bakirkoy's easy. Yeah, if I wasn't looking at just six months I'd go to Bakirkoy.'

'How would you get there?'

'Oh, I don't know. Bribe the prison doctor, or something. If you're really careful and really clever, you can arrange just about anything.'

Our conversation was interrupted by a commotion from the yard. Johann ran over to a corridor and looked out the window. I hobbled slowly behind him, stared out the barred window, and froze. In the yard was the swaggering guard who had pounded the club into my feet. There, too, was his friend with the salt-and-pepper hair. And a third man, small and dapper, dressed in a neat dark suit.

'Who's the big guard?' I asked.

'Hamid. They call him "the Bear". He's the chief guard. He's the only guard who carries a gun. Stay out of his way.'

'Too late.'

'Oh, yeah.'

'Who's the other guard?'

'Arief. They call him "the Bonebreaker". He's second in command to Hamid. Watch out for him, too.'

The two guards stood menacingly in front of a group of kids. But the small man in the suit barked out the questions. Suddenly he reached out and slapped one of the kids across the face.

'He's the worst of the bunch!' Johann muttered.

'Who?'

' "The Weasel". Mamur. The second director. He's the boss around here because the big director never bothers to come inside. If Mamur gets on your case, you've had it.'

Days passed. As my feet healed, my head began to pound. I still hadn't heard from the American consul, or the lawyer

I'd requested. I had no information about my case, or how long I'd be in jail before my trial came up. For all I knew, they were just going to leave me here to rot. Arne told me that the Turkish government was thinking about granting an amnesty to prisoners. He wasn't sure, however, that new prisoners would be included. There were so many questions I wanted to ask. Charles said the people from the consulate didn't come out too often.

I had no books, no writing paper, no money. I borrowed some paper from Charles and tried to write letters to friends. Letters were censored, though not very thoroughly, and I found it hard to express myself, knowing they'd be gone over. And what could I say? I was in jail, but I didn't know what was happening to me. I couldn't say whether I'd be out next week or next month. I scribbled off a note to Patrick and told him I couldn't keep our Halloween appointment at Loch Ness. I wrote another letter to Mom and Dad. Another to my brother Rob. And another to my sister Peg. The words came hard.

Each morning as I woke a choking fear gripped me by the throat. My body ached from the lumpy wood plank bed. The stink that filtered down from the second tier stung my nose. The chorus of coughing, hacking men reminded me all over again that I was living in a cage.

Slowly the strength returned to my legs and feet. I paced the cell each morning until Walter opened the door. Once out of the cell I waited impatiently until the sleepy guard came in and opened the door to the yard. Some days it was six-thirty. Other days not until eight o'clock. Nothing seemed to operate on a strict schedule. But whenever the door was opened, I immediately rushed outside. I sucked in the clear cold air. I stared at the open sky. There were no walls when I looked straight up. Just clouds and birds and blue winter mornings.

Finally, after more than a week of uncertainty, a guard called me one morning. 'Vilyum. Vilyum Hi-yes.' I had a visitor.

I was taken out of the *kogus* and through a corridor to a conference room with long tables and several chairs. My eyes latched onto the view outside the barred windows. There were rolling fields and green trees and great open distances. It was such a treat to gaze off into the distance without having a wall in front of my eyes.

Waiting for me at the table was a fleshy, grinning Turk. Thin black hair, heavily greased, was pushed back in a useless attempt to cover a bald spot. He rose quickly and rushed over to shake my hand.

'William Hayes,' he said in perfect English without a trace of accent. 'I am Necdet Yesil.'

My lawyer. At last.

'Sit down. Sit down.' He offered me an American cigarette. I accepted it nervously. Already I was picking up the prison habit of constantly puffing away on cigarettes. 'The American consul contacted me and I came out here to see you immediately. Is everything all right?'

'Well, no. What's going on? What's going to happen?'

'Don't worry,' he assured me. 'If we act *immediately*, we can get the right court, get the right judge, arrange everything just right. I think we can get you bail. At the very worst, maybe a twenty-month sentence. But I think we can get you bail.'

'I don't want any twenty-month sentence. I want out.'

'I know, I know. I think we can get you bail.' Yesil paused for effect. 'Can you raise the money?'

Sure I could. Couldn't I? I could borrow it from Dad. But would he lend it to me? I shuddered at the memory of our last angry meeting. I'd wanted so much to be on my own. Maybe Dad would leave me that way.

'How much is it going to cost?'

'Maybe twenty-five thousand lira.'

'In dollars?'

'Two thousand, maybe three thousand dollars.'

Somehow I'd get the money. I knew that. I'd make all sorts of promises to Dad if he'd just manage to raise the money. I'd pay him back for sure. I'd even agree to go back to college. Or get a job. Anything. Just to get out of this mess.

'Uh . . . how much money do you have now?' Yesil asked. 'We have to begin quickly.'

'Well, I have about $300. From my airline ticket. They told me they put it in the prison bank.'

'I need $250,' Yesil said abruptly. He pushed a paper in front of me.

My mind raced with thoughts of bail. I signed.

'Who was your visitor?' Johann asked when I returned to the *kogus*.

'My lawyer. He thinks I can get bail.'

'Uh huh.' Johann seemed unimpressed. 'Who is your lawyer?'

'His name is Yesil.'

'Yesil . . . Yesil. I think Max had Yesil for his lawyer.'

'Who's Max?'

'You know that horrible smell from above us? That's Max.'

Johann led me up to the second tier of the *kogus* into a cell directly above mine. The cell was dark, lit only by stray sunlight that filtered in from the corridor window. The bulb in the cell and the one outside in the corridor were both broken. Johann introduced me to Max Van Pelt, a scrawny Dutchman. He peered at me through thick glasses that were set crookedly over his nose I'd seen him briefly around the *kogus*, but never in the yard. He seemed preoccupied, uninterested in small talk. Johann introduced us and asked Max to tell me about Yesil.

Max padded over to his locker. He removed a spoon, a bottle of brown liquid, a candle, and a hypodermic needle. He lit the candle. Then he poured out a spoonful of the liquid. I looked at Johann. He motioned for me to wait.

Max held the spoon over the candle until the liquid bubbled and boiled. I recognized the thick, acrid smell that filtered down into my cell so often.

'What is that stuff?' I asked.

'*Gastro*,' Max said. 'Stomach medicine. Has codeine in it. Best I can do here. Sometimes I can get morphine, but not too often.'

Johann and I watched silently as Max finished cooking the liquid. A slimy black residue lay in the bottom of the spoon. The smell made me queasy. Carefully, so as not to waste a drop, Max sucked the filth up into the hypodermic needle.

'I was busted with this American chick,' Max said quietly.

'We tried to cross the border at Edirne, in the west. Near Greece. We had ten kilos of hash in our car. Yesil was our lawyer.'

Max fumbled with a piece of twine as he tied it around his arm for a tourniquet. Searching for an unused spot amid dirty, infected track marks, he finally plunged the needle into his arm. He pumped the black gunk into his body. Then he loosened the tourniquet. He looked me in the eyes.

'The chick's father came over . . . from America,' he muttered. 'Paid Yesil a whole lot of money. Yesil said everything would be fine.'

Max paused. His eyes took on a faraway stare. 'What?' He looked confused.

'Yesil,' Johann prompted.

'Yesil,' Max repeated. 'Yesil, said it'd be OK. We . . . uh . . . went to court. Yesil . . . bastard . . . stood up . . . said the girl was innocent . . . said it was all my idea.' Max's head began to bob back and forth. 'Girl went free,' he said.

'What about you?' I asked.

Silence.

'What about you?' I repeated.

'What?'

'What's your sentence?'

Max slowly dropped his head forward until it rested upon his knees. His voice was muffled, almost inaudible, as he spoke.

'Thirty years,' he said.

CHAPTER SIX

My feet healed slowly. Each day I hobbled around the yard as much as I could. It measured fourteen by thirty-two paces. How good it would feel to walk in a straight line and not have to stop at the ugly grey wall. I knew now why caged animals pace.

Emin, the trusty, soon found the big metal key to my cell. At nine each evening I was locked into the tiny room where my pacing was limited to five steps up, five steps back. I slept fitfully in the cold cell.

In the mornings I woke with the dawn, several hours before Emin's assistant Walter came around to unlock the cells. I lay there huddled under my blanket. Drifting from a pleasant dream into reality never ceased to be a shock. I kept my eyes closed for a while so I wouldn't see the bars in front of me.

I could hardly breathe in that tiny locked room.

Then one morning a visit card arrived for me at the little porthole in the metal corridor door. It was probably the consul or Yesil. It was enjoyable to walk the long straight length of the corridor without having to turn after the thirty-second pace. The guards at the checkpoints seemed friendly. They tried to speak with me. I smiled and nodded my head. I mumbled 'America' and 'New York' to whatever they asked.

The guard ushered me into a visiting room where the consul stood waiting. Beside him stood a white-haired blue-eyed New York Irishman. His face filled my eyes. We moved towards each other. Our hands locked. His left hand grabbed my arm as though it would never let go. We stared into each other's moistening eyes. He looked so tired. Pain was all over his face. Never before did I realize how much I loved my very own father.

'Dad . . . I'm sorry . . . I . . .'

'Don't worry about it,' he interrupted in a quivering voice. He forced a smile. 'I can punch you in the nose later. Right now we've got to work on getting you out of here. Are you all right?'

'Yeah, under the circumstances.'

'OK. Then let me tell you what's happening on this end.'

We sat down at the table with the consul, and Dad spurted out information.

'I've been in contact with the State Department people. They gave me the names of two Turkish lawyers. They're the best possible people for the situation. I'm going to see them this afternoon.'

'I've already talked to one lawyer. His name is Yesil.'

'We'll get rid of him. I want you to have the best for this. It's important.'

'Be careful, Dad. I've heard a lot of bad stories about the Turkish lawyers.'

'OK. This is why I'm confident about these guys. They're recommended by our people.'

A pause. 'It sounds expensive.'

'Well, don't worry about it now. You can pay me back later when this is over. Right now money doesn't count.'

We both cleared our throats and tried to keep back the tears.

'So . . . uh . . . how're you doing?' I asked. 'Where are you staying?'

'The Hilton.'

'How's Mom?'

'Well, of course she's worried. She would have liked to come see you too, but she didn't think she could stand it.'

'Yeah.' I glanced out the windows towards the green fields. 'Tell her not to worry. I'm all right. Tell her I'll be home by Christmas.'

'. . . Yeah.'

We talked for a while, maybe an hour. Dad said he'd come out again tomorrow after he met with the lawyers. He asked me what I needed, what he could bring me. I felt so bad asking him to buy things for me. He's a proud man. I knew what it meant to him to be here. I knew how it hurt for him to see his son a prisoner, locked up for trying to smuggle hashish onto an airplane. But he brushed all that aside. I needed him. He was there.

60

I found myself filled with a new respect for his ordered existence. Dad knew how to command a situation. He knew how to get things done. That was the kind of man I needed working for me.

Before he left that day we compiled a list . . . pyjamas, toothbrush, note pads, chocolate bars. He said he'd put a hundred dollars into the prison bank for me so I could buy extra food when the cart came around, and maybe some for my friends.

Dad rose to say goodbye.

We shook hands.

I swallowed and worked hard at keeping a smile.

'Have a beer for me at the Hilton,' I said.

'Maybe two,' he replied. 'See you tomorrow, Will.'

'Right, Dad. Thanks.' I ached to walk out the door with him into the sunlight.

Dad came back the next day with news of the lawyers. He had hired Dr Beyaz and Dr Siya, two of Istanbul's top criminal attorneys. They felt they might be able to get me off with a twenty-month sentence, or perhaps even arrange bail. 'If I get bail I get out of the country,' I explained to Dad. 'I hear it's easy to cross the border into Greece.'

He had learned more details from the consulate. The Turks, it seemed, had become concerned over a recent wave of terrorist skyjackings. They had decided to hold unscheduled searches at the airport. I was one of their first successes. I was a showpiece.

Dad brought me a package of food and candy, writing paper, a toothbrush, and a pair of dark green pyjamas with thick black vertical stripes on them.

'These look like a Sing-Sing uniform,' I said.

He smiled and nodded his head. 'I thought you might appreciate them.'

He visited me every day for about a week. We shared bits of memories. I was hungry for news from home. New York seemed so far away now.

'Mom been to bingo lately?'

Dad laughed. 'Sure. You know her. Nothing stops her

61

from going to bingo.' He turned serious. 'It's good for her now. It takes her mind off all this.'

'Do the neighbours know, Dad?'

'No. I don't think so. We don't talk about it to anyone but the family. I've told a lot of people you're in a hospital in Europe.'

I changed the subject. 'So how do you like exotic Istanbul?'

'Well,' he said, 'it's an interesting city, but,' his voice lowered, '. . . to tell you the truth, I think the food is lousy. My God, the crap they sell in those little restaurants. I went out to eat in one of them the first night. I'm still afraid to get too far from a toilet.'

'Toilet? You mean they have toilets there? We've only got a hole in the floor.'

'Right. I learned about that the hard way. And no paper, either, right?'

'Right.'

'But I'm staying at the Hilton. Eating there now, too.

I laughed. 'Uh huh. And we call *this* place the Sagmalcilar Hilton.'

We talked a lot about hashish. Dad was uncomfortable about the subject at first. He seemed genuinely surprised when I explained that it was a derivative of marijuana.

'I don't think I approve of marijuana, either,' he said, 'but at least most people seem to think it's not too dangerous. If you felt you had to do this thing, why didn't you just do it with marijuana?'

'Hashish is more concentrated,' I explained. 'It's easier to hide.'

'Oh.' He was silent. 'It was stupid, Billy. Stupid.'

'I know.'

'Look. Don't do anything else stupid. Just sit here. Let me work with the lawyers. We'll get you out. OK?'

'OK.'

We discussed all the possible legal strategies. I told him Johann's advice to get to Bakirkoy Mental Hospital where escape was easy. Dad was worried about escape. But the lawyers had told him that it might be beneficial to get an official 'crazy report' from Bakirkoy. With a 'crazy report' in

62

my records I couldn t be convicted of any crime. I didn t feel any crazier (or any more sane) than the average human being, but I had one thing going for me. The United States Army had certified me psychologically unfit. That was quite a recommendation. Dad said he wanted to keep as many 'possibility tracks' open as we could. He agreed to send the army report to Beyaz and Siya.

Too soon, it was time for Dad to go home. He said he'd return in two or three months, or whenever it seemed that he could help. He told me to stay calm. I'd go to court in three weeks. We'd see what happened then. He forced a smile and said goodbye.

Beyaz and Siya came out several times in the next few weeks to prepare the case. Beyaz was a pudgy little man less than five feet tall with white, wispy hair along the edges of his balding head. He had thick bushy eyebrows. Siya was tall and pear-shaped. He let Beyaz do most of the talking Neither of them spoke good English so we needed a translator. This job was eagerly filled by the grinning Yesil, who refused to let my father take him off the case. Yesil had $250 of my money. He was willing to stick around to see if he could get more. Anyway, we needed a translator.

The lawyers wanted me to emphasize that I just wanted the hashish for my own use. In truth I'd planned to sell a good bit of it, but Beyaz and Siya told me to lie about that. The judge would probably see through the story. But we had to keep the court transcript clean. It would mean a lot when the high court in Ankara, the capital, reviewed the case.

I sat in Charles's cell the night before the trial. Arne, Charles and I discussed my testimony.

'First of all, keep it simple,' Charles said. 'Everything you say has to be translated into Turkish. You have to make each word clear. It's a weird system here. You're guilty until proven innocent.

'You're kidding.'

'Hell, no! Maybe it's not that way on the books, but that's the way it is. These guys will even bust you for a traffic accident.'

'No. Come on. For a traffic accident?'

'They busted a Bulgarian guy for an accident. He spent six months here.'

'What happened in the accident? Anybody die?'

'Yeah. The driver of the other car.'

'Well, there you go. It was a serious accident. Maybe he deserved it.'

Charles looked tired. 'Right. Maybe he did. Except that he was eating lunch in the Pudding Shoppe when a drunken Turk smashed into his parked car.'

'What? He wasn't even in the car?'

Charles nodded.

'They gave him six months?'

He nodded again.

'Uh . . . well . . . maybe I should practise my testimony a bit more.'

He nodded a third time. 'Simple,' he reminded me. 'Gotta keep it simple for these simpletons. Short sentences. Compact ideas. If you get complicated you'll lose them.'

'I've got to make a good impression,' I said. 'I've just *got* to.'

'Damn right,' Charles agreed.

'Maybe they'll give me bail.'

Arne looked up from his book. 'Maybe,' he agreed quietly.

Popeye poked his head into the cell. 'Stop thinking about bail. Just hope you get off with four or five years.'

'You're a real positive thinker, aren't you?' I was annoyed.

He looked at me hard for a moment, then laughed. 'William, William. You just don't know. And you don't like me, I can tell. Doesn't matter. But I also tell you we'll be friends this time next year. For your sake I hope you're gone, but I think you're going to eat a lot of fasoulia beans before you taste a hamburger again.'

There was an uncomfortable silence. Finally Arne spoke. 'Yes, well, no sense worrying today about what might happen tomorrow.'

I looked at Arne. He sat there so quietly, with his long thin hands folded together in his lap. I really didn't understand his calm acceptance of his fate. He spoke again.

'But tonight you have to get ready for court.'

Popeye remembered. 'Right. That's why I came to see you. You got a good pair of pants?'

I shrugged.

'Wear these tomorrow.' He handed me a pair of dark green slacks. I'd have to hitch them up high, but they'd be an improvement over my blue jeans.

'Thanks.'

Popeye whistled. 'They're my lucky pants. I wore them at my trial.'

'But you got fifteen years.'

'*Only* fifteen.'

'That's lucky?'

'Hoo, boy!' Popeye laughed. 'Lucky, lucky, lucky.' He ran off down the hall.

'Don't let him bother you,' Arne said. 'He's just a little stir crazy. He always expects the worst. But he means well. He just doesn't want you to be disappointed tomorrow.'

The others helped me complete my outfit. Charles loaned me a shirt and tie. Arne gave me a coat. Johann stopped by with a pair of shiny black shoes. It was an international ensemble.

The next morning soldiers took three truckloads of prisoners to court. They unloaded us back at the room where I'd done my juggling act. The air was thick with the smoke of cheap tobacco. I went to the bathroom. The door squeaked on rusty hinges as I pushed it open. The floor inside was wet and slimy. Over in one corner an old blanket was spread over the stone. Several well-dressed Turks squatted on it in a circle. They were rolling dice. Money flowed freely across the blanket amid shouts of excitement and anger. The room stank from the toilets. The air reeked of hashish.

'Joe!' someone shouted. I recognized the smiling Turk who befriended me at the police station the night of my arrest. Again he offered me hashish. I refused as politely as I could. I wanted my head clear in the courtroom. He shrugged, took a generous swig from a vodka bottle and continued his game.

This man's influence amazed me. I couldn't understand how he got away with all this.

Out in the waiting room someone called my name. Two

soldiers handcuffed me and led the way through a maze of underground passages and up several flights of dark, narrow stairs. When we reached an upper level they unchained me and placed me alone in a small room, not much bigger than a cupboard. There were no windows. It was bare except for a heating pipe. The walls were covered with more graffiti than a New York subway train. I found one small blank spot took out a pen and wrote, *William Hayes, New York, 11/10/70.*

Then I was called into court and placed in the prisoner s dock. My eyes immediately settled upon a good-looking girl in the spectators' seats. It had been a long time since I'd seen a woman. She had a yellow legal pad on her lap. I loved her legs.

Beyaz and Siya sat at a table in front of me. Yesil babbled something to them. I looked over to the spot where Charles had told me the prosecutor would sit. I was concerned about him. I didn't want a Turkish F. Lee Bailey tearing me apart on cross examination. He caught my gaze and scowled at me behind dark green glasses.

The chief judge walked in. He solemnly took his place behind the high desk up on the podium in the centre of the three-man panel. His long black robes had a flaring scarlet collar. He had a kindly, if sagging, face under his short grey hair.

A young man sat behind an ancient typewriter on a small table in front of the podium. For about twenty minutes various people stood up, chattered in Turkish, and sat back down. The typewriter clattered behind the sound of their words. Beyaz and Siya both spoke briefly. The American consul said something. The three judges conferred. Finally Yesil motioned for me to stand up. 'The judge wants you to explain your story,' he said.

'I am a student at Marquette University,' I began Yesil translating. 'That is in Milwaukee, a city in the United States of America. I am studying English. I am almost ready to graduate. I only need to finish my thesis. I want to be a writer. I have been smoking hashish for several years. I believe that it stimulates my mind and helps my creative powers. When I smoke I write better. I was travelling in Europe on vacation. I wanted to bring back some hashish

66

because it is so expensive in the United States and I don't have much money. And I wanted enough hashish to last me until I finish my thesis. I heard that it is very cheap in Istanbul, so I came here by train. I wanted to buy a small amount – maybe half a kilo. I spoke to some Turkish boys with long hair. I said I wanted a small amount. They took me to a room and showed me a lot of hashish. I have never seen so much hashish. They said they would give me two kilos for $200. In the United States this would be very, very cheap. I thought, well, I'll take these two kilos and they will last me a long time.'

The judge was silent for a few moments. Hashish stories had floated in and out of his courtroom for decades. We carried on the conversation through Yesil.

'You were taking this back for your own personal use?' he asked.

'Yes.'

'You weren't going to sell any of it?

'Oh, no,' I lied.

'Were you going to give any of it away to your friends?'

The lawyers had coached me on this one. 'I think hashish is a very strong thing and it could be dangerous for some people. I think it's a good thing for me because it stimulates my creative powers and helps me to write. But for other people maybe it's not such a good thing. So I don't know. I think each person has to decide for himself if he should smoke or not. So I don't want to give any to my friends. Maybe for them it wouldn't be so good.'

'Two kilos is a lot of hashish to smoke yourself.'

'Well, I didn't want two kilos. I only wanted half a kilo. But then they offered me all of it so I was foolish. I decided I'd take it. Then I'd have a lot when I got back to the United States.'

'But not to sell it?'

'No. To smoke it myself.'

'Do you smoke a lot?'

'Yes. I've been smoking it for years.'

The judge paused. He conferred with the judges on either side of him. Then he spoke to Beyaz. Suddenly he fired another question at Yesil, and the translation caught me off guard.

'What is the subject of your thesis?' the judge wanted to know.

No one had coached me for that question. I wasn't really writing a thesis. An answer popped into my mind. 'The effects of drugs on literature and music in contemporary America,' I blurted out.

Yesil stared at me in disbelief, then slowly translated. There was a moment of calm in the courtroom. The chief judge suppressed a grin, then slowly shook his head at his colleagues. He set a trial date for December.

There was nothing I could do but wait, and as I waited I slowly settled into the drab grey routine that is prison. Charles, Popeye, Arne, and Johann had all been through the same process. The shock of the arrest, the stupid hope of the miracle of a quick release, then the sinking into the reality of prison. In his own way, each man helped me adjust to life in the *kogus*.

Charles worked hard, almost in a fury. He kept to a rigid schedule. Throughout the night, locked into his cell, he laboured over his short stories and poems. He tried to convince me of the need to keep to my own schedule in prison, to have a plan for each day That way time had a positive meaning to it rather than just a negative one.

'You can drift away in here and never know you're gone,' Charles warned me. 'You can fade so far out that you don't know where you're at or where anything else is at, either. And you don't come back to reality for days or weeks or months.'

'Some people,' he said quietly, 'get so lost in here they don't ever find their way out.'

I thought of Max, but was Charles describing himself, too, without knowing it?

'It can get real spooky inside,' said Charles.

I nodded.

Popeye was the eternal pessimist. He repeatedly warned me to expect a long stay in Sagmalcilar. He was wrong, I felt certain, but his attitude balanced against my optimism. He

68

tried to mask his gloomy outlook on life behind a happy-go-lucky façade. His laughter and his Harpo Marx whistle constantly disturbed whatever peace there was in the *kogus*. As he'd predicted, I found myself liking him. His constant chatter helped pass the time.

Arne taught me perhaps the most important lesson of all. Arne was a most unusual prisoner. There were spies and informers all around, eager to gain an advantage over you by learning anything that might give them a lever. For this reason alone, people inside were suspicious of each other. Trust was not easily given. The result was that when your body was locked up, you imprisoned your feelings, too. Arne understood the need to protect his feelings. But he equally understood the need to express them. In long evening talks in his cell, he cautioned me not to close off my emotions. If I did, he warned, I'd have real problems relating to people. Both in prison and out.

Johann was the one who had made no adjustment to prison life at all. From his first moments he had thought only of escape. Johann was a spur-of-the-moment person, however. Long-range planning was difficult for him. He never seemed to follow through on his dreams of a scam, an escape. Now his sentence was so short that escape was no longer practical for him.

'But *you've* got to do something, Willie,' he urged. 'Don't trust the courts. Don't trust the Turkish lawyers. Don't even trust your friends. Just count on yourself.'

Sampling all of this advice I created my own routine. Morning became a ritual. I learned to wake myself at five-thirty. For about two years I'd been experimenting with the postures and positions of yoga. Now I really worked at it. I lay on my belly, my back arched stiffly, feet raised off the ground. I held the position for several minutes. Then I relaxed, breathing deeply. Next, I sat on the floor. Slowly I pulled one leg up towards my head. With practice I was able to bring my leg up behind my neck. The discipline of the postures woke my body. It woke my mind.

As soon as the cells were unlocked and the yard door opened, I raced outside into the cool air. Usually I was in time to watch the sun rise over the artificial horizon of the high stone wall. I'd sit against the wall and meditate or draw pictures. I studied the shadow patterns in the yard. I watched the pigeons whirl around above me. When the wind was right I could smell the sea. If I listened hard enough I thought I could hear it. After breakfast I'd write letters or play chess or read a book. In the afternoon I'd join one of the football or volley-ball games in the crowded, cramped yard. In the evenings I'd talk with friends or just sit around thinking and dreaming. At night after our cells were locked I began to carve chess pieces out of soap, using my nail file as a knife.

But even though I was settling down, I remembered Johann's words. I kept my eyes and ears open.

Evening. Arne and I sat with Charles in his cell in the upper tier of the *kogus*. Arne strummed his guitar. Charles slapped his bongo drums. We relaxed with our thoughts. The lights flickered, then dimmed, then went dark. Arne lit a candle and placed it on the rickety wooden tabletop.

'It happens a lot,' he explained. '*Turk-mali*.'

'What's that mean?' I asked.

' "Made in Turkey." It's our own little joke. Nothing seems to work right here. Turk electricity isn't very reliable. You'll have to get some candles next time they come around.'

'They sell candles here?'

'Yeah. In that cart that comes with the supplies. I think the Turks flick out the lights on purpose, just so people will buy candles.'

'How long do the lights stay out?' I asked curiously. Maybe a blackout would provide a good escape opportunity.

Charles must have noticed the edge of my question. He answered without missing a beat on the bongo. 'Not long enough.'

'For what?' I asked innocently.

'For anything,' he replied. 'Sometimes they're out for twenty minutes, sometimes for twenty seconds. You never know.' He tapped out a rhythm on the drum. 'And we hear that the soldier patrols around the wall are immediately doubled when the lights go out.'

'Well, anyway, the darkness is nice for a change.'

70

'So keep quiet and dig it.'

'Right.'

For some reason the darkness caused prisoners to lower the volume on their battery-powered radios. Arne picked his guitar softly. A rare moment of tranquillity settled over the *kogus*. I sat watching the patterns of the candle flame flickering against the wall. I was warm. My belly was full. It was pleasant in the darkness with my friends. I forgot about the bars and the court and the big question mark hanging over my head. Sharing the quiet moment was enough.

Ten minutes later, all too soon, the lights came back on. With them, the constant undertone of noise in the *kogus* began again. Radios blared. Prisoners argued. The kids yelled across the yard. We tried to savour the mood a bit longer. But with the darkness gone, the magic was gone. We were in prison again.

Suddenly there was commotion in the children's *kogus*. It drew us into the corridor. From the windows in the upper tier we looked down into the bottom room of the children's *kogus*. It was identical to ours except there were no individual cells. It was just two long rectangular rooms, one above the other like an army barracks.

We watched the children scurrying downstairs, prompted along by several yelling guards. They lined up. None of them seemed to want to be up front near the door.

Then I saw Mamur the Weasel, staring in icy silence. Arief the Bonebreaker and Hamid the Bear flanked him. The shouting and turmoil of the upstairs room ended at the bottom of the stairs. Each kid fell silent at the sight of Mamur.

There was an exceptionally young child there, cowering at Mamur's side, holding his hand.

'Who's that little kid next to Mamur?' I asked.

'That's his own son,' Arne said. 'He's around the prison a lot.'

The boy was only about five years old. He seemed frightened at the commotion his father's presence caused. Mamur stood motionless until the children had all been routed out of their hiding places upstairs and lined up before him. The children were silent. The guards fell silent. Mamur gave his son over to Hamid. Hamid's huge paw engulfed the little boy's hand. Mamur slowly paced out in front of the straggled line of children. He stared up and down for a moment. Then he spat out one word that ripped the silence apart.

'PIS!' he screamed. It means filthy or obscene.

The whole line of kids shuddered.

Mamur waved his arms in the air. He marched up and down the line screaming into faces. He seemed to be questioning individual kids, slapping and shaking and screaming at them. One crying child pointed at some others. Mamur separated about five of them. He dragged them out of line by the hair and threw them to the waiting guards. He barked a command. The rest of the children fled to the other end of the *kogus*.

Guards threw their victims to the floor. Other guards grabbed a long wooden bench with metal legs. The kids screamed and struggled. The guards slapped them down. They managed to clamp the rungs of the bench over the upturned legs of the children. The kids were pinned on their backs on the floor, bent over double, their squirming feet in the air. A guard sat on either end of the bench.

Most of us in the *turist kogus* were at the windows, watching. News travels fast on the prison grapevine. Ziat, the prisoner who ran the tea shop, relayed the information. 'They raped one of the new kids while the lights were out.'

Mamur removed his coat and handed it to a guard. He pulled off his cuff links and rolled up his sleeves. He loosened his tie. The kids on the ground were silent again, except for a few whimpering cries. Mamur grabbed a *falaka* stick and smashed it down across a pair of wriggling feet.

My own feet ached at the memory.

He flailed away at the screaming, struggling children. The guards on the bench spread their legs to keep balanced. Other guards leaned on the ends. The kids squirmed and struggled, wailing beneath Mamur's rage. He beat them on the feet, on the buttocks, on their legs. He paused occasionally to yell something at the other children huddled against the wall in the back of the room.

He worked his way up and down the line in an absolute frenzy. One boy wriggled free. Mamur was on him instantly.

72

The boy fell to the floor and cringed. Mamur smashed the boy's upturned hands. He beat his legs.

Finally the Weasel finished. He threw down the *falaka* stick and nodded to the guards. They picked up the bench. The children lay sobbing on the floor. Mamur stood there for a moment, catching his breath. He glared at the kids. He turned, received his jacket from a guard, put it over one arm, and walked across to his son. The boy still stood half-hidden behind Hamid. The second director of Sagmalcilar prison grabbed his son by the hand. Silently he walked out of the *kogus*.

CHAPTER SEVEN

There is a Turkish expression: *sula bula* (pronounced 'shirla birla') which means 'like this, like that'.

Everything about Sagmalcilar *ceza evi* ('house of punishment') and its three thousand inmates was *sula bula*. It wasn't so good and it wasn't so bad. There were all sorts of rules and there were no rules at all. There were guards who couldn't leave certain areas and prisoners who roamed freely about the prison. Gambling was illegal, but all the Turks rolled dice and most of the foreigners played poker. There were strict laws against drugs and prisoners could buy hashish, opium, LSD, morphine, and pills of every shape, colour, and description. Homosexuality was a legal and moral crime but it was rampant in the prison. The very guards who were supposed to be in control of this situation seemed to gain sexual pleasure from binding and beating a man with his pants off. Money was not allowed inside. A prisoner could draw credit from his account or he could carry special prison markers. Despite the rule, most longtime prisoners had cash hidden among the belongings. Or they carried it in their jockstraps. Depending upon the changing moods of the prison authorities and the shifting situations of fate, it was an easy place to do time, or it was hell.

Just as there was a hierarchy in the administration, headed by Mamur, Arief, and Hamid, there was also a hierarchy of prisoners. At the very top were the big-time gangsters, the Turkish counterpart of the American Mafiosi. These heavyweight criminals were called *kapidiye*. They were feared and respected both outside and inside prison. They were rich and ruthless. A prison sentence seemed nothing more than a minor inconvenience to most *kapidiye*. No matter the charge, a little money here and there, a new court, a new judge, new statements, new papers, new police records or doctors' reports and they were free. They would spend a year, maybe eighteen months, inside. No more.

While they were inside they lived like kings. They didn't

want to escape because then they'd have to leave the country and all their power was in Turkey. They spent their time running the prison rackets – gambling, drugs, contraband items. The profits were high, but so were the risks. Violence was the accepted method of competition among various power groups.

Just a rung below the *kapidiye* were a great number of lesser gangsters. They were the up-and-coming criminals, brash young killers out to make reputations for themselves. Murderers were highly regarded. Murder is considered an *erkek* ('manly') crime in Turkey.

Common street thieves and pickpockets were near the bottom of the social structure. But right at the bottom, as far as the Turks were concerned, were the foreign, non-Moslem, hippie hashish smokers.

I couldn't quite get used to it all. But I tried. The morning and evening yoga seemed to help. I also developed my own particular form of meditation. After yoga in the morning I'd sit on my bed in the darkness and listen to the sounds of the prison waking around me.

The stillness before daybreak was the best time. I could hear the hollow flapping wingbeats of the pigeons as they pushed off the eaves above our *kogus*. Sometimes the low mournful call of a ship out in the harbour floated in on the dawn. I'd dream of the sea. Of riding a steamer down the Marmara until we came to the Greek islands. I could drift out of the prison so easily on my thoughts. But when the other prisoners woke I couldn't maintain my good mood. I had to watch my temper carefully. Moods could transfer from individuals to whole groups without anyone even realizing it until too late. The *kogus* was an emotional tinder-box. Fights could happen at any time.

Since eating was one of the few sensual experiences in prison, it was taken very seriously, and our little kitchen was a focal point of much of the trouble. There was a bottled-gas stove provided by the prison authorities. Tea and coffee were brewed there. Food was prepared when food was available. The small flat metal stove, with its three burners, was presided over by the *chi-gee*, *chi* meaning 'tea' in Turkish, and *gee* being 'guy' who worked the *chi*. The *chi-gee* bought packages of tea, coffee, and sugar from the prison authorities at inflated prices, which he passed on to us. Prison was literally a captive market. Everyone drank endless quantities of tea and coffee. Water wasn't always available and wasn't very good anyway.

The *chi-gee* sold his brew in small glasses for fifty *kurus* apiece (about three cents). He worked twelve to fourteen hours per day during his month. But he made a good profit, especially if he brewed weak tea and coloured it with carbonate.

A prisoner named Ziat was running the *chi* shop when I arrived. Although Johann told me the job was supposed to rotate, Ziat was still brewing tea in December. Ziat was a swarthy-looking Jordanian. He was about my height, five-foot-nine, but much broader. He had yellow-stained teeth. I distrusted his grin at first sight. Johann told me that Ziat loved nothing in the world more than money, and there were constant arguments over the quality of his *chi*.

By the time the guard came in to unlock the yard door and call out for the Iranian prisoner who carried the bread up from the prison kitchen each morning, the tea was ready. Other prisoners were up by then. They arrived at the stove with bits of green pepper or onions or maybe an egg to fry. A line formed. Inevitably, the men pushed and shoved. Ziat was reluctant to give up use of the burners. He made tea on two of them and only allowed one for cooking. You might only have an egg to fry. But in front of you someone else would slowly fry onions or boil water in a big pot to cook some potatoes. Then Ziat might let one of his friends use one of the other burners. This would spark an argument. Prisoners speaking a variety of tongues chattered and complained. If the circumstances were right, the *chi* shop turned into a minor battlefield. Glasses would fly. Maybe a knife would flash. The guards would rush in. It happened all the time.

I learned a lot about Ziat from Johann. Ziat had been a police informer on the outside. He spoke Turkish, English, and German almost as well as his native Arabic. He'd meet *turists* in the Pudding Shoppe or around Sultan Ahmet square and ask if they'd like drugs. He'd make all the arrangements

76

with them. Then he'd contact the police. After the *turist* received the hashish or whatever else he was buying, Ziat left and the police arrived. The *turist* went to jail. The police had another arrest. Ziat got paid off, either in money or in goods.

But according to Johann, Ziat became greedy. He held back seventeen kilos of opium in a deal that involved a Turkish *kapidiye*. He received a five-year sentence.

Several prisoners were in Sagmalcilar due to Ziat's treachery. He was a very careful man. He'd already been stabbed once, fifteen months ago.

His greediness surfaced immediately in prison. As an informer, he had many influential contacts. By the time I arrived he was the major supplier of drugs for the *turist kogus*. He was a good friend of Arief and of Mamur. They warned him whenever there was going to be a 'control' – an unexpected search by guards or soldiers. He always managed to protect his supplies of drugs. And no one could find the money he must have accumulated.

The amount of cash flowing around prison surprised me. At first I drew prison markers from my account and used them to buy things from the food cart. Then I discovered the endless world of prison gambling. Poker was forbidden, but we played constantly when the guards weren't around. Even the soccer or volley-ball games in the yard were often played for money. Like the others, I was soon walking around with cash stuffed into my jockstrap. It was the one place the prison guards seldom searched – maybe there was some sort of rule against it.

I found myself drifting more heavily into smoking hashish. It was easy to get from Ziat. Reality was stagnant. The drug produced a haze that helped the time pass. The water pipe near the toilet hole in my room was *Turk-mali*. It was broken, rusty, and corroded. But the inside was just large enough so that I could slip in a small piece of hashish. The Moslem guards considered the toilet area *ayip*, 'unclean', so it was a most effective hiding place. They never stuck their fingers up that dirty pipe.

I was becoming a con.

It seemed that everyone was always waiting for something in prison. You waited for the cell to be unlocked and for the bread to come in the morning. You waited for the food at noon. You waited for the water to come on so you could use the toilet hole or wash your face. You waited for visits. You waited for court.

You waited to go free.

And every day you waited for mail. It usually came in the late afternoon. At the shouted call of *Mektup* a score of prisoners would bolt down the stairs. A guard or one of the Turkish trusties would stuff letters and packages through the small square hole in the metal corridor door. Someone would read the envelopes and shout out names. There was always confusion. The postal system was *Turk-mali* too. Many letters from the outside world never seemed to arrive. Or they came weeks late. Often the stamps were missing.

My correspondence gradually grew. Sometimes I focused the whole day upon the possibility of receiving a letter. Any letter. If nothing arrived the disappointment was bitter. I felt so isolated, locked away in a strange country with such a different culture. I felt forgotten. Days and days would pass without a letter and each day I'd stand alone by the door after all the mail had been given out.

Then sometimes whole groups of letters would arrive at once. I'd soar on them. Dad wrote regularly, even though his letters arrived unpredictably. Sometimes Mom added a line or two, to tell me that she loved me. Mom never did like to talk much, but her support was always there in the background. Dad would tell me about winning a trophy in the company handball tournament. Rob and Peggy, my brother and sister, also wrote. Rob's grades at Brown University were good. He thought maybe Dad could get him a job with Metropolitan when he graduated. Peg gushed about boyfriends, cheer-leading, new clothes. Each letter was packed with little details of everyday life. And that hurt. Back on Long Island life was going on. I ripped each letter open eagerly, then lingered over it as the ache grew. And between the lines of each letter was their poorly hidden anguish over the lost member of the family.

There were other letters, too. Many of my old friends at Marquette wrote. And a letter finally arrived from Patrick. He'd been working on a tuna boat off the Oregon coast for the past several months, catching fish during the day and writing mad poetry at night, so it had been a while before he heard of my predicament. He wanted to know all about the legal situation. And then he wrote, 'Have you read *The Count of Monte Cristo* lately?' Typically Patrick. He always leaned towards the swashbuckling solution to things. If it ever came down to it, I knew I could count on him.

Then one day I was surprised by an envelope addressed in fine-lined, loose-flowing handwriting. It brought a quick stirring deep inside me. I had grown up with Lillian Reed. She'd been my date for the freshman dance at St Anthony's High School several centuries before. She wore a red velvet dress that night, I remembered. Dad drove us to the dance. We were in love off and on during our teen years, then somehow drifted apart. So many years were bridged by the envelope in my hands, the image in my mind. Her long brown hair framing deep brown eyes. A late summer evening, in that suspended time between high school graduation and the beginning of college. Soft young love and whispered words. We had both dreamed of travelling the world. But Lillian got married. To a wrong guy. It lasted less than a year. She was in Cambridge now, working as a legal secretary at Harvard. Her divorce had just become official.

She touched me with her words. Her thoughts reached around the globe and warmed me. I read her letter several times before writing her a long emotional reply that night. I encouraged her to pick up the pieces of her life and live it fully. We both had our problems. It was strange how two old friends could both mess up their lives so badly. Maybe we could help one another.

Court was set for 19 December. I hoped that something definite would happen. If I didn't make bail I wanted a sentence Then at least I would know. Rumours of amnesty were stronger now. Some prisoners thought the government might drop ten years off everyone's sentence. If the court sentenced me – even for ten years – maybe I'd be free soon anyway.

Again I rehearsed my story carefully the night before the trial. Again my friends helped me dress. Everything depended upon a good impression. If I could make bail, maybe I'd even be home for Christmas.

The morning arrived. Soldiers drove me to court. I was more nervous this time. Prison life was becoming more difficult to handle. This day was one of the most important in my life. I wished the proceedings were in English so I could follow them.

My lawyers were in their booth once again. Beyaz and Siya nodded politely as I entered the room. Yesil gave me a big reassuring grin. I smiled back. I recognized several other faces – the consul and some of the spectators. The girl with the yellow legal pad and the nice legs was there.

There was more unintelligible Turkish conversation between my lawyers and the judge. I sat quietly, prepared for a long session.

The prosecutor got up and made an impassioned speech to the court. Suddenly, before I realized what was happening, the soldiers chained my hands together and started to take me away.

'What happened?' I yelled across to Yesil. 'Why are they chaining me? Why are they taking me back already?'

'It's not important,' he said.

'What do you mean it's not important! I want bail. I don't want to spend one more night in that place.'

'Yes, yes. OK, we'll be out to talk to you tomorrow.'

'What did the prosecutor say?' I asked. 'What's going on?'

'It's not important, just technical things.'

The soldiers pulled at my arms.

'Like what?'

'Well, he presented to the court what he wanted, you know, what he wanted to charge you with.'

If my hands had been free I might have grabbed Yesil by the lapels. My fate was decided in Turkish and Yesil wouldn't translate.

'What did he want?' I asked again.

'It's not important. We'll tell you tomorrow.'

Now the soldiers were dragging me off my feet. I jerked my head around to look at Yesil. 'What the hell did the prosecutor want? Yesil!'

'He's asking for a life sentence.'

Spinning and weaving and churning inside my head. The evening lights of Istanbul through the slats in the side of the prison van. Life!

Back in the *kogus* I babbled the news to Johann. He tried to calm me. He assured me that it was standard procedure for a prosecutor to try to look tough. It was just a formality, he said. Charles and Arne were reassuring, too. Popeye levelled an 'I told you so' stare. I needed some straight information. What were my chances? Would the court seriously consider the prosecutor's suggestion?

'Why don't you ask Max?' Johann suggested. 'He probably knows more about it than anyone.'

Together we went to see the Dutch junkie. He was sitting on the edge of his bed, fidgeting and scratching at his arms. 'Out of *Gastro*,' he explained simply. 'Gotta get some shit.

While Johann and I watched, Max fumbled under his bed and pulled out a long thin stick. Squinting through his thick glasses, he stumbled out into the hallway. He checked to see if the corridor was empty. Then he began swinging the stick wildly at the overhead light. He had difficulty hitting the target, but finally the light bulb smashed. Glass scattered all over the hallway. Max trotted to the edge of the stairway and yelled, 'Hey Walter, the light's broken up here. Tell Emin to send the electrician.'

Max returned to his cell and continued to scratch at his arms.

I told him about my court. He shook his head. 'Who knows? I don't think they'll give you life, but I didn't think they were gonna give me thirty years. I think you oughta get your ass outta here any way you can,'

'What about Bakirkoy?'

Max twisted his face into a grimace. 'Aaaaah. I was at Bakirkoy for a while. In Section 12. For the junkies. It's no good. You have to have friends. Do you know any *kapidiye*?'

'Huh?'

'*Kapidiye*. If you know one of them maybe you can arrange to bribe a guard or something at Bakirkoy. It's easy to get out, but you've gotta have clothes and money, some way to get over to Greece.'

I told Max about the Turk who befriended me at the police

station. Max assured me he was a *kapidiye*. 'They have a lot of friends inside and out. They have a lot of money. The guards are so poor it's easy to bribe them. But if you're not careful, they'll double-cross you. That's why the *kapidiye* are important. Nobody double-crosses a *kapidiye*. If he does, he gets a knife in the belly.'

The electrician arrived and set up his ladder to replace the light bulb. Max padded over to him, whispered something, and slipped some Turkish lira out of his underwear. Casually the electrician passed him a bottle of dark brown liquid.

'Ah, medicine time,' Max muttered. Conversation ceased while he cooked up his fix and shot it into a vein. He closed his eyes and leaned back against the wall. Johann and I sat for a few minutes, wondering if he was conscious . . alive, even. Then Max suddenly began speaking as though in the midst of a heated discussion.

'. . . No man, don't try to cross at Edirne.' He opened his eyes, leaned forward and grabbed my arm, falling off his bunk in the process. He lowered his voice. 'Look,' he said, 'there's this strip of land south of Edirne. If you get ahold of a Turkish map, study it. There's an old railroad track that runs from Edirne to Uzun Kopru. It was built a long time ago before one of the wars screwed up the border. For a couple of miles it actually runs into Greece and then back out again. The train doesn't stop anywhere, but you could just jump off into Greece. Remember it.'

I left Max to enjoy his high. Would it really come to that, I wondered?

Yesil came out the next day and assured me that I had nothing to worry about. The prosecutor was 'a shit', he said, in a rare break from his cultured English. The judge would probably give me twenty months . . . maybe even bail. We'd find out soon.

At any rate it looked as if I would spend the holiday season in most unusual surroundings. Then I had an idea. Perhaps I could spend New Year's Eve in Cambridge. I wrote to Lily and asked her to sit down on December thirty-first, at three-thirty in the afternoon. It would be eleven-thirty p.m. in Istanbul. I would sit on my bunk and meditate. Together we would try to tune our brainwaves to the same frequency and

82

transport my mind halfway across the world so that I could spend the holiday back home in America. I knew the letter would arrive in time, but she wouldn't have a chance to reply. I could only hope that she'd go along with the plan. It might even work.

The *kogus* settled into a holiday mood. Though the Turks didn't celebrate Christmas, New Year's Eve was a big holiday for them. So they were relaxed and happy all week. They allowed us to buy jams and jellies and even a little flour. Arne, never ceasing to amaze me, mixed them all up and baked Christmas tarts on one of the gas burners. Several of us gathered in his room on Christmas Eve. Arne lit candles. He played his guitar softly. Johann joked and rough-housed. He had six weeks left on his sentence. He passed around some very potent hashish that he bought from Ziat. At midnight Arne brought out the tarts. They were very tasty, once they got past the lump in my throat.

Eleven-thirty at night. New Year's Eve. There was a party again. Emin didn't bother to lock the cells, so little groups of friends clustered together. They smoked hashish and celebrated.

I left my friends and walked softly towards my cell. I stripped naked, just in case my body transported to Lillian as well as my mind. I wrapped myself in a blanket. I sat cross-legged in the cell and closed my eyes. I relaxed, let my thoughts flow. They flowed towards Lily. Her long brown hair. Her brown eyes. Her smooth legs. Minutes passed. I could touch her. An erection grew. I'd been a long time without a woman. But I kept my hands on my knees. Masturbation was boring. Arne was right, one of the worst dangers of prison was the way it taught you to seal up emotions. I wanted to be close to a woman. So from seven thousand miles away I tried to reach into Lillian's mind.

Suddenly I realized I wasn't alone. Was I with Lillian? Where was I? I blinked and stared straight into the dark eyes of Arief. I blinked hard to make sure. It was Arief all right, scowling fiercely at me through the bars. Then he stepped back into the corridor, steadied himself drunkenly against the wall and moved away.

I realized that the *kogus* was full of noise. Several other guards ran by, shoving prisoners into their cells. We were having a 'control' a search, really more like a guard riot. Hamid's ugly voice screamed down the hallway. He raced into my cell. He, too, seemed drunk. I jumped up and stood against the wall, wrapped in my blanket. His eyes settled on the unfinished chess pieces I was carving in soap.

'Arrgghh!' he roared. His big hand swept them off the top of my locker. They crashed to the floor. Then he stamped them into powder with his feet.

He threw open the door of the locker and grabbed a handful of books. He shook them violently. Pages flew all over. Then he searched the clothing in my locker, ripping into pockets, tearing off buttons. I was worried about a tiny piece of hashish stashed in the plumbing, but Hamid didn't search there.

He turned, cocked his arm, and smashed me in the face. Then, as quickly as it began, the control ended. The guards rushed out. Emin locked the cells. All was quiet.

Happy New Year, Lil. Welcome to 1971.

A few days into the new year the *kogus* door opened and guards threw a new prisoner inside. His name was Wilhelm Weber, a German. He spent his first few days travelling from cell to cell bragging to each prisoner in German or English or halting Turkish.

'Ya, ya,' he told Popeye. 'I race sports cars at Monte Carlo. Ya, I dive off the cliffs at Acapulco.'

'Hoo, boy!' Popeye said. 'Don't tell me, let me guess. I bet you climbed the Matterhorn, too.'

'Ya, ya. Dat too. Ya.'

'This guy's the biggest crock of bull in the world!' Popeye moaned. Coming from Popeye that was quite a compliment.

Within a few days no one in the *kogus* could stand Weber. Nobody wanted to be around him or talk to him. Suddenly he stopped bragging, settled down in his cell, and wrote letters.

No one bothered him. No one seemed to worry about him. Was I the only one who could see? Weber had a game going. He'd deliberately made everyone mad at him. Maybe he wanted to be left alone. Quietly I asked my friends about

84

their talks with Weber. Just as I suspected, no one knew any personal details. Weber hadn't even told anyone why he was arrested. Just a lot of gibberish.

'He's an idiot,' Popeye said.

I wasn't so sure.

I never really knew about cold until winter in prison.

The stone walls and iron bars held no warmth. A few coil-pipe radiators were scattered around under the windows but they worked poorly. And quite often, not at all. Most mornings when I woke my breath would steam the air. I found that the coarse prison blankets didn't really hold in any body heat. I tried dressing in long underwear and socks before I went to bed. This didn't help much. I'd just sweat and get even colder from the chill of evaporation. Eventually, I came to sleep in a curled-up foetal position, totally wrapped in a blanket-and-sheet cocoon.

To wake up cold in the morning, day after day, was so depressing. And then never to really warm up, even as the weak winter sun crossed the sky; to have cold feet and hands all day, even when I was active and moving around; to face another long locked night in the cell – it all froze my mind as well as my body.

Patrick sent a book – Solzhenitsyn's *One Day in the Life of Ivan Denisovich*. Siberia was *really* cold. How I empathized with Ivan.

The highlight of the week was my night for a hot bath. Groups of prisoners were assigned various nights. Arne spoke to Emin. I was put in with his group. Six or seven of us gathered down in the kitchen after *Sayim*. Cold water spurted out of the faucet. We waited for the glorious moment when the hot water was turned on.

It was hard to tell how long the hot water would run. Some nights it hardly filled the sink. Other nights it didn't come on at all. But one night it poured steaming out of the faucet endlessly. Billows of vapour filled the small stone room. A warm fog wrapped around us. All the aches and tensions of the day seemed to ooze out of me. I poured pitchers full of hot water over my head. I savoured the warmth. Tight muscles relaxed. As I stood there in my soggy underwear, the heat was sensual.

Arne and I stayed in the kitchen long after the other members of our group went back to their cells. It felt like a sauna. I washed myself until my skin squeaked. Arne had a coarse washing sponge that his folks sent from Sweden. He washed my back with it. It was pleasant. The sponge invigorated my skin. I washed his pale, bony back and watched it turn red beneath the sponge.

'Arne, you're so skinny. Were you always this thin or is it just Turkish cuisine?'

'No. I've always been on the slim side. I used to run a lot, too. Cross-country stuff.'

I could see that by his long wiry legs.

'I ran a lot myself. On the beach in New York.'

'You look like a swimmer to me,' Arne said.

'Did a lot of that, too. Life-guarding and surfing. I love the ocean.'

'Yeah, and now we've got the sink.'

I looked through the fog. A few prisoners were lolling around near the door. Watching us.

'Yeah. The sink and the Arabs.'

Arne glanced over briefly, unconcerned. 'They get off by watching guys wash in their wet underwear.'

It didn't matter to me. 'We should charge admission.'

'I could care less,' Arne said. 'Finished for tonight.'

'Yeah. I'm waterlogged. But I feel great.'

'Nice to have your back scrubbed and your body clean once in a while. But God! How I wish I was naked on a beach in the sun somewhere.'

'Dream on, I said.

'I do,' Arne replied. 'I do.'

Johann's grin outshone the morning sun. After two years, he had finally completed his sentence. He handed me his Persian bedspread that he'd gotten from an Iranian.

'Be careful with it, Billy,' he said. 'there's a special present inside. I've been saving it just in case they screwed me and didn't let me go.'

'I'll write,' he promised. 'I'll keep in touch. If you need

anything let me know. I mean it, man. I'll help you out all I can.'

'Have a good time travelling,' I said. 'Let me know when you settle down.'

'Sure will.'

I watched Johann walk out of the *kogus* to his freedom. For several moments the glow of his happiness remained with me. Then my mind made the obvious comparison. I was still inside. I unfolded the bedspread curiously. There was nothing in it. Carefully I examined it. A rough braid decorated the edges. In one spot it was hard. I turned toward the wall to hide my actions from the corridor. Carefully I pulled at the threads holding the braid in place. A file! How did Johann get it? It didn't matter. There it was.

Late that night I tested it against the metal of my bed. It seemed to cut easily. I decided to keep it. It was like money in the bank. I slipped it inside the binding of my diary.

I sank deeper into depression the next day. Johann's empty cell next to mine would be a constant reminder. On an impulse I trotted down to ask Emin if I could move my cell up to the second tier. There was an empty spot between Popeye and Max. Emin said yes, and in twenty minutes I was living upstairs. Popeye was happy, and his chatter helped the day pass by. But by night time I was back in my low mood. I'd now been in prison for six months and still didn't even know the length of my sentence. The Turkish court system was moving incredibly slowly. I was stupid to have believed that I could get out early. I thought of Max in the next cell. I promised myself that I would talk to him more about escape . . . more about that border crossing into Greece. I knew one thing, for sure. I couldn't spend much more time in this prison. I was twenty-three years old. The best years were ahead. The Turks were slowly taking my life away.

Finally I dropped into sleep. I woke in the middle of the night and heard a low mumbling coming from Max's cell. I wondered who could possibly be over there at this time of night. Cautiously I crept towards the bars. I strained to listen to the voices next door. There was only once voice – Max. I could see his reflection in the glass of the barred corridor window. He was standing in front of his open locker, talking quietly into it. He giggled.

'Max,' I whispered. 'Who are you talking to?

He wheeled in surprise. 'Uh . . . it's strange . . . my friend's in there.'

'Oh, really?'

'Yeah.' He turned back to the locker and giggled.

'Well, do you think you could talk a little softer? Your friend is keeping me awake. OK?'

'Right, sorry.' He peered into his locker and said, 'Shhhh.'

For the next couple of weeks Johann's release remained constantly on my mind. Arne could tell I was preoccupied. I had never talked with him about escape. I knew he would never seriously consider it. He would sit in his cell passively and do his time until the Turks let him go. Charles was too near the end of his sentence. And I could never trust Popeye to keep a secret.

That left Max. I asked him again about Bakirkoy. He was doubtful. But he agreed with me that if the court sent me to the mental hospital for observation, I should watch carefully for any opportunity.

Court came once again. And I was determined to see some action. When the day finally arrived and the soldiers took me into the courtroom, I rushed over to Yesil.

'I want you to ask for bail today,' I said. 'Do you think our chances are good?'

'*Sula bula,*' Yesil said, lapsing into Turkish. 'I'm not so sure it's the right time to ask.'

'Look, I've been in this prison for six months and you haven't asked for bail yet. Tell Beyaz and Siya that I want them to ask for bail today.'

Yesil was thoughtful. 'Maybe it would be better if *you* asked,' he suggested.

'Fine. That's what I am going to do.'

Once again court was a gibberish of Turkish law. The judge spoke, my lawyers spoke, the prosecutor spoke, the judge spoke again. No one asked me anything. So I picked a lull in the proceedings. I stood up and raised my hand. The judge looked over in surprise. He spoke to Yesil.

'What do you want?' Yesil asked.

'You know what I want.'

'All right. Speak to the court.'

'I've been in jail six months now,' I said. 'My health is getting bad. My teeth are very bad. I have problems with my stomach. I'm getting very depressed. I would like the court to grant me bail so that I can be outside and take care of my physical health.'

Yesil translated my speech and the judge simply laughed out loud. He spoke some more with my lawyers. Once again the soldiers prepared to take me away.

'What happened?' I asked Yesil.

'It's very good,' he grinned. 'The judge looked at your reports from the United States Army. He is sending you to Bakirkoy for observation. Maybe you'll get a crazy report!'

Or maybe I'll just run like crazy.

CHAPTER EIGHT

Freedom beckoned to me through the slats in the side of the red panel truck that hauled the prisoners towards Bakirkoy. In the dimming light of dusk I could see that there were still such wonderful things in life as women, trees, and open horizons. But the truck banged into a rut and my head cracked against hard wood. I remembered that the women and trees and open horizons were for the lucky masses who probably took them all for granted. Meantime, I bounced along in a prison wagon, chained to an emaciated young lunatic who dripped a constant stream of spittle from the side of his mouth.

But at least I was on the move. I'd accomplished nothing during six months of rotting at Sagmalcilar. The only real step I'd taken was to hide Johann's file. It was still in the binding of my diary, locked inside my cell along with my few other possessions. Now, with luck, I would never need it. The court had ordered me to Bakirkoy for seventeen days of observation. I expected that would be enough time to arrange something.

The bouncing ride in the squeaky cramped truck created an illusion of progress. I would never go back to Sagmalcilar, I was sure. I would get my 'crazy report' and stay in Bakirkoy until I could plan an escape. This was my big chance.

It was nearly dark as the truck pulled up alongside the wall of the mental hospital. I could see a large tree inside the court, with huge overhanging branches that rocked in the winter wind. Surely I could skip up that tree and lower myself to the ground outside.

Several hospital attendants dressed in grimy white smocks took charge of our group as we entered an administration office. The oldest looked about sixty, but he was the largest of them and still very strong. A lifeguard's silver whistle dangled from his neck. The others called him *Policebaba*. They obviously respected his authority.

'Lira? Lira?' the attendants asked.

I pretended not to notice. This was the beginning of my crazy act; I intended to be sullen and withdrawn.

'Lira?' one attendant asked again, pointing his big hook-nose directly in my face.

I shrugged and slowly pulled a hundred lira note out of my pocket. He pointed at my watch. He gestured to explain that it would be stolen inside. He took that, too, and placed it in a bag with my name on it.

Policebaba watched closely. Here was a crazy *turist* with a hundred lira note and a fancy watch. There must be more money where that came from. He glided over towards me and motioned for me to follow. The drooling lunatic and I led the way into Bakirkoy.

The grounds were wilder than I had imagined from Max's description. Pathways wound up and down rolling hills. Abundant clumps of trees and overgrown bushes would make for easy hiding. If only I could get loose into the park, I was certain I could escape the main complex. I tried to memorize the route we were taking to Section 13. But the early February night had completely closed in. The air was fresh and cold, invigorating. This was the first time I had seen the night in six months.

Ahead of us loomed a huge, formidable, grey stone wall, perhaps fifteen feet high. We walked towards a large iron gate; rounded into an arch at the top, it reached nearly as high as the wall. Big brass bolts dotted the strong iron surface. Set into the gate were two smaller doors also made of iron. One of the attendants withdrew a large, old-fashioned iron key from his pocket. He twisted it in the lock. A small door swung open on squeaky hinges.

Policebaba unshackled me and gently pushed me inside. I found myself in a large yard of hard-packed earth. In the centre, wrapped in darkness, was a long, squat rectangular grey building. Section 13, the section for the criminally insane. It was my new home.

We crossed to the building. Another key in another lock. The metal door opened and the attendants crowded us into a small room. They forced us all to strip to our underwear. Then they issued thin, faded pairs of shorty pyjamas that seemed ridiculously inadequate for the winter night. They

91

took our shoes and socks and gave us each a pair of old shower sandals. All the floors and walls of the building were fashioned from stone. Smooth, cold, stone. It seemed no warmer inside the building than out.

Policebaba led me through a ward that was dirtier and grimier than anything I had seen in prison. The walls were covered with a whitewash that was now dark grey, even black in the corners. Walls and ceilings joined in arches rather than right angles. The building looked like a medieval dungeon. I shivered in the cold damp air.

Several attendants sat on one bed playing a two-card game called *kulach*. My protector led me past them through an open archway into a second room. I was struck immediately by the noise level of the room and the sense of ceaseless jumbled movement.

In the near corner, just around the wall from where the attendants were playing *kulach* in the first room, Policebaba showed me a bed. It was occupied by a fat-faced man in filthy pyjamas. He snored contentedly in spite of the general uproar in the room. Policebaba indicated that I could have this bed. I simply stood there, trying to force a vague look into my startled eyes. The bed was in a favoured position, close to the protection of the attendants. I wanted it. But could I risk appearing sane enough to offer the old attendant a bribe?

'*Nebu?*' said a scruffy-looking man at my elbow. He tugged at the sleeve of my pyjamas.

'*Nebu?*' grunted another madman standing behind me. He pulled at my blond hair.

Policebaba growled and chased them away. He smiled at me. Again he indicated that I could have this bed. Then for the first time he seemed to realize that it was occupied. This was no problem. He just reached down with his huge arms and rolled the sleeping man onto the floor.

'*Allah!*' the fat madman cried in a frightened voice. Policebaba growled. The man scuttled away.

I looked down at the bed. Yellow urine stains were in abundance. There was undoubtedly a lice convention amid the folds of torn linen.

'*Pis*' ('Dirty') I muttered. I wasn't crazy enough to sleep in that filth.

'Eh?' Policebaba said, looking puzzled. Then it flashed on him. His grizzled face again cracked into a gold-toothed smile. He yelled. An eager old man in frayed pyjamas ran off, returning in a moment with a torn, thin bit of grey cloth that I supposed was a clean sheet. He ripped the old filthy sheet off the bed and replaced it with the new filthy sheet.

Policebaba indicated twenty lira. I grunted, which he apparently took as an admission of the debt. He could collect from my hundred lira note later. Then he turned and yelled a string of harsh words at some other inmates near by. The word *turist* came through clearly. He seemed to be telling them that this was my bed and that they shouldn't bother me.

I sat down on my bed and pressed my back securely into the corner of the wall. I studied my new home.

'*Cigare?*' a naked man asked. He held his hand out towards me. '*Cigare? Cigare?*'

I gave no response.

He was thin and young and sickly looking. His bones showed through his nakedness. His left hand was tightly cupped over his crotch while his right hand stood out in front of me. The fingertips were chewed raw.

In a steady monotone he asked, '*Cigare? Cigare? Cigare? . . .*' A few others gathered around and joined him, '*Cigare? Cigare?*'

Minutes passed. When I failed to respond with cigarettes several of the men shuffled off. But the naked man stood his ground '*Cigare?*' he said softly. I shook my head. He gave no response to that. He continued to stand there in front of my bed, shivering from the cold, staring down at me with a vacant look in his eyes.

I avoided his gaze and glanced around the room. It seemed like a circus freak show – except that I was in the show rather than the audience. The noise had always been bad at Sagmalcilar, but it was worse here. Various chants and droning singsong monotones seemed to be under way. They formed a steady background hum behind the shouting emotional conversations. Sporadic shattering screams tore the atmosphere. Men yelled at others in fights over sheets, blankets,

beds, cigarettes. Others merely sat there on their beds babbling to themselves ... rocking, screaming, chuckling,
crying. Filthy, smelly men, some stark naked, some wrapped
in torn blackened sheets, moved around the room in mean-
ingless syncopated activity. There was some sort of routine to
it. Many seemed to follow a strange awkward rhythm.
Others patrolled the room like quick ferrets. They moved
smoothly among the crowded disorderly rows of beds, sharp
eyes open for anything they might find. Still others plodded
around in staring, blank-eyed silence.

A few beds down from me was a pale-complexioned old
Turk with a bristly broom-moustache, the sort a Swedish
janitor would wear. He looked like Mr Swenson, the janitor
in the 'Archie' comics. On the left side of his face, just under
the eye, was a large round lump that appeared to be solid,
like a big fleshy walnut in his cheek. He was a quick, nervous
little man. He looked at the lump from every possible angle,
checking it in a small round pocket mirror. With three fingers
of his left hand he constantly rubbed at the offending knob in
flurries of motion.

Across from me one man sat on the edge of his bunk
muttering *'Omina koydum.'* I'd heard the expression before,
back at Sagmalcilar. (Literally, it means 'I put it in her
cunt'; but the Turks in prison use the expression much like
an American would say 'Ya know? Ya know?') *'Omina koydum,'* he muttered to his bed. *'Omina koydum'* to his feet.
'Omina koydum' to the ceiling. *'Omina koydum'* to the old white-
haired man next to him, a retired judge who had gone insane
and now spent all his time painstakingly copying legal
papers and putting the copies in a pile. Across from their
beds another man sat muttering an incantation to his string
of olive-pit *tespe* beads. They all ignored each other.

As I watched all this, the naked man continued to glare
down at me. Occasionally he muttered, *'Cigare?'* under his
breath.

To escape his annoying stare I slid off my bed for a tour of
Section 13. I wanted to know the routine. I wanted to locate
the attendant with the key. I wanted to find windows or
doors that might be hidden from view.

I ducked back into the first room. Immediately I realized

that it had a very different aura from the one I was in. The first area, though filthy by American standards, was a Hilton hotel compared to my own room. Forty or fifty beds were lined up neatly in three rows. Most had clean sheets tucked into their mattresses. No one was naked. Men dressed in clean faded pyjamas sat on their beds in apparent control of their senses.

Suddenly I stopped in amazement. There was Memet Celik, whom I had seen in court. And Ali Aslan, who had been pointed out to me in prison. Both were *kapidiye*, Turkish gangsters. They were vicious and crazy-mean but not insane. They sat on their beds in their own pyjamas, not the hospital issue, playing *kulach* with some attendants. What were they doing in Bakirkoy? Certainly they weren't here to escape. They really couldn't afford to escape and become fugitives. What, then, were these *kapidiye* doing in Bakirkoy?

Pondering this mystery, I walked back to my own room. It was quite a contrast – filthy naked men screaming and jumping around on the beds. The same naked madman still stood in front of my bed so I decided to move on and explore further. I walked slowly between the beds, looking into faces along the way. Most eyes avoided mine. Some glared back burning bright. A few men reached out to touch me. I smiled and moved along. Ahead of me was another arched entrance into still another room. I stepped into it.

It was as though I had lifted a stone and discovered hundreds of white maggots crawling around. The stench stopped me in my tracks. The room was cramped with beds and bodies. Bunks were pushed together in clusters of three and four, and perhaps nine or ten men slept together on them. There seemed to be perpetual jungle warfare. One man threw another off a bed and the other returned screaming to reclaim his place.

There was crying and cursing and fighting everywhere. The heavy ammonia fumes, the horrible stench of human waste, were inescapable. And the stench was worst at the opening to what could only be the bathroom.

The bathroom was one of the chief goals of my search. Not so much for immediate use but because it might have a window isolated from the view of the attendants. I walked over and stuck my head inside but saw nothing. The smell was so overwhelming I had to pull back quickly. Tomorrow, I decided, would be soon enough to survey the toilet.

Next to the bathroom was a table where a grinning Turk in faded pyjamas guarded several cartons of cigarettes. '*Cigare?*' he asked. '*Birinici?*' He indicated a price of one lira, seventy-five *kurus* – about twelve cents for a package of Birinici cigarettes. I walked away and turned towards the wall. I waited until I was sure no one was watching. Gently I slipped a five lira note out of my underwear. Then I went back to the cigarette vendor. Now, at least, I could chase away the naked man hovering over my bed.

As night approached, one of the attendants walked through the ward with a big apron containing several pockets bulging with red, blue, green, and white pills. '*Hop, hop,*' ('Pill, pill'), he cried. I shrugged. I didn't like barbiturates. But just about everyone else gobbled them as if they were candy. The attendant gave them out by the handful.

As the pills took effect on most of the inmates, the noise lowered considerably to a steady rumbling punctuated by only occasional screaming. The attendants drifted back to their card game. Section 13 settled down for the night.

I lay down, shivering under my thin sheet as the cold wind blew in through a broken window pane at the foot of my bed. I struggled to clear my mind of the incredible sights I had seen during my first hours at Bakirkoy. The weird events of the day kept distracting me from the real purpose of my visit. I was here to get a 'crazy report', I remembered. Then to engineer a spectacular escape. But which attendant had the key? And how could I get over that huge wall in the yard? And where would I go dressed only in these thin cotton pyjamas? Tomorrow, I decided, tomorrow I would settle down to some serious planning. After what must have been two or three hours I fell asleep.

In the middle of the night I sensed someone's presence quite near by. I rolled over and looked into a dark face. It was a young man in his early twenties. He was tall and extremely thin and wore a wild grin. A blackened old rag of a sheet was all he had on. It was wrapped around his head, and he

96

clutched it under his chin like a peasant lady holding her shawl. I know that human eyes can't be yellow, but his were.

He smirked when he saw the surprise and fear on my face. He opened his mouth slightly. He ran his tongue along dry chapped lips. His shifty eyes moved up and down my body. His meaning was only too obvious. I turned away and pulled the sheet up over my head. But he just stood there.

'*Cigare?*' I heard him say softly.

I didn't respond.

'*Cigare?*'

I would have tried to wait him out but his presence made me uneasy. I uncovered my head and looked him in the face. He smirked again. He held out his palm.

'*Cigare,*' he said, in a soft easy voice. '*Cigare?*' A pause. '*S'il vous plaît.*'

His unexpected French so surprised me that I pulled the pack of Birinici out from under my pillow and gave him one. He asked for a light. I lit his cigarette. Then he ran his tongue around his mouth one more time. Finally he left, fading into the shadows.

I awoke early to the drone of Moslem prayers drifting in from the third room. No one in the first two rooms seemed inclined to join them, religion apparently being reserved for the craziest. I lay in my bed, shivering. I tried to clear my head. I'd been afraid that I would crack under the pressure of confinement back at Sagmalcilar; what then would the madness of Bakirkoy do to me? If I stayed here too long would my already susceptible mind begin to absorb the insanity that surrounded it?

The attendants came around at seven a.m., poking everyone away with short wooden clubs. Everyone, that is, except the *kapidiye* and a few human vegetables who were incapable of leaving their beds. They herded us like cattle to a post near the dining area. Then they made us wait while they poked around under beds and into corners to send stragglers scurrying. One by one the attendants shoved us into the small dining area as they counted. Quickly the room, only about twenty-five feet square, became jammed with men. Perhaps two hundred of us were packed in tightly. I found it nearly impossible to move. It was unpleasant even to breathe. The stench of unwashed bodies and foul mouths was overpowering. I felt a hand rub my behind. Then it reached down to caress my testicles. I quickly turned to see a Turk leering at me. I brought my knee up swiftly between his legs. To the sound of cursing Turks I elbowed my way over to the wall for protection. The attendants checked their numbers slowly, going back into the rooms to count the *kapidiye* and the vegetables. For more than half an hour we were packed into the stinking smoke-filled little room.

Finally they got their numbers straight and allowed us to come pouring back out. Someone shoved a bowl into my hands and filled it with a weak gruel that had a few lentils floating in the bottom. I ate the lukewarm mixture hungrily. I'd missed dinner the night before.

Then, inevitably, nature called. I had postponed a trip to the bathroom until I'd just above reached the limits of my endurance. So drawing a deep breath, I stepped into the dark room. Almost the entire floor was covered with piles of faeces and puddles of urine. Cat-stepping carefully in my sandals, I ventured towards one of the four holes cut into the floor and squatted, Turkish style.

Immediately a scrawny Turk came over and squatted down in front of me. He began to masturbate while he stared at my penis.

'Yaaahh!' I yelled at him. He hopped away. But as soon as I settled back into a squat again, back he came. I had no choice but to ignore him. I wanted to get away from the incredible stench as soon as possible. Then a vacant-eyed barefoot Turk shuffled in, stepping squarely into a pile of wet faeces. He looked around as if realizing for the first time where he was. A knowing look crossed his features. And then a dark stain dripped down his pyjama leg and a puddle of urine formed on the floor at his feet. Finished, he turned and shuffled out, tracking footprints.

What I needed then was air. Fortunately the attendants chose that moment to open the door and allow us out into the yard.

The winter air blew right through my thin pyjamas. But its

fresh aroma was desperately welcome. I drew in deep draughts of it as I began my study of outside security.

The wall was more than twice my height. It was constructed of stone and mortar in the same style as the old building. In several places the mortar had fallen out, leaving huge gaps between the stones. I scanned the wall carefully, looking for a pattern of gaps that might allow me to climb.

The top of the wall was covered with an ancient wire fence. Its broken, rusted strands of barbs tangled and twisted within an overhanging weight of thick green dangling ivy.

I began a slow walk around the base of the wall. I studied the mortar chinks carefully. Many of the huge stone blocks were smooth near the base of the wall. The rubbing of how many madmen? In the rear of the barracks, stairs led to a basement door. It was bolted from the outside. A short wall about chest high jutted out from the stairwell. I wondered if I could jump from there to the top of the larger wall. Trying to appear inconspicuous, I eased myself up onto the low wall and counted the steps. With a running start I could leap towards the high wall. If I had a short length of rope with a rock or piece of wood attached, I might be able to lunge for the wall, throw the weighted rope up and catch it in the barbed wire. Then the barbed wire would have to hold the weight of my body as I climbed. The scheme wasn't much, but it was a possibility.

Then as I turned the third corner I saw my chance at the west wall. Enough chunks of mortar had dropped out from several spots, I felt, that I could scale this part of the wall easily. I had no idea what was on the other side. But it wasn't Section 13. This wall just might be the beginning of my flight to freedom.

In the yard a young man named Yakub came over and offered me a cigarette. He spoke reasonably good English. We talked together for a while. He volunteered the information that he was here because the court had ordered him examined. He had killed his sister because she was a prostitute. I could understand that, couldn't I? Yes, of course, I told him slowly, trying to move away. But he did seem fairly sane and very knowledgeable about Section 13. The *kapidiye*, he explained, often use Bakirkoy for a sort of vacation.

Occasionally they are faced with a court problem which will take a year or so to fix. Meanwhile, they bribe their way into this hospital. There are fewer hassles for them here. With their reputations and their money, they live like kings in Bakirkoy. They stay in the first room. They don't let the filthy madmen near them. 'The crazier you are, the further you sleep from the *kapidiye*,' Yakub said.

A fluttering sound came from the top of the wall. A huge peacock was landing on the ivy-covered barbed wire. He screeched and preened the rainbow of his long tail feathers, then flew off. That was the most beautiful thing about him – his freedom. I was breathless.

Yakub waved away my awe scornfully. 'They're all over the park.'

The walk outside was invigorating, but we were soon shivering uncontrollably. We went back inside. There was a vendor's table near the bathroom. Yakub explained that a few of the inmates were assigned to jobs outside the wall. They bought food and resold it here for a profit. Today there were oranges, onions, bread, and yogurt. And lots of cigarettes, always.

I bought a yogurt and an orange for lunch, ignoring the hospital's offering of watered-down potato soup. I left Yakub and went to my bed. After I peeled the orange I threw the peels onto the floor. Three men leaped for them. They beat each other to get the peels. Then they moved away and watched with hungry eyes while I ate my yogurt. I left a little in the bottom of the cup. I offered it to one man crouched down on his haunches at the foot of my bed. He jumped towards me, but then hesitated for a moment. I held out the cup. He snatched it. Then he scurried off into a corner somewhere to lick it clean.

At the far end of the building, between the vendors and the toilets, was a stairway. When I had pointed to it, Yakub said, *'Pis'* and walked off. I decided to explore.

The circular steps were dark, damp, and slippery like moss-covered rock. As I moved slowly down, darkness closed in around me. I found myself floating into a gloomy medieval dungeon, a low oppressive room that seemed packed with lost souls. Two tiny bare light bulbs gave faint illumination to one side of the chamber. Across on the other side a pot-bellied stove flickered; it etched the shadowy forms of gaunt-faced men in a strange orange glow. My glance caught on sets of fire-lit eyes staring into nothingness.

The low ceiling pressed in on me. My first impulse was to run. But I swallowed my fear and moved to one side of the room. My back was defensively against the wall. As my eyes adjusted to the dim light I could see the circular movement of scores of men as they trudged slowly, silently in a counter-clockwise flow around a pillar in the centre of the room. Others huddled near the pot-bellied stove. Still others were jammed into a low L-shaped wooden platform that ran the length of two walls.

Many were naked, open sores covering their scrawny knees, elbows, and buttocks. Others clutched scraps of blackened sheets. They were quieter than the upstairs crowd. I realized that I had reached the lowest pecking order of the madmen of Bakirkoy. This was the bottom of the bird cage. These were the men who weren't even fit for the third room upstairs. These, indeed, were the damned.

There was a scream as a naked man jostled for position near the pot-bellied stove and was pushed against the hot metal. He snarled and swung his fists. Several people shoved at him in anger. He fought back weakly, finally retreating with a whimper.

The pillar dominated the basement. Grim and squat, it bore the weight of the threatening ceiling. The silent, relent-less shuffle of men around it drew my attention almost hypnotically. It was a wheel, I thought. But the spokes – the men – were broken. I watched in fascination as the wheel of broken spokes turned on its journey to nowhere. Slowly, slowly, I found myself drawn to it. I moved from the shelter of the wall and joined the procession. I slid easily into the circle of shuffling men. We flowed like the current of some sluggish, mindless river. I let my eyes hang loosely on the floor. I watched the soothing rhythm that our feet assumed as we scraped along at that numbing yet comforting pace. I looked at the men around me. They seemed like old plough-horses, still trudging the same path long after the reins of control had been dropped. It was easy to become a cog in this circle of insanity.

I shuffled along for about an hour. But I didn't want to stay away from my bed too long. Perhaps the doctors would call for me. I went back to my bed and rehearsed the paranoid blabber I was going to throw at them.

The day dragged on. Afternoon blurred into evening. Still the doctors didn't come.

From a crack in the wooden cover of my broken window I stared at the west wall, the chinks in its mortar beckoning me to make the climb. I watched the sun drop down behind the wall to light up the other side of the world that I missed so much.

But Section 13 quickly intruded upon my thoughts. A couple of men eased close to one of my neighbours . . . the one sitting on his bed rocking and chanting relentlessly to his *tespe* beads. Suddenly one of them grabbed the beads. He flung them across the room to another man.

'*Allah!*' the old man moaned in disgust. He pushed up off the bed to chase after his beads. '*Yok, yok, yok,*' he pleaded to his tormentors as he clambered among the beds.

Several other men joined in the game, passing the beads around the room, keeping them just out of their owner's reach.

'*Brack!*' he called, his puffy nose growing red.

The poor man was frantic. He just *had* to have his beads back. Sweat broke out on his shiny bald head. His movements speeded up. He grew violent. The joke had ended for him. He erupted with a bellow and leaped after his beads, shoving beds and bodies out of his way. He jumped onto sleeping men, kicking anyone who tried to stop him.

Howling with rage he ran back and forth. The beads flew from the hands of one tormentor to another. In his wake men battled each other, yelling and punching whoever was near.

An attendant finally responded to the uproar and called out 'Ossman!' From the first room, dressed in inmate pyjamas, came the brawniest Turk I had ever seen. He resembled a gorilla, with the same faint spark of intelligence hovering behind his furrowed eyes. He lumbered over to the owner of the beads. He was obviously the troublemaker. Ossman grabbed the screaming old man by the shoulders. He smashed him violently against the wall. The old madman collapsed instantly. Then Ossman picked up the limp body and carried it into the first room. The attendants treated the man's cuts and bruises.

'Ossman. Ossman,' the attendant said approvingly.

Ossman grinned.

Between the endless requests for cigarettes, the never-ending hum of *'Omina koydum'* from across the way, and the general bedlam of the place, I could get little clear thinking done. I had to evaluate my situation, plan my actions. But where in this madhouse could I think?

Yes, the wheel. There I could pace in solitude, I could sort out my jumbled thoughts. Down I went to the cellar. I joined the procession marching steadfastly towards counter-clockwise oblivion. My thoughts continually crept back to the west wall. Those huge footholds in the mortar. I was sure I could climb that wall. I was like a monkey when it came to climbing. But could I find clothes? Could I get a passport? Most important, if I escaped from here, would I have enough time to cross the border before I was discovered? To be free I had to escape from Turkey, not just this hospital. My blond hair and my shorty pyjamas would make me a bit conspicuous out in Istanbul. I decided to wait for the doctors' decision.

A hand on my shoulder interrupted my thought.

'You're an Englishman?' a gruff voice asked.

I turned to see a tall cadaverous-looking Turk with a grizzled beard and greying leathery skin. His silver hair was matted down on his head, accentuating the shape of his skull. Big clumps of hair had fallen, or been pulled, out.

'You're an Englishman?' he repeated, in a clipped British accent. It seemed so improbable coming from his yellowed mouth.

'American,' I answered.

'Ah, yes, America. My name is Ahmet,' he smiled. 'I studied in London for many, many years.'

He shuffled along next to me for about twenty minutes, chattering about his trips to London and Vienna years ago.

He had studied economics. He had worked all over Europe. I told him about my own studies and how I had abandoned them to travel the world instead.

He looked at me knowingly. 'You've travelled too far,' he said.

'Yeah, it sure looks like it,' I admitted sadly.

Then my curiosity got the best of me. 'How long have you been here?' I asked. 'Why are you here now?'

His face betrayed no change of emotion. Quietly he said, 'I think we have spoken enough today. I say good night to you now.'

Then, while I stared after him, Ahmet wrapped his rags around himself. He dropped to his hands and knees, and crawled into the filthy darkness under the L-shaped wooden platform.

Three Turkish doctors called me into the office the next morning. They all seemed to speak reasonably good English.

'Good morning. How are you, William?' said the one who was obviously in charge.

I said nothing.

'Why are you here, William?' he asked.

Still I said nothing. My eyes were cast down. I stood in the middle of the small room working myself into a tense state. Considering the circumstances, that was rather easy to do. My body began to twitch.

'Would you like to sit down?'

'No.' I backed into a corner.

'What's the matter, William? Why are you here?'

'They sent me.'

'Who sent you?'

Silence.

'Are you sick? Are you ill? Do you have a problem? Can we help you?' The questions were calm and deliberate. A second doctor wrote information on a chart.

'They sent me from the prison. No, from the court,' I roared suddenly. 'From the prison. I don't know. I don't know. What are they doing to me?!'

'Do you have problems?'

'I have this . . .' I faded out. Then suddenly I lunged at the doctor writing on the chart. 'What the hell is he writing all this down for?!' I screamed. 'Do you think I'm an animal? What are you doing to me? I'm not some animal you lock up in a cage!'

'Calm down, William. What's the problem? We're here to help you.'

'My problem is . . . they locked me up in this prison . . . I'm trying to write notes . . . I used to be smart . . . I went to university . . I was writing . . . I can't read a book now . . . they're always looking at me . . . I can't write a letter to my parents . . . I forget . . .'

I ran to the corner and faced against the wall, hiding from them.

The doctors spoke among themselves in Turkish. I couldn't understand what they were saying. I wondered if my act was working, whether I was laying it on thick enough. I wondered if I should leap on the doctor and bite off his nose, maybe, just for effect.

'What do you want us to do, William? Do you want to stay here?'

'I don't want to stay here.'

'Do you want to go back to prison?'

'I don't want to go back to prison. They want to kill me there. They lock me up in a cage like an animal!'

'Why don't you sit down in the chair?' he asked gently.

'I don't want to sit in your goddamn chair!' I screamed, kicking it across the room. The attendant at the door made a move towards me. The doctor held up a hand to restrain him.

'You people don't give a shit. You don't care if I live or die. You're just like the others. You all want to lock me away and kill me. I don't want to be here!'

I crashed through the door, pulled away from the attendant's grasp, and ran back into the second room. I huddled on my bed, not quite believing what I had done.

In a few moments one of the doctors came for me. He'd been quiet during the session. Now he tried to reassure me. 'Come back,' he said. 'It's all right. Come back.' I followed him back. He drew me aside into another room.

He motioned me to a chair. He sat down facing me. He placed both his hands on my bare knees and spoke gently 'I think I can help you. I would like to contact your American consul and speak with him. I can't help you here, not in this section. I would like to take you over to my section. But I can't do that unless the consul will come out and vouch for your behaviour.'

I kept a blank look on my face, even though my head was whirling. *If the consul would vouch for me!* This meant that his section must be open. No bars, no walls. Just doctors to help poor sick men like myself. Oh yes, I could picture it. I'd stay a few days, walk around the park, talk with the friendly doctor who still had his hands on my knees. Then I'd be gone like the wind. No more Bakirkoy. No more Sagmalcilar. No more Turkey!

The doctor allowed me to use the phone. I called Willard Johnson, the vice-consul. Trying to keep the excitement from my voice, I explained the situation. If he would come out here and speak with the doctors, they would help me. He said he'd be in touch soon.

Back on my bed I could almost taste freedom. I didn't need the footholds in the west wall. All I had to do was keep the doctor convinced that I needed help badly and I would soon be moved to within an inch of freedom.

Under the able instruction of Section 13's four hundred and fifty madmen I began to add more and more craziness to my act. I wanted to make the proper impression in case the doctors were having me watched. Soon I began to wet my bed and defecate on the floor. Most of the craziest inmates were always stark naked. So several mornings in a row I hid my money in a tear in the mattress, ripped off my pyjamas, and raced out into the yard. It seemed like the thing to do. If it would help my act then all the hassles of being naked among these madmen would be worth it. But the attendants didn't care. One more naked fool didn't make any difference to them. Only Policebaba seemed concerned. I ignored his protests. But the only people interested in my nakedness were interested for the wrong reasons. So I abandoned this approach.

I walked the wheel for hours.

Day after day passed. Nothing happened. Why didn't the consul come? Maybe he had come and they didn't let him in to see me. Why hadn't I heard any news? Why was I still in Section 13? Slowly, my thoughts turned from fantasies of flight into lingering doubts.

I bribed one of the attendants to use the phone again. Again I called Willard Johnson. Again he promised to relay my message.

Then one afternoon as I sat on my bunk a short, creepy-looking Turk walked up to me. He might have been thirty. He was thin but not emaciated. His pyjamas were neat and fairly clean, a sure sign that he was more sane than the average inmate. He had bright, shiny, scary eyes. He approached, looking directly into my face. In perfect English he said, 'You'll never get out of here.'

I froze. Who was this man? What did he know?

'You think that you'll just stay a little while and then go free,' he continued. 'But it's not true.'

'Who knows?' I shrugged, trying to appear nonchalant. My muscles tensed. 'Where'd you learn to speak English?'

'I studied. Outside.'

'What are you doing in here?' I asked.

'They put me here.'

'Who did?'

'*They* did.'

'Oh. Well, have you been here a long time?'

'Yes, a very long time.'

He was quite a conversationalist.

'Well, why don't you leave?'

'Can't. *They* won't let me.'

I couldn't say I blamed *them*. He was definitely nuts. His eyes gave me the creeps. They were red-veined and protruding, like little raw egg embryos. Just talking with him made me feel uneasy.

'And they won't let *you* go either.'

I wasn't sure where he got his information. But the smug certainty of his manner annoyed me.

'What do you know? They'll let me out.'

'No, they'll never let you go. They tell you that but you stay. You never go from here.'

I turned away, hoping he'd leave. This conversation was not to my liking. The man was obviously a lunatic.

Otherwise he wouldn't be here. So what was I doing arguing with him?

Uninvited, he sat down on my bed His name, he said, was Ibrahim. After bumming a cigarette he continued his gloomy chatter. I desperately wanted to chase him away. But that would seem like an admission that I couldn't cope with his argument. I continually assured him that while *he* might be stuck here for ever, *I* would soon leave.

He tried to explain the situation to me. 'We all come from a factory,' he said, like a father lecturing to a child. 'Sometimes the factory makes bad machines that don't work right. They put them here. The bad machines don't know that they're bad machines, but the people at the factory know. They put us here and they keep us here.'

'They're keeping you here, maybe, but I'll go.'

'No. You'll never go. You're one of the machines that doesn't work.'

CHAPTER NINE

Each day at Bakirkoy I felt myself becoming more isolated from reality. The insanity around me seemed to be infectious. The walls pressed in. The constant babbling and screaming of the inmates tormented me. I had to get out of Section 13. And I had to get out fast.

For a fifty-lira bribe Policebaba agreed to send a telegram for me. It was to Willard Johnson at the American consulate. I tried to make it sound crazy-desperate. He *had* to come out and persuade the doctor that I was trustworthy. Then I could be transferred to the open section, a step away from freedom. Johnson was evasive.

Days passed. Ibrahim kept coming back over to my bed. He told me that I didn't know what *they* were doing to me. Because a bad machine doesn't know that it's a bad machine.

It almost seemed as though Ibrahim were right. Willard Johnson was strangely silent. The doctors didn't bother with me any more. I found myself studying the west wall. Should I try it now or wait? If they gave me a 'crazy report' then I'd have time later to try the wall. In fact, maybe I'd *have* to go out that way. If they really thought I was crazy, they wouldn't let me out any other way. It seemed strange that I was actually trying to create the very situation Ibrahim was predicting.

One morning when I was awakened early by the Moslem prayers, I slipped out of bed to walk the wheel alone and think. As I passed through the third room I saw the madmen at prayer, led by an old white-bearded *Hoja* who had long been the spiritual leader of Section 13. Some of the men had prayer mats. Others merely had a scrap of sheet or blanket. Two spastic inmates on the end had difficulty following the routine of bending and kneeling. They got tangled up and often fell to the floor.

Downstairs I found the wheel at a standstill. The night-walkers had left and the day-walkers were still asleep. Rag-wrapped figures lay strewn around the corners of the room. They huddled in clumps in the darkness under the platform. The wheel was empty. It looked strange. I'd never seen it stopped before. It had always been moving and always in the same direction. But why, I wondered? Why do things always have to be the same? What if I started walking in the other direction? What if I moved clockwise? When others woke would they fall in step behind my wrong-way leadership? I decided to try it.

So the first spoke of the wheel began turning slowly in the wrong direction that morning. I moved alone around the great stone hub of the wheel at a steady hypnotic pace. It was very soothing, a slow circular movement in the gloom. I might have continued for quite a while. But two Turks came over and began walking in the usual direction. They motioned me to turn around. I shook my head. I motioned them in my direction.

'*Gower!*' they grunted, and continued counter-clockwise.

I was on the inside track. Each time we passed they tried to block my way. But I was determined to hold my position and force them to step outside of me. For some reason this seemed important. It became an issue. I had to fight against the insanity around me.

Ahmet approached from the darkness. He drew me over to the side. More Turks were waking and moving into the flow of the wheel. 'A good Turk always walks to the right,' Ahmet explained. 'Left is Communist. Right is good. You must go this way. There will be trouble if you go the other way.'

So I turned to the right. In a way it was better, all of us flowed together on our journey to nowhere. I seemed to fit in well with the silent madmen. Around and around we moved with a soothing rhythm. We tried to hold back the flow of time. Years from now these same madmen would probably be walking this same wheel in the same direction, the only difference being that I wouldn't walk with them. That was for sure. Or was it? I had a quick flash of a blithering blond-haired idiot wrapped in a scrap of linen and a cloak of madness circling endlessly around the wheel. Suddenly the dungeon felt very spooky. I quickly climbed back upstairs.

Ibrahim cornered me later that morning. In all of Turkey

he was the greatest expert on good machines and bad ma chines. I was almost definitely a bad machine, he assured me. I would never leave Bakirkoy. I found myself really troubled by the sight of him. There was a strange light in his eyes that upset me far more than I would have thought possible. It was becoming more difficult to ignore his ravings.

I lay on my bunk that night, peering through the crack in the window cover. A pale full moon rose in the sky over Section 13. The screaming grew louder. Normally calm inmates became violent. Normally violent ones got worse. There was an electricity in the air. I could feel it running through me.

Yakub, the man who had murdered his sister, ran into the room. That very afternoon we had shared a cigarette. He had been clean and neat in his pyjamas. Now he was naked, enraged and screaming in frenzy. Blood dripped from raw scratch marks on his face. Attendants raced in and wrestled him to the ground. They clamped his hands into a *kiyis*, a thick leather belt that screwed tightly around the waist. It held his hands out front in leather cuffs. Naked except for the *kiyis* belt, screaming curses at the guards, Yakub was hauled down to the cellar.

I waited a few minutes. When the guards returned I went downstairs.

I could hear his screams from a back room near some punishment cells. But as I walked past the wheel and into the back room I saw he wasn't locked in a cell. Instead he was hog-tied to a bed against a wall. Several inmates were gathered around him. One knelt on the bed, pulling at Yakub's penis; he yanked on it as if it were made of rubber. Another felt around underneath him, trying to work his fingers up into Yakub's anus. A third guy, naked and also in *kiyis*, leaned over jabbering and drooling in his face. This seemed to enrage Yakub the most. He lunged up to bite the man's face. He cursed and struggled against the rope and the *kiyis* belt to no avail. The attendants had made sure he wouldn't be upstairs again that night.

I raced in. I smashed at his tormentors and threw them off. They scattered. But they'd be back as soon as I left. I tried to talk to Yakub, to tell him I would untie the ropes. But he

111

didn't recognize me. And I really didn't recognize him. He didn't seem to be the same person I'd been with the past few days, the same person I had talked with and eaten with.

His body arched up against the bindings. He roared at me. His neck strained, his mouth sputtered. His teeth snapped the air.

I didn't untie the ropes. What could I do? I left him down there to his fate.

Violent roaring continued throughout the evening, a hymn to the full moon. The attendants passed out extra doses of pills that night. An uneasy quiet settled over Section 13. I lay on my bed and wondered about the legends of werewolves in the mountains.

I awoke in the middle of the night to the sound of angry screams coming from the area of the attendants' card game. A naked inmate, his hands in *kiyis*, stumbled back into the second room. He crashed against my bed. Then he picked himself up and raced back towards the attendants, shouting at the top of his voice.

'Ossman,' one attendant called. The huge bouncer came running like a faithful puppy dog. He grabbed the naked man and flung him towards the third room. With no hands to break his fall, the man smashed heavily against some beds. He crumpled to the floor. Ossman stood his ground for a moment, then turned back into the first room.

But a moment later the man rose from the stone floor. He began moving towards the attendants again. His face was swollen. His mouth bled. He stopped beside my bed, just short of the first room. He wasn't screaming now. He was crying. He tried to say something to the attendants, but shallow sobs broke his voice. He seemed to be pleading for someone to listen to him. Other men from near-by beds yelled, shouting for him to be quiet. He turned towards them, still sobbing, still trying to explain something that seemed so important he was willing to get beaten for telling it.

Ossman came up. He caught the man from behind. He smashed his face up against the wall at the foot of my bed. The tormented madman twisted around and sank his teeth into Ossman's massive shoulder. Ossman bellowed. Then he grabbed the inmate by the hair and yanked his head back.

The man would have crumbled after Ossman's knee smashed up between his legs but Ossman held him by the hair. Again and again his huge hand crashed into the madman's face. Ossman hit backhanded, the same way Hamid liked to hit. The sheet at the foot of my bed was splattered with blood.

Finally Ossman grabbed the *kiyis* belt in one hand and the man's hair in the other. Dragging him down the hallway, Ossman stopped at the circular stairwell. With a mighty heave he pitched the man towards the dungeon. The body rumbled and clattered against the stone. It rolled to the cellar. Ossman slammed the barred gate shut. All was quiet from below.

Is that the way it happened? I wondered. Maybe they never let anyone out of here. They just let bad machines get worse and then dumped them into the cellar.

An unearthly high-pitched scream woke the barracks the next morning. Hung over from its encounter with the full moon, the madhouse came to life slowly. Inmates looked quizzically at one another. Again a wild scream.

But it came from outside the building.

I ran over to a window. Several others joined me. There, on top of the wall next to the main gate, was a peacock. It thrashed in agony. It was trapped in twisted swirls of rusted barbed wire within the ivy. Blood dripped onto its beautiful feathers. It squirmed and tore its flesh on the murderous barbs. The more it struggled, the more helplessly it became enmeshed. Several men yelled and cheered, laughing hysterically. I watched quietly as it screamed and struggled for perhaps half an hour. Finally it sank into a merciful death.

That same morning the attendants discovered that one of the old vegetables had died during the night. They wrapped him in his dirty sheet and hauled him away to spend the rest of eternity embalmed in his own wastes.

I thought again of the west wall. Its convenient footholds seemed even more inviting. But where would I go? What would I do? I was a prisoner not merely in Bakirkoy but in all of Turkey. I needed a passport. I needed friends on the outside who knew what they were doing.

113

And what I did not need was Ibrahim s relentless taunt-ing.

Each time I saw his smirking face the low ceilings of Bakirkoy seemed to inch even lower. I was smothering in madmen. The filth, the stench, the lice, the screaming and raving, the stares of men with burnt-out brains, all drew me deeper into depression. Ibrahim kept telling me I was one of the factory rejects, and I was beginning to believe him. The power of suggestion, added to the outrageous reality that surrounded me, was pushing me to the edge.

Then while walking the wheel in the early hours of the morning, an answer floated into my mind. Yes, an answer that would make me solid against Ibrahim's argument

Shortly after breakfast he sought me out.

'You still don't believe it, that you're a bad machine? You'll see. You'll find out. Later on, you'll *know*.'

'Ibrahim,' I said, 'I already *know*. I know that you're a bad machine. That's why the factory keeps you here.' I lowered my voice. 'I know because I'm from the factory. I make the machines. I'm here just checking up on you . . .'

Ibrahim narrowed his eyes. Quickly he rose from my bed and walked away.

CHAPTER TEN

I woke up expectantly. It was the seventeenth day of my visit to Bakirkoy. The court order ended today. The doctors had to make a decision. I knew they would send me back to Sagmalcilar prison. I was sane. I didn't belong at Bakirkoy. It was obvious.

Soldiers came for me. They loaded me into the back of a van and drove to the prison. Strangely, I looked forward to arriving back in my old *kogus*. If I had to be locked up, I wanted to be with my friends.

As the guard pushed me into the *kogus* I was greeted by a Harpo Marx whistle.

'Popeye!'

'Hoooo, Willie,' he yelled. 'How is the nuthouse? Any broads there? What happened? You ain't gonna tell me you're sane, are you?'

I laughed.

Popeye lowered his voice. 'Didn't you get a chance to run?'

'Well. I could've got out, I think. But what could I do then?'

'What do you mean?'

'Where could I have gone? I was in pyjamas.'

'Willie!' Arne ran over and patted me on the shoulder. He thrust a cup of tea into my hands. I tasted it. '*Aaaah!* Weak.'

Arne shrugged. 'Ziat,' he said. 'What can you do?' The Jordanian dope-peddler was still monopolizing the tea concession.

'C'mon,' Popeye said, tugging at my arm. 'Volley-ball. We can get one hundred lira apiece from these two new Danish guys I've been setting up.'

'Wait a minute. I want to say hello to everybody. Where's Charles?'

'Upstairs,' Arne said. 'Packing.'

'Packing?'

'He's been transferred. To a prison island.'

I went upstairs. Charles was bent over his bed, sorting through a pile of books.

'Hi, Charles.'

He looked up. 'Hi, Willie. So you're back. How was it?'

'*Sula bula*. What's this about an island?'

Charles grabbed a map. 'Imrali,' he said, pointing to a dot in the Sea of Marmara. 'I requested it months ago. The consul came out with a form. He said I could request a transfer. The Turks let you do that when your sentence is approved by the high court in Ankara. But I didn't hear anything for a long time. I figured they'd refused. Suddenly they said OK. I'll be leaving sometime in the next week or so.'

'Why do you want to go there?'

'Work. They can vegetables and fruits there. Gonna spend some time in the sunshine.'

'Any other Americans there?'

Charles shrugged. 'I don't know. I don't think there are any other foreigners, but I don't care. I need some exercise. Gotta get out of this dump.'

'Well, I hope you like it.'

Charles grinned. 'Just remember me next Christmas. If you have jam tarts, remember that I canned the jam.'

Next Christmas. Surely I wouldn't spend another Christmas here. My good mood faded. I was still in prison, and my big plan had failed.

I went towards the smell of *Gastro*. Max and I analysed my trip to Bakirkoy. He thought I'd made a mistake in the way I talked to the doctors. By answering their questions I proved myself sane, at least too sane for Bakirkoy, too rational to get a 'crazy report'.

'I should've climbed the wall,' I said.

'Which wall?'

'The one facing west. It had big holes in the mortar. I could've climbed it easily.'

'West. West,' Max muttered. 'It's a good thing you didn't.'

'Why?'

'That's the wall that connects to Section 12. The junkies.

That's where I was for a while. You would've dropped right down inside Section 12. Jumped from the criminally insane to the junkies.'

Emin the trusty unlocked my cell. Then he brought me a letter that had arrived while I was gone. I felt warm inside when I saw it. I stared down at the envelope for a few minutes before I opened it. I sat down quietly on my bunk and read it over and over. 'Your letters helped me get through a difficult time,' Lillian wrote. 'The break-up of a marriage – even a bad marriage – brings a terrible sense of failure. You've helped me see my self-worth. You rekindled the spirit of adventure in me. Lillian had quit her job at Harvard. She was joining a mountain climbing expedition to British Columbia. Good for her. At least one of us could enjoy the outdoors. Maybe through her letters I could escape this hell.

The biggest surprise of my return was Weber, the new German prisoner who could outboast even Popeye. Weber strutted around as if he owned the *kogus*. He wore an electrician's tool pouch filled with screwdrivers and pliers and other handy items. I couldn't believe it. Popeye told me that Weber somehow had got a job helping the Turkish electricians and plumbers. No one knew how he got the job. The Turks normally didn't like the foreigners to work. So now, every day, Weber was allowed outside the *kogus*. 'The director, he making me boss. Over the whole prison work. Ya, ya,' Weber told Popeye. 'I do good work. Ya, ya. Fix, fix.'

'I'd like to bust that guy right in his "ya, ya",' Popeye muttered.

Weber walked away. He certainly was obnoxious. But still I didn't think he was as stupid as he acted. Weber was up to something.

A few days before Charles was to leave for Imrali, his girlfriend Mary Ann came over from America for a visit. She was coming to the prison with Willard Johnson from the American consulate. Charles asked me if I would come to the visiting room and keep Willard busy in some sort of discussion while he and Mary Ann sat at the other end of the long table.

She was a beautiful woman. Pale white skin and long

117

brown hair. My eyes kept straying to her as I threw questions at Willard.

'What's going on?' I said angrily. 'Why didn't you call the psychiatrist? Why didn't you help? Do you want me to rot here in prison all my life?'

Willard was a bit flustered. He struck me as an Ivy League-type, well-meaning but obviously uncomfortable in prison and in the company of convicts. In his seersucker suit and striped tie he would have seemed more at place in a New York men's club or on the floor of the stock exchange. His plump face had turned red. 'Hold on a minute, Billy. It's not that easy.'

'Don't you want them to help me? Don't you care about me at all?'

'It's not that simple, Billy,' Willard said firmly. 'The doctor wanted me to guarantee that you wouldn't try to escape. That's an open section where they wanted to take you.'

'So?'

'So, how could we give them a guarantee? How did we know that you wouldn't try to escape?'

'I wouldn't do that.'

Willard levelled a knowing stare at me. I decided to change the subject.

'I need some stuff from the canteen. I need a carton of filter cigarettes.'

'You're smoking now?'

'Yeah. It gets to you inside. There's smoke all around anyway. Might as well.'

'OK. Carton of cigarettes.'

'And some chocolate bars.'

'OK. Is that all?'

I could see that Mary Ann had slipped her hand under the edge of the table. It looked like it was in Charles's lap. Her arm moved back and forth slowly.

'Uh . . . more,' I stammered. 'I need . . . uh . . . a toothbrush.'

'Toothbrush?'

'Yeah . . and . . . uh, soap.'

118

'Soap. OK.' Willard turned suddenly. 'Charles, you need anything from the canteen?'

Charles jumped. 'No,' he said quickly.

'What about my trial?' I asked. 'It's been more than six months now. I still don't know my sentence.'

'Well, the court has received your report from Bakirkoy. They've set a new trial date of May 31.'

'Will they sentence me then?'

'I think so.'

Mary Ann's arm was moving faster now.

'How long do you think I'll get?' I asked Willard.

'I don't think it will be too bad,' he replied. 'Maybe thirty months. Maybe five years.'

Charles's eyes were closed.

'Sounds bad to me,' I said.

'Yeah, I suppose it does from your viewpoint. But it's really not a tough sentence for hashish smuggling.' The consul turned and glanced across the table. 'What do you think, Charles?'

Charles opened his eyes and blinked. 'Huh?' Oh, yeah. Imrali's really nice, man. Yeah. It'll be fine.'

The consul looked confused. Mary Ann grinned shyly and put her hand back on the table.

Prison life took on a different perspective after the darkness of Bakirkoy. My balance was disrupted. Yoga and meditation helped, but I found myself reacting more quickly to the tensions of the *kogus*. Charles made me a present of his Turkish-English dictionary. Speaking to the guards was difficult, so I determined to study the language. But my concentration wavered. I began to smoke more heavily, both tobacco and hashish. I depended more and more upon both habits to keep my nerves under control. Ziat was the source of most hashish in the *kogus*. But his prices were outrageous. I discovered that Max, through his friend the electrician, could provide cheaper, better hash.

The evening after Charles left for Imrali, Popeye, Max, and I sat in Max's cell feeling a bit lonely. Max was already wasted away on his *Gastro*, but never needed an excuse to smoke hashish. He walked unsteadily over to his toilet hole.

He reached underneath and returned with half a plaque. He broke off small bits and rolled them into joints. Max nodded softly to himself. I listened to Popeye's endless chatter about the possibility of a revolution in Turkey. If a new government came in, I thought, maybe it would declare an amnesty.

Suddenly I heard the door open to the *kogus*. A measured walk came to the bottom of the stairs. *'Eskilet!'* a voice called out. It was the Turkish word for 'skeleton', the Turks' nickname for Max.

Max didn't want guards coming up to his room. Quickly he stumbled out into the corridor and down the stairs. Popeye and I dropped our hashish down the toilet hole and slipped back into our rooms. Suddenly I heard Max yelling. I raced down the corridor and arrived at the top of the stairs to see two guards twisting Max's arms behind him. Arief reached into the pocket of Max's robe and pulled out hashish. The guards dragged Max off to the basement. Then I saw Arief mutter something to Ziat, who stood near the door with a grin on his face.

Max returned a few days later. He limped slightly. His wrists were bandaged. His glasses were missing. He squinted painfully at me when he talked. They had taken him downstairs, beaten him for a few minutes, and then run to get Hamid, Max said. While the guards were gone, Max broke his glasses and used a sliver of the glass to slash his wrists. The guards were forced to drag him to the *revere*, the prison dispensary, instead of beating him further.

'It was Ziat,' I told him.

'I know, I know. Damn him! But I learned a great truth from this.'

'What?'

Max leaned closer to me and lowered his voice. 'Man, there's all kinds of drugs in that *revere*.'

Arne studied his astrological charts carefully. He had made a survey of all the men in the *kogus*. He was not at all surprised to find that I was Aries. It was the most common sign in prison. Aries tend to act rashly and impetuously. That was me, all right.

Every morning when I bought a cup of Ziat's watered·

down tea his smirk reminded me of how he squealed on Max. I began to wonder why Ziat was still running the *chi* shop. The job was supposed to go to a new prisoner every month. Some of us didn't need it, because fifty dollars from home would supply all our needs for months. But there were others around who had no contact with their families. They could use the money, too. So one day when I was in a particularly rotten mood I wrote a letter to the prison director. I complained that Ziat was Emin's friend, that he bribed Emin to keep him working the *chi* shop each month. Because of this no one else could get the concession. I took the petition first to Weber, because he seemed to speak good Turkish as well as English. I needed a translation. Weber refused to get involved. He had a good thing going. He was a construction supervisor for the prison now. He didn't want to upset his job.

So Max did the best he could to translate the note into Turkish. I took the letter around to see if I could get other prisoners to sign it.

Ziat, of course, heard about it immediately. I was standing in the corridor talking to Arne about the petition when Ziat came running up to me. 'Nobody sign,' Ziat raged. 'You waste your stupid time.'

Before I knew what was happening I had grabbed Ziat. I threw him out into the yard.

'I don't care what happens but you and I are gonna settle this,' I screamed. 'I'm going to kick you all over the yard.'

Ziat was calm. 'Fine,' he said. 'Good. Man to man. We settle this right now. But I tell you now, whatever happens, when this is finished I bring in the guards and they break you to pieces.'

'What! You and I are settling this, not the guards. What's this about the guards?'

'Right. I fix you afterwards.'

The soles of my feet told me to stop a minute and think this over. Ziat had connections. Arief! The *falaka* stick.

Ziat said calmly, 'Look. You don't bother me, I don't bother you. Right?'

'But you bother me. You bother me all the time. You make crummy tea. And you got Max into trouble. He's my friend.'

'I will leave you completely alone,' Ziat promised. 'Your friends, too. I make special tea for you. We have to live like brothers. We have to be in here together.'

I wanted to smash him in the face. I wanted to pay him back for Max. But reason returned. A fight would only bring me more trouble. I made the only sensible decision.

I relaxed my fist. 'OK,' I agreed. 'You stay out of my way and I'll stay out of yours.'

The door opened downstairs one morning. A hush fell over the *kogus*. Word spread quickly that one of the members of the Turkish mafia had come to live with us.

His name was Memet Mirza. He moved his bulky body around in an insolent swagger, much like Hamid. He was only in his early twenties, but he had a reputation. His father and uncle were big-time gangsters. Memet had already shot and killed a couple of men on his own. If he were an ordinary Turk he might have been hanged for his crimes. As a *kapidiye* he would probably serve twelve to eighteen months at the most. For the first few days everyone stepped politely aside whenever Memet approached. Ziat was deathly afraid that he might have one time informed on one of Memet's friends. Memet simply paced around the corridors and the yard like a hungry grizzly bear.

Popeye and I were upstairs one day, trying to interpret the *Hurriyet* newspaper for news of the anarchist rebellions, when we heard a raging scream from the yard. We raced to the window to look out. We saw Memet swinging wildly at two foreigners. They were Peter and Ibo. I didn't know them very well, except that the two of them were good friends.

Memet may have been a killer with a gun, but he was lousy with his slow-moving fists. Ibo punched him in the side of the belly. When Memet glanced down Peter caught him squarely in the eye.

'Aaaaah!' Memet roared. He reached for both men, trying to clamp them together in a bear hug. But Peter and Ibo squirmed loose. They raced for their rooms and hid under their beds until Memet's temper quieted down.

Later, Popeye and I sat in the kitchen when Memet came in to buy a cup of tea. Popeye snickered. He gave a loud Harpo Marx whistle and nudged me in the ribs. Big, tough Memet was wearing dark glasses to cover up a huge shiner over his left eye.

That evening I glanced into Max's cell. He was curled up on his bunk reading a book. I almost walked on past, until I realized that he was holding the book upside-down. Even for him this was a bit unusual.

'Max, what are you doing? You must be really stoned.'

Max jerked his head up. He saw it was me, and brought a finger to his lips. 'Shhhh. Willie, come here.'

The book was Nietzsche's *Beyond Good and Evil*. Max studied the blank page of the inside back cover carefully.

'Got this in the mail today,' he whispered. He walked over to his locker. He knelt down, pushing his weight against it. Nothing happened. 'Shit,' he muttered. 'Willie, give me a hand here. Push the locker back at an angle.'

I leaned my weight against the top of the locker, rocking it backwards on its base. Max's fingers fumbled for something underneath. He brought out a broken bit of razor blade. We sat together on his bunk, hiding the book between us. Carefully Max slit into the edge of the back cover, right at the seams. Then he peeled back the heavy paper to expose the cardboard of the cover. Holes were gouged into it. Packets of aluminium foil were set carefully into them. Max laid them out on his bed and opened them. He glanced at the accompanying letter.

'This must be the hash. This is the grass. This is speed. This is the morphine! . . . This has got to be acid,' he said. 'Want some of it?'

'No.' LSD is a whole different type of drug. Marijuana and hashish I knew were relatively harmless. LSD could be rough.

Max scraped a bit of it into a piece of foil and pressed it into my hand. 'Keep it,' he said. 'You never know when you'll want it.'

I went to my cell. I slipped the tiny piece of foil into the binding of my diary, next to the file. Then I joined a poker game in Popeye's cell.

A bomb was planted in the American embassy. Soldiers were gunned down in the streets. Anarchists declared open war on the Turkish government. The military took power. They imposed a heavy curfew throughout the country. The streets were said to be filled with armed guards.

We were all happy to see any change in the government, for it might bring an amnesty. But the only thing it brought was anarchist prisoners. Scores of them were shipped in each day. The prison administration wanted to keep the leaders separated. But there was only one *kogus* in the prison with separate cells, and that was reserved for foreigners.

We heard the commotion downstairs in the morning. The guards told us to hurry, to gather our things together. We were moving out. We were being transferred to another *kogus*. Once again I learned that I rarely appreciated anything until I'd lost it. Gone was the privacy of my individual cell. Now we were jammed together in a barracks-type arrangement. There were forty-eight bunk beds on the second floor and, for some strange reason, nothing on the first floor.

I scrambled for a bed in the corner, where I could keep my back to the wall. I took an upper bunk so I could have a little extra privacy. Popeye dumped his things on the bed below me, cussing nonstop about the new *kogus*. Some of the men immediately screened off their lower bunks by hanging sheets from the top bunks.

Turks had been living there, so it was filthy. The floors were covered with thick grime. Paper scraps, filthy rags, and cigarette butts lay scattered around. Smoke had discoloured the yellow plaster walls. Some windows were broken and the others hadn't been cleaned in months. Dirty cotton mattress stuffing was strewn about the floor. The stench was overpowering. And at the far end the stinking bathroom was little better than the accommodations at Bakirkoy.

We shared a new yard with a *kogus* of Turkish prisoners, and the first glimpse of them was a real surprise. Several of them were playing volley-ball. But they were dressed in suits

124

and ties, jumping around in the hot sun. *'Kapidiye,'* Max muttered.

Memet seemed terribly upset. I realized that he was embarrassed to be around other *kapidiye* while his eye was blackened.

'Hoo, boy!' Popeye snickered. 'Big, tough fighter. Big, tough *kapidiye*. Big tough black eye.' He whistled and danced around. Memet swore at him.

Every man had developed his routine in prison. Hassles began when someone or something disrupted that routine. Now, everyone's routine was messed up. The air seemed charged with electricity.

The next morning I tried to re-establish my own routine. I got up early and practised my yoga in the emptiness of the new downstairs room. Ziat, at the far end, brewed his tea. I went into the yard and watched the new patterns of sun and shadow on the unfamiliar walls.

My head snapped around when I heard cries coming from the kitchen area. There was yelling and shouting and cursing. I heard people running. Suddenly the noises stopped and it grew deathly quiet. Slowly, carefully, I moved back inside.

Two men were dragging Popeye towards the *kogus* door, while outside a guard called for a stretcher. Popeye's T-shirt was stained with huge blotches of bright red that dripped onto the floor in puddles. He was conscious but seemed to be in shock. I watched the men carry him out of the *kogus*. Then I turned towards the kitchen area. Men were sitting around at the tables, silent. Some still ate their bread. One table was empty. It was covered with blood.

'What happened?' I asked.

'Memet,' someone said simply. 'He just came up from behind and stabbed Popeye.'

'Where's Memet?'

'He's out in the yard.'

'What? Didn't anyone do anything?'

'What could we do?'

A curtain of hot red anger dropped in front of my eyes.

'What's the matter with you guys?' I yelled. 'You gonna let the Turks just kill us all, slice us all up? Why didn't you jump on him or throw something? How can you sit there and eat your bread?'

Arne tried to calm me down. But I pushed away from him. I raced out into the yard. If I wasn't crazy at Bakirkoy, I was now. Memet walked up and down in the yard, his hands in his pockets. Some of his *kapidiye* friends stood near by.

'*Deli!*' I screamed at him across the yard. 'Crazy!' '*Ipnay*' ('Queer'). I searched for the most vicious words I knew. I was frustrated that I hadn't learned to curse well in Turkish.

Memet stared at me anyway. You couldn't call many Turks crazy queers and get away with it. But when the Turk was a *kapidiye* with a bloated opinion of himself and his friends were watching, it was a really serious move. Emin rushed over to calm me down. But I pushed at him. He stumbled to the concrete. Memet stopped pacing. He turned to face me across the yard.

'Willie,' it was Arne's voice behind me. 'He's still got the knife.'

Oh, God. It wouldn't help Popeye if I got sliced up, too. I needed a club. Or something. Anything.

Memet took a step in my direction. The knife flashed in his hand. Suddenly huge arms grabbed me from behind and I was dragged backwards and slammed into the concrete wall. It knocked the breath out of me. Dimly I saw Hamid's grizzly face. His huge hammy hand was cocked in my direction.

Wham! he hit with full force. I bounced hard against the wall. *Wham!* he caught me backhanded. Flashes of pain and whirling lights filled my head. Then he yelled orders to Emin and the other guards. They herded all the foreigners back into the *kogus* and locked us inside. That afternoon we were to be moved to another similar barracks-type *kogus*, on the other side of the children's *kogus*. Once again we would share the yard with the kids.

The director, Mamur, gave strict orders. No more Turks in the foreigners' *kogus*. That was a bonus. Emin had to go. Mamur appointed a Syrian named Necdet as the new *memi sir*, the trusty in charge of the *kogus*. He spoke many languages well and was a highly educated man. He was serving twelve and a half years for spying on the Turkish army. He was the only prisoner in the foreigners' *kogus* with nothing to hide. He wasn't interested in drugs or sex. He didn't even play cards.

My head ached from Hamid's blows. I gathered my things together. I choked back tears for Popeye. But soon Max padded over with the news. 'Necdet heard from the *revere*,' he said. 'They say Popeye's going to be all right. He won't die. They're sure of it.'

I sat down on the bed in relief. Max bent over and examined my puffy face where Hamid had struck.

'That Hamid is an animal. But he did you a favour today,' Max muttered.

'What are you talking about?'

'He saved your life, man. Don't you realize that?'

I closed my eyes and remembered the flash of Memet's knife.

Court. Another session of confusing Turkish words flying all around me. My destiny was decided in front of me. I was powerless to speak. Yesil motioned for me to rise. Solemnly I heard the judge say the word *dort*, 'four'.

'Four years and two months,' Yesil told me. 'For possession of hashish. That's good. The prosecutor wanted to charge you with smuggling.'

Fifty months. I'd get one-third off for good behaviour. So I would serve thirty-three and one-third months. I would be free on 17 July 1973. More than two years to go.

I was horrified. I felt nausea building inside me as the soldiers chained my hands. I stared in glassy-eyed silence as I was driven back through the streets of Istanbul to Sagmal-cilar.

Arief searched me roughly. Another guard grabbed my arm and pulled me down the corridor to the foreigners' *kogus*. A key rattled. The door opened. The guard pushed me inside.

The heavy metal door slammed shut behind me.

CHAPTER ELEVEN

Day after day passed. A whole summer of my life down the drain.

Charles wrote from Imrali and seemed really happy working out his sentence on the island. He could swim on his lunch hour. He could take long walks around the island on Fridays. The food was good. Since he worked with fresh fruits and vegetables all day long, canning them, he could eat as much as he liked.

His letter started me thinking.

'Max, what about Imrali?' I asked.

'It's fine, I guess. If you like to work.'

'No. I mean to run from.'

'You mean scam?'

'Yeah. Bust out.'

'Naaah. You're twenty miles from the land. And even if you get to the shore you're still in Turkey. What're you gonna do then? You're better off at Imros.'

Imros was another island prison. But it was located off the west coast of Turkey in the Aegean Sea. Some of the Greek islands were less than ten miles away. There was a catch. Imros was classified as an 'open' prison. I probably couldn't get a transfer there until my sentence was too short to make an escape worth trying. By that time it wouldn't matter.

Max and I settled down to some ambitious scamming, planning all sorts of wild escape attempts. Some of the time he was too incoherent to talk. But at other times he really seemed ready to try something. He peered through his thick glasses. He complained that the *Gastro* was making him go blind. He said he needed some real morphine for a change. When he furtively pulled out a Turkish map I was astounded; then I realized it meant that Max finally trusted me.

He surprised me again one day by pulling a set of drawings from among a pack of letters. 'The plans to the prison,' he announced matter-of-factly.

'How'd you get them?'

'There was an Austrian guy here a while back. An architect. He was helping the Turks build some things here. He let me copy the plans.'

We studied them carefully. The dumbwaiter shaft led downstairs. Then nowhere. There would still be plenty of guards and bullets in the way of freedom. If we could somehow get to the roof of the *kogus*, however, we might have a chance. We could walk along to the edge of the main wall and drop over. We'd need a rope. And how could we get to the roof?

We agreed reluctantly that escape directly from Sagmalcilar would be almost impossible. The bullet percentage seemed high. Any plan would be too intricate. And the guards in the watch-towers had machine guns. Nevertheless, I copied the plans and kept them with the jumble of papers in my diary.

We developed the 'acid' plan. We could request a transfer to Kars, a prison all the way across the country, near the eastern border of Turkey. That would require a two-day train ride. There would probably be two soldiers guarding each of us. Max still had his supply of LSD from the drugs that were mailed to him in *Beyond Good and Evil*. I still had the other bit of LSD in the lining of my diary. If we could somehow slip it into the food or drinks of the soldiers, we might be able to run. We might be able to just say, 'Excuse us,' and walk away while the guards enjoyed the colours of the railroad tracks. There wouldn't be any need for violence, either. The difficulty would be that we would probably leave Sagmalcilar in the morning. It would be best to wait until night to make our move. That, however, would leave us in the middle of Turkey. The Black Sea would be to the north. Russia would be to the east. Anyway, I couldn't transfer anywhere until my *tastik* arrived, the piece of paper that said the high court in Ankara had formally approved my sentence. But the 'acid' plan remained in reserve. I made myself a copy of the plans and the map.

Max favoured the idea of going to a hospital and trying an escape from there. Max, for that matter, just favoured the idea of going to a hospital.

129

I thought again of Bakirkoy. If I could get back there, somehow, I really felt that I could escape. Maybe I could climb the west wall and walk across it to the front of Section 13.

But no matter how long we talked we always came back to the same problem. Once out of prison, we were still in Turkey. And we had no friends in Turkey. Maybe I could persuade Patrick to be my outside man. I knew what his reaction would be. Visions of *The Count of Monte Cristo* would fly through his head.

Max translated the story from the newspaper. A young British hippie was arrested trying to sell twenty-six kilos of hashish to three undercover policemen. I looked at the photo. Long, dark hair streamed wildly over his shoulders. He and his mother had driven a van from India to Istanbul. The van was full of trinkets, bangles, and bells. There was a picture of the boy's pet monkey named Beano.

The boy's name was Timothy Davie. He was fourteen years old.

He arrived at our *kogus* a few days later, already a celebrity. Necdet tried to tell him the rules, but a horde of men gathered around to stare at his lanky young body. Someone wanted to know if Beano liked hash.

'Awl-right. Awl-right now,' Timothy said. 'Hold on a bloody minute here. Let us rest a bit, mates. He backed inside a cell and sat down on the bed.

Amazing. Fourteen years old and he wouldn't let anyone push him around.

Within a few days I discovered that he had learned yoga while he was in India. I lent him a few books. We quickly became friends.

In a few weeks Timmy went to court. The prosecutor demanded fifteen years. Immediately the British press picked up the story. The British were outraged that a fourteen-year-old boy would be held in prison with older hardened criminals. Like me.

'*Mektup!*'

The mail.

'Timmy,' the guard said, and handed the boy a package. 'Timmy,' another. 'Tim-o-tee. Timmy. Timmy.'

'Blimey!' Timmy muttered. 'They're all bloody Bibles. Why's everybody sending me Bibles?'

'To protect your bloody morals,' I said.

'Blimey. Why don't they send me some science fiction?'

The *kogus* door opened one day and from upstairs I could hear the Harpo Marx whistle. I raced down the stairs.

'Popeye!'

He grinned, whistled, and patted me on the back.

'Look!' He pulled up his shirt. He had one scar on his back, low. Another high, near the neck. Memet's last blow had caught him in front, just above the heart.

'You were lucky. But I guess you know that.'

Popeye whistled.

The grapevine carried the story to our *kogus*. The guards had 'controlled' one of the cell blocks. They noticed freshly dug earth in the middle of the yard near the drainage grate. They dug up the hole and found a gun, several knives, thousands of pills, and a big Samurai sword. I think the Samurai sword was too much for them. So the prison administration decided to fill in the unpaved section of each yard with concrete. Two days later a huge crane appeared on the other side of the wall. Workers came in to dig up the old facilities and replace them with a new concrete pad. Several of the workers paced back and forth on top of the wall. Our entire *kogus* was surprised to hear a German accent ordering the Turkish workers around. 'Ya, ya,' the voice yelled. Then it chattered in Turkish Weber. He was supervising the entire project!

I sat out in the yard for hours that afternoon. I watched Weber swagger back and forth on the wall as he gave orders to the Turkish workers. He had grown about as powerful as any prisoner could.

The construction continued for several days. But one afternoon I noticed that Weber wasn't at his usual command post on top of the wall.

Weber didn't show up for *Sayim* that night. That wasn't unusual. He often worked late around the prison. The follow-

131

ing morning Necdet, the trusty, broke the news. Weber had escaped. He told the director he had to go into the city to get supplies – something he had done several times in the past. So the director was not upset until Weber was many hours overdue. If he had a car and a passport arranged, he was probably over the border into Greece by the time the director even became suspicious.

Good for Weber. He had us all fooled. He played his own game from the moment he stepped into our *kogus*. He made sure that we all hated him so we would leave him alone – alone to work hard and build up his power with the director.

Then, bye-bye.

I was jealous as hell.

On August 2, the three hundredth day after my arrest, I sat quietly on my bunk trying to meditate. I thought hard about Lillian as she climbed the rugged, beautiful mountains in British Columbia. I hoped she was thinking of me. I hoped she felt my presence. But I was strangely sad, worried. I couldn't understand it.

Weeks later a letter arrived. Lily was in a hospital in Salt Lake City. She had lost her footing halfway up a mountain. She tumbled down the edge of a glacier. Her pickaxe jammed into her right cheekbone, underneath the eye. The accident had happened on August 2.

She was flown to Salt Lake City for treatment by a plastic surgeon. She assured me that her face would be patched up properly by the time I saw her again.

Time passed. Grey days, black nights. Then one day Willard Johnson came out from the American consulate. He seemed concerned. 'It looks like you're going to have a new court,' he said.

'What do you mean?'

'Well, it seems the prosecutor objected to your sentence. So the high court in Ankara wants the lower court to review the case once more.'

'What's going to happen now?'

'Probably nothing at all. You'll go back to the same court.

The same judge. He liked you. He'll probably give you the exact same sentence.'

'Yeah, but what if the prosecutor objects again?'

'It won't matter. When the lower court gives the same sentence twice, Ankara will approve it.'

I tried to figure it all out as I walked back to the *kogus*. I was scared. All the prisoners had horror stories to tell about Turkish justice. A fifty-month sentence was bad enough. I knew I couldn't cope with anything worse.

I slept badly all week. I had a recurring nightmare. I was standing in the yard. Weber directed bulldozers to push the concrete walls in on me. I had nowhere to run. The grey stone pushed in close until it pressed against my chest . . . I would wake up, bathed in sweat, shivering in the autumn air.

A visitor. Maybe it was Willard with more news. The guard ushered me into the lawyer's visiting room and I stepped squarely into a bear hug.

'Johann! You son of a bitch. What are you doing here?'

'Hi, Billy. I've got a surprise for you. I'm going to live here now.'

'Where?'

'In Istanbul. I got a job. In a hotel. I'll come to visit you all the time.' He pressed chocolate bars into my hands. And packs of Marlboros for all of his friends in the *kogus*.

'Billy,' he went on, 'I want you to meet someone. This is Madam Kelibek. She's a lawyer.'

She quietly shook my hand. She was about fifty years old. She must have been quite beautiful in her younger days.

Johann lowered his voice. 'Billy, she can do things for you.'

'Can she get me to Bakirkoy?'

Johann translated the question. The answer was easy to understand even in Turkish. She wanted four thousand lira. About three hundred dollars.

'Can she guarantee it?' I asked.

Johann nodded.

'Explain to her that I can arrange for the money. But she doesn't get a single *kurus* until after I'm there. Everything's C.O.D., understand?'

133

Johann translated. Madam Kelibek indicated her approval.

'Johann, can you get me clothes . . . a car?'

Johann put his broad hands on my shoulder. 'I'll do anything to get you out of here.'

'OK. It'll take me a while to get the money. I'll write to Dad today.'

We talked a bit more, exchanging news about our friends. Johann promised to visit me the following week. I rushed back to the *kogus* to write home. To fool the censor I used words with double meanings. I talked about 'possibility-tracks' and the trains that run on them. First there was the Legal Local. I would ride it if I had to. But it moved slowly. And I didn't trust the engineer. There was also the Midnight Express, I said. It was a fast train. I admitted that it could be a dangerous ride, but I said I had someone waiting for me at the station. It was an expensive train, though. To make sure I had enough money to cover the entire fare I figured I needed about fifteen pictures of Benjamin Franklin (printed, of course, on the faces of one hundred dollar bills).

On 6 December 1971, I was back in the Turkish courtroom. Despite the assurances of Beyaz, Siya, and Yesil, I was worried. What if something went wrong? I would die if they added a single day to my sentence. Again I heard the word *dort*. The same judge gave me the same sentence for the same crime – four years and two months for possession of hashish. Then the same prosecutor lodged the same objection. Beyaz, through Yesil, explained to me that there was absolutely no problem. Now that the lower court had reviewed the evidence twice and reaffirmed the sentence, Ankara would accept its decision. He was sure my sentence would be approved. My *tastik* would arrive soon.

Nineteen more months was nineteen too many.

So I sat on my behind in the *kogus*. I waited impatiently for an answer to my letter. I could see freedom clearly now. A quick bribe to get to Bakirkoy. Then over the wall, into Johann's waiting car and into Greece. Simple. All I needed was a little help from my friends.

Then Dad wrote. His letter reflected anguish and pain.

'Your mother and I have talked about this over and over,

he wrote. 'We've prayed about it. We've cried about it. From our perspective, nineteen months isn't worth the risk of getting killed. We've made our decision out of love. We pray that it's the right decision. We have to say no.'

I was upset. My own family was rejecting me. I threw the letter onto my bed and stormed out into the yard. I walked and smoked all afternoon.

Then I reread the letter. I realized that I couldn't blame them. They loved me. They didn't want me to get hurt.

I sat down and wrote a letter to Patrick.

CHAPTER TWELVE

The last time I had seen Patrick he'd come to visit me in Milwaukee, just before I quit school. He was a small, wiry, black-bearded elf dressed in blue jeans and a green-and-black lumberjack shirt. An old black stove-pipe hat perched on his head. A canvas duffle-bag was slung over his shoulders. His eyes sparkled.

For more than a year I'd been writing to him, taunting him. I wanted him to join a special club that a half-dozen of us at Marquette had started. It involved a certain game, a ritual, out at the city zoo.

The zoo was almost deserted when we arrived.

'This is it?' Patrick asked.

'Uh huh.'

He stared down into the rhinoceros pit. Two huge gray animals lay asleep in the sun at the far end. A third rubbed his thick hide lazily against the rough stone wall.

Patrick laughed. He hopped up onto the thick wall. Once more he checked the three animals. He leaped into the pit and ran to the centre.

The rhinos hadn't moved. Patrick stopped and turned to look at me, a big grin on his bearded face. He held out his hands and shrugged.

The ears of a big bull rhino twitched. In an instant he huffed up to his feet and was running full speed. The ground shuddered.

Patrick was a sprinter in high school. He beat the rhino to the wall by a good twenty yards. He leaped and scrambled for a hold. Then his thighs crashed into the stone, he tottered for an instant, balanced in the air. Then he fell back into the pit.

My heart stopped. Suddenly the game wasn't funny. What a stupid way to die.

Patrick bounced off the ground and seemed to slither up the wall like a lizard. The rhino skidded to an incredible halt beneath him, huffing and snorting. Patrick was so close he could have reached down and touched the horn, but he'd had enough for that day. Careful not to overbalance and fall into the elephant pit on the other side, he scrambled along the narrow wall and leaped off. He grabbed me and then whooped with laughter. Then we ran quickly out of the zoo before the security people arrived.

Patrick stayed in Milwaukee for a few days more. Then he flexed his hitch-hiking thumb in a westerly direction. He was on his way to Alaska to seek his fortune. Jack London had done it. Why not Patrick?

My path lay east. We were both off to see the world. We planned to meet at Loch Ness in little more than a year. We would compare our fortunes.

But the meeting had had to be postponed. Now, more than two years later, he reappeared on the other side of the world.

The visit was no accident.

He came out to Sagmalcilar accompanied by Willard Johnson from the consulate. If a visitor came alone, he was directed to one of many cabins partitioned off from the prisoner by thick glass. But if a lawyer or someone from the consulate was present, the visitor was brought into the same room as the prisoner. Willard's presence allowed me to pump Patrick's hand. But I didn't want the consul to learn our plans. I still didn't know if I could trust Willard.

Patrick chatted casually while Willard sat quietly off to one side of the room, only half listening to our conversation.

'I got a job,' Patrick announced.

'You're kidding. You? Where?'

'John Deere. Tractor factory. Mannheim, Germany.'

'I can't imagine you in a tractor factory.'

Patrick laughed. 'Neither can I. I figure maybe I can tough it out for six months. Mr Franklin should be in good shape by then. I'll bring him along to see you next time. Should I bring any things for you? What will you need?'

'A .45 Magnum . . . three full clips of shells . . .'

Willard stiffened. Then he realized our joke and laughed.

'No, really, I'll need some shoes by then,' I said. 'Sneakers. For playing volley-ball in the summer. And be sure they've got a lot of sole support. Mr Franklin can help you with that.'

Patrick scribbled in his note-pad.

137

'Can you send me some books?' I asked. 'I'm reading *Death in the Afternoon* right now.'

'Ah, Hemingway. *The Old Man and the Sea*. *Death in the Afternoon*. Halloween on Loch Ness and . . .'

'. . . and all I need is a tall ship and a star to steer her by,' I concluded.

Willard was confused.

'Do you like Masefield?' I asked.

'Well, yes.'

'What about Alfred Noyes, Englishman though he be?' Patrick boomed. 'Ah, *The Highwayman*. Excuse us. We're both English majors. We get carried away. It's our Irish heritage. Our ancestors were Gaels, you know. Used to strip naked before going into battle. Stained their bodies blue with wild berries. A fearsome sight they must have been. Screaming blue men charging down the hill at you with naught but their beards and bludgeons.'

Willard Johnson squirmed restlessly in his chair. Patrick had that effect on some people.

Patrick turned back to me. 'So how's your love life?' he asked abruptly.

I laughed. 'It could be better. What are you up to?'

'Same old stuff. I met this fantastic lady in Mannheim. And with a boldness to match my imagination! Mmmmm. Too bad she's married.'

'Is she German?'

'No, American. Her old man is a sergeant in the army.'

'You sure know how to pick them. Better watch yourself.'

'Sure. It makes life interesting.'

By the time Patrick left Istanbul we knew exactly what we were doing. He'd work at the tractor factory until he saved about $1500. Then he'd return to Turkey and smuggle money to me inside the soles of a pair of sneakers. Then he would wait for me outside Bakirkoy.

The plan was right for him. He always pictured himself as one of the Musketeers.

Letters came from Lillian more frequently. They brightened the waiting time. She slowly recovered from her mountain climbing accident and travelled back east to recuperate. She sent me a picture of herself. The scar was no more than a beauty mark. I kept the photo in an honoured position on top of my locker.

She stopped in to see Mom and Dad. She even tried to explain to them such things as differences in life style. They'd heard it all before from me. She was happy. She enjoyed the visit. Soon she set out for the West Coast once again, where the mountains were.

I learned to save her letters. It didn't seem right to open them during the day when the madness of the *kogus* was heavy in the air. So I'd slip her letters inside my shirt and wait until night when the *kogus* was quiet. Once, long ago in a different world, I was in love with a girl named Kathleen. The thought of her always brought a strange stirring deep inside. I got the same feeling from Lillian's letters.

It was a time of waiting. Patrick wrote frequently. Slowly the money accumulated. But reading between the lines, I could tell that some of it was siphoned off for the entertainment of the sergeant's wife. I hoped he was careful. He didn't need his nose broken again.

Timmy was sentenced to fifteen years. Headlines in the British press called the Turks barbarians. The Turkish press denounced Britain's attempts to influence the judicial system of the glorious Turkish republic. Premier Demirel cancelled a planned visit to London.

'A load of bullshit,' Timmy said about the whole thing. 'It doesn't get me out of here for all the bluster.'

But all the bluster did get Timmy's sentence reduced to seven years, counting good behaviour time.

'Too bloody much,' he said.

I agreed.

I got tired of waiting, sitting around doing nothing to help myself get out. Then one afternoon Popeye, Arne, and I were busy winning one hundred lira from three Frenchmen in a volley-ball game. I went up high to block a shot. I lost my footing and got tangled up in the net. Suddenly I had an idea.

In the middle of the next morning a grumbling rose from

the yard. The volley-ball net was lost. It had disappeared during the night from its storage place under the stairs. No one could understand what happened. A couple of men ran through the *kogus* looking into lockers. Voices rose in anger.

Necdet, Emin's replacement, stepped in to calm things down. He didn't care if the net was gone. Prisoners always played the volley-ball games for cigarettes or money. Under those conditions they took the game seriously. Maybe if the net was gone there wouldn't be so many fights.

Then men grumbled, but at Necdet's urging they went outside to play soccer instead. I sat quietly on my bed. Underneath me, stuffed inside a pile of dirty laundry on the floor, was the net.

Night after night I worked under my blanket. Slowly, painstakingly, I unravelled the nylon net. I wove the thin strong strands into a rope that would hold my body weight. I used an old 'barrel stitch' weaving pattern that I learned while making key chains as a boy.

I laboured slowly I jumped at every noise. If the guards staged a control I would be caught for sure. The rope grew in inches.

My friends couldn't understand why I slept so much during the day. I began to work even more feverishly. Until I finished the rope and had it hidden safely away I was vulnerable. If Ziat – or some other stool-pigeon – saw me he would be sure to report me.

Finally it was finished. I guessed that it measured maybe forty feet. According to the prison plans there was an antenna in the centre of the prison roof. If I could somehow get to the roof, I could tie the rope to the antenna, drag the other end to the wall and slide over. Maybe the rope would come in handy some day.

But I couldn't hide it in my locker. A control would find it. So in the middle of one night I sneaked to the far end of the *kogus* near the bathroom. There was an unused locker. I tipped it up and slid the rope underneath.

A few days later Patrick wrote from Germany. He was almost ready.

CHAPTER THIRTEEN

15 June 1972
Patrick,

I'm reading Death in the Afternoon, *by Hemingway. In it he speaks of the moment of truth. I expect you to receive this letter on Monday afternoon. It is the moment of truth – the time to make the clean kill and pass over the horns. Monday night is not too soon for you to don your winged sandals and gather Mercury's swiftness in your Gobbledom Flight.*

With all the exercise I do here I am in need of a new pair of sneaks – the size is forty-two. I think you should purchase these before meeting Mr Franklin. I'd be most happy to see you out here with the consul for a visit. I hope you can contact him on Tuesday and come out on Wed. or Thursday. Please bring me a Herald-Tribune *as I have little access to the news here. And harken, my friend, remember to bring my sneaks with Mr Franklin's warm inner sole – this will be the first movement of the muleta with the left hand – the ploy that keeps the bull's head down before the sword slips in. Afterwards it will be a party.*

My eyes await your grinning face and my feet are tingling in anticipation of the P. F. Flyers.

The Buddhists speak of an inner sole (note sp.) and I firmly believe in this. But the inner sole must be glued with the intelligent hand and the substance of it all comes down to mazuma. But perhaps I speak in too metaphoric a tongue. And then I think not. I am sure you see the light and I await your presence.

Tempus fugit and so do you and your friend, I hope.

I remain,
Willie

I opened the throttle wide. The wind lashed the brim of my lucky hat. I skimmed the big motorcycle along the tree-lined road, past familiar places and faces. I saw Lillian waving at me and smiling. Patrick stood there, grinning as always. I flew by Dad, who shouted at me to be careful.

On an impulse I pulled back on the handlebars. The bike eased off the ground. We glided above the trees. The wind had stopped now. The cycle floated through the calm morning air. I realized I could steer the bike by leaning my weight to one side or the other. I swooped down low over the tree tops, flowing like the wind over the road. Lily tore her clothes off and waited there on the grass for me to land. Dad shouted out a warning. But I couldn't find Patrick. I looked and looked but I couldn't see him. . . .

I woke. It was Tuesday. Had Patrick received my letter yet? Would I hear from him today? How soon before we moved? I was choking on time. I had to get out.

I paced outside in the yard, waiting for something to happen. The fine weather made it even more difficult to stare at the ugly stone. Summer was upon the earth. The morning ration of bread was distributed. It was stale. Mail arrived later. Nothing for me. I tried to write a letter to Lily. I wanted to tell her how much her letters meant to me . . . how much I longed – ached – to see her again. But it was no good. Freedom beckoned to me. It was too close. I couldn't concentrate.

'Vilyum. Vilyum Hi-yes.'

A telegram? For me? Was it Patrick?

I ripped open the yellow envelope and read:

NORTH BABYLON, N.Y.   JUNE 20, 1972
TO WILLIAM HAYES
SAG MALCILAR CEZA EVI
ISTANBUL, TURKEY
PATRICK DEAD. LETTER TO FOLLOW.
DAD

My mind stopped. A gaping crack opened inside me. All my thoughts tumbled into the abyss. I was hollow, emptied of breath as if I'd been kicked in the stomach. The hollow filled with aching pain. I was numb. I stood in the corridor and stared at the telegram. I walked out into the yard and sat down in a corridor against the wall. Patrick dead? How? Why? I pulled my legs up against my chest and wrapped my arms around my knees.

I cried.

Two days later a special delivery letter arrived from Dad. He'd heard the news from Patrick's father. Patrick had been found by the German police in his apartment, in bed, a bayonet thrust through his chest. Among his few remaining personal effects was a train ticket to Istanbul. In his mailbox, unopened, was my letter of June 15. The German police ignored the obvious evidence of the bayonet. They declared Patrick's death a suicide. He was buried by the time his father arrived in Mannheim

His parents were torn. The stigma of the suicide report weighed heavily on their minds. I selected a few of Patrick's most recent letters to me and mailed them home to his parents. I wanted them to read the letters of their son just before he died, to feel the strength and determination in his letters. And the happiness. The sensitivity. Patrick did not pull the bayonet into his own chest. I knew that for sure. Patrick's parents asked American officials to apply pressure to re-open the investigation. The German police finally changed the ruling to homicide. But they had no clues or evidence. The case remained unsolved. Patrick's father wanted to trace down the murderer himself and avenge his son's death.

I decided not to tell anyone about Patrick and the sergeant's wife. I couldn't see the sense. It wouldn't bring him back.

I never felt more depressed. Even the idea of my freedom wasn't as great as the loss of my friend. It took something out of life. But each morning I still scrambled from my bunk to pace the downstairs floor until a grumbling guard finally decided to open the door to the yard. I was still determined to escape. I just had to! Somehow I had to get the money to return to Bakirkoy. I had to rely on the strongest possible ties now. It had to be Dad. Some way I had to persuade him to change his mind.

I wrote to him in code. I needed at least six pictures of Ben Franklin, I said. That was the absolute minimum. Dad wrote back quickly and said he was coming for a visit in a few weeks. He said he would talk with Mr Franklin at the bank before he came. Patrick's death must have shaken Dad, too.

I wrote to Johann at the hotel, suggesting a visit. He came

out the following week. In a guarded conversation I hinted to him that I needed a driver to wait for me outside Bakirkoy. He said he would be glad to do it. All I had to do was send him a postcard with the dates in a coded message.

Once again, things looked as if they were shaping up.

Max wished me luck as he carefully packed his belongings together and moved them out of the *kogus*. He had persuaded the doctor to let him live in the *revere*, the prison dispensary, for a while. There, with plenty of *Gastro* and all sorts of drugs, Max could handle prison time more easily.

Lillian, fully recovered now from her accident on the mountain, wrote to tell me she had lined up a job for the winter at Howling Dog Farm in some place called Willow, Alaska. She would spend the cold winter months working with dog-sledge teams. So it seemed that we could share a kind of spiritual kinship in those months. She would clean the dog pens. I would shuffle around Sagmalcilar.

I grew more dependent upon her letters. Lillian was my eyes to the beauty of the outside world. She was my woman. She did wonderful things to my body whenever I dreamed or fantasized. She was an emotional rock for me. She really cared about me. I treasured her letters more than ever.

Weeks passed. I found a strange haze settling over me. Patrick's death continued to depress me. Maybe I should just sit still and try to figure out the *why* behind all of this. I practised yoga more intently than ever before. I spent hours in the yard, meditating.

I tried to copy Arne's slow, steady, confident pace. His relaxed attitude amazed me. Through many long late-night discussions Arne explained to me the philosophy he was studying. He had been reading the works of Gurdjieff and Ouspensky. Man, they said, is composed of three centres – the intellectual, the emotional, and the physical. All of these centres are guided by the being, the life force within you. The important thing in life is to bring all three of these centres into alignment. When one centre is out of control, you blow the others.

He touched a nerve. My own emotional centre seemed as if it had been totally out of control And had I ever blown it!

Arne tried to convince me that I wasn't conscious. He

forced me to think back. Sure, I could remember the high and low points of my life. But everything in between was blurred into dull shades of grey. According to Arne that proved that I was not conscious. If I were, life would be a never ending series of vivid, real experiences.

We talked a lot about religion. He recommended a series of books titled *Mystic Christianity*. He loaned me some. For the first time I began to realize that Jesus Christ was a man. A real man. A conscious man. A super-conscious, aware, together, no-nonsense, experiencing, individual man. It was a far different concept from what I was raised with.

'When I was thirteen,' I told Arne, 'a priest came to school. He had a talk with all of us boys. He used a lot of fancy words, but we finally realized what he was telling us. He was saying that if we masturbated, we were going to hell. It was impossible *not* to masturbate. But afterwards I was in agony. I knew I had just committed a mortal sin.'

'How sad,' Arne said.

'Right. I finally just had to say to this priest, in my mind, "Come on!" How could he tell me something is a mortal sin when it felt so good? And then, as if that wasn't bad enough, he said it was a mortal sin even to *think* about masturbating. Even if you don't do it. How can you think of anything else when you're thirteen years old? So if you deserve eternal hell fire whether you do it or just think about it . . . what difference does it make? You might as well do it. At least you'll be guilty of something worthy of the name of sin.'

'Sex is vital,' Arne said. 'All energy comes from your physical centre. That's sex. You have to direct and channel that energy. If you don't control it, it can blow you apart. But you can't waste it, either. You have to keep all your centres in balance. Too little sex, too much sex – either will throw you out of balance. It's the same with your mind and your emotions. You've got to keep them balanced. Aligned.'

He levelled a stare at me.

'Your intellectual centre is a mess,' he said. 'You cloud it. I used to cloud mine, too.'

'What?'

'The hash. You use it to become less conscious of reality. What you really need is to become more conscious.'

145

I thought about his words carefully. I'd been smoking hashish for a long time. During the last couple years of college, and during a year or so of bumming around the world, it had been almost a daily part of my life. In prison it was sometimes difficult to get and always risky. But there was enough of it provided by Ziat and others to make it a fairly regular practice. I looked forward to it as an emotional if not physical escape from prison. What would it be like to stop smoking it? It wasn't physically addictive, but it could hang me up emotionally. And when I looked at the situation objectively, I realized that hashish was the cause of a lot of my trouble. And if I kept smoking it, I risked more beatings and more time on my sentence.

So I sat cross-legged on my bunk. Calmly I considered the facts. 'OK,' I said to Arne. 'I won't promise to stay off for ever. But let's see what it's like not to smoke.'

'While you're at it,' Arne suggested, 'throw the stupid cigarettes away, too.'

A visitor's slip. Dad. I ran into the room. He stood there behind the table. Willard Johnson was next to him. I was so caught up in my own plans that I didn't even say hello.

'Dad! Have you seen Mr Franklin? I want you to call this guy Johann for me. You've got to meet him and talk to him. And call Madam Kelibek. And . . .'

'Hey, slow down,' Dad interrupted. 'You haven't even asked about your mother.' Dad sat me down in a chair. He forced me to make small talk. I could read the betrayal in his tired face.

'You didn't see Mr Franklin, did you?'

He shook his head. I almost screamed at him.

'Dad . . . why?'

'I spoke with the priest about it. He said that if I gave you the money I'd be sealing your death. I thought and thought about it. Mother and I have done a lot of crying and praying about it. No, Billy. No. You've got only one more year We can't let you.'

Red floated in front of my eyes. I didn't care if Willard understood the conversation. 'Dad, I'm going to do it, I promised. 'I'm going to get out of here one way or another With your help or without it.'

He was near tears. 'Please, Billy,' he pleaded. 'Wait. Please wait. I've been talking with people from the State Department. Our ambassador here, Macomber, is following your case closely. He thinks he might be able to persuade the Turkish government to release you early.'

'Why haven't you told me this before?'

'I only heard about it myself a couple days ago.'

'It's not sure?'

'No.'

A pause. 'Dad, I've learned a lot about the Turks. I don't trust them. This isn't the good old United States.'

'Oh, so now you appreciate your own country.'

'Yeah.' I gulped. 'All it takes is a few years in a fascist prison.'

'I'm sorry, Billy. I didn't mean to hurt you.' Dad's eyes moistened. Willard got up from the table and walked over to a window. 'Billy,' Dad said, 'try to understand. Your mother and I have died a little each day during these past two years. You're our oldest son. We would gladly trade places with you if we could. All we want is a chance for you to start your life all over again. You can make something of yourself. I know you can. It's only one more year, Billy. That's not too long. Wait it out. Then you can start fresh. We'll be there to help you. We love you, Billy. We . . .' he choked and wiped at his eyes.

CHAPTER FOURTEEN

20 November 1972
Lily,

What to say about being lonely in the night? I am a man. At night the emptiness surrounds me.

You asked about my sex life. For the first year I could speak to you of strange frustrations, of dreams and sweat-soaked mornings and wasted energy. For the past year or so I've been celibate. Hard to believe, even harder to accomplish. Difficult under these conditions but then life is easy only for those who set themselves an easy goal.

And now I look around and the loneliness is still there, hovering like a shadow in the corner. But it doesn't press so on my chest. Talking to you helps. So I store the sorrow inside of me to laugh that much more someday. And I mean to say that I do have some laughing to do. Because aside from what I have been storing up, there's also the thing that I decided about Patrick – which is that, seeing as how he's not around, then I'll just have to laugh for both of us.

> *Night Lil.*
> *Touching you,*
> *Billy*

In the early morning hours of 10 December, three vans drove across the border from Syria into Turkey. They were stopped by guards at the Cilvegozu checkpoint. The guards were suspicious of the long-haired young man driving one van and enchanted with the six beautiful American women riding with him in the caravan. They politely offered tea to the *turists* while one of them inspected the vans. He poked a stick at the ceiling of one van. It broke through a false top. Bricks of hashish fell out. The three vans were stripped. The hash piled up. There was an official total of 99.7 kilos, which is about 219 pounds. The Turkish newspapers estimated its street value in the U.S. at $950,000.

The man, Robert Hubbard, said he had met the girls at various places in Europe and the Middle East. He invited them along on his trip to buy 'stuff' for his store in Munich.

He claimed the girls were all innocent. But he and Kathryn Zenz, Terry Grocki, Jo Ann McDaniel, Penny Czarnecki, Margaret Engle, and Paula Gibson were taken to the prison at Antakya in southern Turkey, near the shores of the Mediterranean.

I followed the newspaper stories carefully. I sympathized with them. The girls were also quite good-looking. I wondered if the publicity surrounding their case would finally get the message across to other Americans: It's a serious thing to get arrested for hashish in Turkey; it can cost you a lot of years of your life.

If they'd managed to smuggle any of that hashish into Sagmalcilar, I wouldn't have been a customer. As time passed I was enjoying the fresher, brighter outlook on life that seemed to grow within me. Whether it was the lack of hashish, my new spiritual awareness, the vigour of my exercise programme – or a combination of them all, I didn't know. But I was calmer now and I was more eager than ever to rejoin the world. Yet I felt better prepared to accept my fate, whatever that was to be.

Just before Christmas another American prisoner arrived at the *kogus*. He was new to Sagmalcilar, but he'd been in the Izmir prison on the Aegean Coast for one year longer than I'd been in Sagmalcilar. (Izmir used to be called Smyrna before the Turks captured it from the Greeks.) His name was Joey Mazarott. He had bright blue piercing eyes and a long black handlebar moustache. On his right arm, just beneath the rolled edge of his faded purple T-shirt, was a tattoo. It showed a tiny, grinning red devil holding a pitchfork. Joey was a lively, friendly man. He came into the cell block and bought a bunk right out from under a young Italian prisoner, then he lay down to sleep almost nonstop for two days.

He was serving ten years for smuggling about eighty kilos of hashish.

'Got any hash?' he asked me as soon as he woke up.

I shook my head.

'I gotta have some hash.'

I told him about Ziat. Joey went to the *chi* shop to speak with the Jordanian. He came back with a little piece of hashish and a scowl. 'Too damn expensive,' he muttered 'Gotta get a better source.'

We had a poker game that night. Joey bet me his suit against a 125-lira pot. I drew a queen to an inside straight. I wouldn't have to borrow clothes for my next court appearance.

It took Joey and Ziat no time at all to become bitter enemies. Joey and I were out in the yard one morning when we heard a commotion. Ziat yelled at one of the children for bumping into him, causing him to spill a glass of tea he was carrying out to a customer. Several kids followed Ziat back towards our *kogus*. They peered inside the window. They teased him. One of them called him *ipnay* (queer).

Ziat ran out into the yard, enraged. He pushed the kids away from the window. One of them fell to the ground. Ziat aimed a kick at his stomach. Suddenly a banzai-like scream came from the children's *kogus* and out rushed Chabran, the self-proclaimed leader of the Turkish delinquents. Chabran was a fifteen-year-old weightlifter. Not too many of the grown men in our *kogus* wanted to tangle with him. Chabran ripped into Ziat. With flailing fists he backed him to the wall. Ziat screamed in pain. Chabran's fists found his stomach, his groin, then an eye. Necdet finally arrived and broke up the fight. He ordered us into our *kogus* and locked the door, leaving the children out in the yard. But Chabran, his rage unfulfilled, walked out into the yard and smashed the glass in all the windows. He yelled and screamed Turkish curses. Not a guard bothered him. Necdet kept us inside until the blood from Chabran's sliced hands overcame his anger and he agreed to let Necdet send him to the *revere*.

Necdet let us into the yard once more. Ziat went back to his *chi* shop. But children milled around the yard, stepping over slivers of shattered glass. They muttered under their breath at Ziat.

As usual, Necdet tried to apply logic to an illogical situation. He confronted an angry group of children and attempted to sort out their stories. The chattering urchins couldn't seem to make him understand. Necdet angrily accused one of them of spitting at Ziat through the window.

Joey raced over 'This is ridiculous, man,' he said to

Necdet. 'Ziat's terrorizing those kids. He's beating up on them. And he cheats us all on the tea, anyway. He puts water in it. These kids were just complaining about his tea.'

Ziat ran out and tried to swear at Joey in his clumsy English. 'You goddamn, you shut up,' he spluttered.

Wham! Joey's fist flew up without a moment's hesitation. It caught Ziat in the nose and knocked him into a crowd of kids. They squealed in delight. From that moment on, Joey was their hero.

Still another newcomer arrived at the *kogus*. His name was Jean-Claude LeRoche. He was being held for extradition to France on an embezzlement charge. He was a dapper, distinguished-looking gentleman in his forties. Though he seemed the picture of health, he immediately told Necdet he had tuberculosis and needed to go see the doctor. Thereafter, once a week, he went to see the doctor. Sometimes he spent all day there. He also received long visits from a man named Sagmir who was supposed to be a big *kapidiye* lawyer. It was rumoured that Sagmir could arrange almost anything.

One day when I was visiting with the consul, Jean-Claude had a visit with Sagmir. Jean-Claude's wife was there too. She was a slim, tiny Vietnamese woman with long, black, straight hair. Her skin was pure cream. I fell in love with her immediately.

After four or five weeks Jean-Claude announced that he was being sent to the hospital across the street from the prison. His tuberculosis was worse. He needed special treatment. He still looked healthy to me.

Ten days after he went to the hospital, Jean-Claude escaped. No one seemed to know how. One night he just disappeared from the locked, guarded prisoners' wing. It was another week or so before I heard the full story when Max shuffled over from the *revere* for a visit. According to Max's *kapidiye* friends, the escape was planned by Sagmir. The first night in the hospital, Sagmir appeared at the door to the prisoners' wing. Jean-Claude's gorgeous Vietnamese wife was with him. They had a basket of food. What could the guard say? He stared at the luscious woman and allowed Jean-Claude to come to the door for his basket of goodies.

Every night for ten nights Sagmir drove the woman to the hospital in Jean-Claude's very own Porsche. The guards looked forward to the visits by the elegant young woman. Then one night Jean-Claude said to the guard, 'Look, I'd like to be with my wife for a while. Know what I mean? But I can't do that here. I want to go downstairs in the car with her. As a guarantee that I'll return here's ten thousand lira to hold onto.'

Very clean. Very neat. No one took the blame. Jean-Claude left Turkey in style. And Sagmir was still driving his client's Porsche around Istanbul.

The emotional coldness of prison life was worse than the physical cold. Loneliness is an aching pain. It hurts all over. You can't isolate it in one part of your body.

The weekly bath came to mean more to me than just washing and hot water. It meant a chance to touch another human being. To be touched. I soaped the muscles of Arne's shoulders with my hands. He washed my back. It seemed strange that I was enjoying the touch of a man's hands on my body. I never had before. This wasn't supposed to be right.

Then why did it feel right?

We began to give each other massages in the evening. I'd take off my T-shirt and stretch out across Arne's bed. He had hung a sheet down from my bunk above for privacy. Arne's long fingers felt good kneading the tired muscles of my back and shoulders. I liked the human warmth of his hands on my back. He was Swedish, and he knew how to give a massage. He handled my body like he handled his guitar. Gentle strength. Easy rhythm.

Some days the pressure of prison was so great I thought I'd burst inside. I lay on Arne's bed after just such a day. He knew how I felt. My head was turned to the side. My eyes were closed.

His hands stopped moving.

'Willie?' he questioned.

I opened my eyes. A long erection stood up out of his shorts.

I rolled over on my back. He held me in his hands and lowered himself onto the bed.

'It's all right, Willie. It's only love,' he said.

CHAPTER FIFTEEN

21 January 1973
Folks,

Long time we're waiting now, isn't it? I know about waiting but this is getting a bit trying on the old central nervous system.

Another American came up here a few weeks ago. He's been in prison down in Izmir for three years now. Izmir is an exceptional prison. The facilities are new, like this Istanbul jail, but there all the similarities stop. Down there, tourists are a rarity and treated especially well. Tourists have their own rooms. Food can be bought outside each day and brought into the jail. Each day a helping of milk and yogurt plus three!!! meals are brought in for the Americans there. Four guys now in residence. Each gets bacon-eggs breakfast, packages of oatmeal, pota toes, steak!! etc. There is a library where nonworking prisoners can go. What a joy compared to this barracks room set-up.

So . . . I've hired a lawyer to effect this transfer down to Izmir. Only one problem. To get transferred down there for the remaining months, I must first have received my approval from Ankara. I've seen this lawyer work — believe me, he does a good job. He says my case is delayed due to a backlog and the difficult 'adjustment problems' of the current government. But he also says he could get my case to court, and, most important, approved, with relative ease and speed. He asks payment of six thousand Turkish lira. But not one lira until after completion and I'm at Izmir. And since the only way I can be transferred is for my four-year sentence to be approved, I find this arrangement trustworthy.

Perhaps you are wondering why. Easy to answer — I think our other lawyers are doing absolutely nothing. They have failed to even reply to my three letters (one to Yesil in English, two to Beyaz in Turkish). I believe it to be essential to have someone in Ankara working on the case. I have less than six months left. If the case does not come up in Ankara by then, I remain here. I do not go free until a decision is made. You may find it hard to believe that could happen. You're wrong — this is Turkey — I've seen it happen. So I've hired this guy. I want to know when I will have a degree of privacy and liberty; and where I will be able to prepare myself for going out.

I consider this step to be a sort of compromise between the foolishness

154

*of excessive action and the equal foolishness of sitting back awaiting the
vagaries of chance.*

The hundred arrived. I thank you. My love to all.

Billy

My new lawyer was none other than Sagmir, who did such
fine work for Jean-Claude. With him on my case I knew it
would take little time for Ankara to approve my second court
sentence. My *tastik*, the approval of my sentence by Ankara,
would arrive soon. I could almost taste the good food at
Izmir.

The privacy, too, would be beautiful for the last six
months, though I would miss Arne. I was teaching him yoga.
We had developed a morning routine.

I woke first, and slipped on my shorts. I walked barefoot
over to Arne's bunk and laid a hand on his shoulder. He woke
quiet and smiling. We gathered up our blankets and slipped
downstairs to the empty lower room. I stood by the window
and drew fresh morning air deep into my lungs. Arne smiled.

He stood silent, balanced lightly on his feet. His palms
were pressed together beneath his chin. Slowly he rose on to
his toes and stretched his arms out above his head. It was the
beginning posture, his body greeting the day. I balanced
myself and slowly rose onto my toes. My arms stretched up
and out, high enough to reach the sun. We moved through a
series of postures.

An hour or so later, Arne finished. He sat silently in the
lotus position, waiting for me. I finished and sat facing him.
We breathed slowly. Our bodies were relaxed. Our minds
were still. We were centred inside ourselves. We looked into
each other's eyes. The smile came to his face. And mine.

'A prison, a monastery, a cloister, a cage . . .' Arne had
once said.

I knew what he meant. Prison can be any one of those
things. Perspective. Everything depended upon that.

Sometimes, in the early morning, we just sat. Sometimes
we made love. Then Ziat woke and clomped down the stairs.
The magical time of day was over. The monastery was a
prison once again.

*   *   *

British and Turkish officials finally came to an agreement on the case of young Timothy Davie. He was to be transferred to a minimum security children's prison on the outskirts of Ankara.

'Should be a bloomin' breeze,' he said as he packed. 'A couple of months, I figure. Mom'll have me out.'

'Good luck, Timmy. Keep cool. Keep quiet. I'll be waiting to read about you in the papers again.'

'Thanks, Willie. The best to you, too. Ta . . .' He waved.

On 8 April 1973, I ripped a big sheet of drawing paper off of a tablet the consul had brought me. Carefully I drew numbers in descending order from one hundred to one. With coloured pencils borrowed from Arne I drew a wild rainbow flowing from the last day. I taped the paper prominently onto the side of my locker and sat down to admire it. Each day from now on I would cross out one of the numbers. On July 17 I would go free.

I had forgotten, almost, about the rope hidden under the locker. The prison plans and the file hidden in my diary didn't seem necessary any more. But I held them anyway. Maybe I'd give them to Popeye or Joey or Max before I left. Someone could put them to good use.

Lillian wrote me a sweet letter from Alaska, where she was finishing her work with the sledge dogs. She talked about going to Switzerland and getting a job in the Alps where she could climb and ski all the time. In the summer, she said, maybe she could meet me. We could spend some time together in Morocco, perhaps. Lying on the beach together in the sun. Wonderful. Lying in a bed together in the dark. Fantastic.

Life became a dream. I watched myself rise, go through the motions of the day, go to sleep at night. Soon I would wake up after three long years. I'd be free. The world would be fresh and open to me. I could wait a few more months.

Incredible. Amazing news. Arne was going home! The guards came around suddenly and told him to pack his things.

'Arne. What's happening?' I asked in amazement.

'They did it, Willie!' he said. 'They're going to transfer me back to a Swedish jail. The Swedish ambassador has been working on it for more than a year. I can't believe it.'

'Why didn't you tell me about it?'

He looked at me and stopped smiling. 'I wasn't sure. I didn't want to speak about it in case it didn't happen. You know what I mean?'

'Yeah, I know. But it's just so sudden. I . . . I'm going to miss you, Arne.'

He smiled again. 'I know, Willie. I'll miss you, too. But you'll be OK. You don't have much longer.'

'I know. Listen, how long do you think you'll stay in jail there?'

He laughed and whispered to me. 'The way the jails are in Sweden, people don't want to leave. But I guess a few months, just for show. Then they'll let me out.'

He didn't pack much. He gave almost everything away. I got his guitar. 'I expect you to be good on that thing when we meet again,' he said.

I laughed.

He finished packing and made his way around the *kogus*, shaking hands with everyone. I waited down by the corridor door. There were tears in his eyes as we embraced.

'Keep smiling, Willie.'

'I will, Arne.'

Then he waved his hand and was gone.

'Timmy has escaped!' Necdet said to me one morning. 'I heard it on the radio.'

'Fantastic! How'd he do it?'

'I'm not sure. The radio says he just walked away from the children's prison last night after *Sayim*. No one's heard from him since.'

'Just great! I knew he'd get out. He was a real smart kid.'

But not smart enough. The news that evening had the sensational story of the escape and capture of Timothy Davie. It seems his mother and a friend arranged the escape. They met Timmy after he walked away from the minimum security prison. They dressed him in a long-haired wig and women's clothes. They had a false passport for him. They tried to get him across a checkpoint on the Iranian border. But the passport they obtained was on a list of wanted items. Timmy's mother and friend crossed first. But Timmy was caught.

The Turks sent him to another children's prison in Izmir. This one was maximum security.

A little later we heard that four of the girls who had been imprisoned last December at Antakya were freed on bail. Good for them. But the three who were driving the vans – Robert Hubbard, Kathy Zenz, and Jo Ann McDaniel – were still in the Antakya prison. Hubbard claimed the two girls were innocent. But the courts wouldn't believe him.

The days passed in a slow, methodical march. My *tastik* still hadn't arrived. When I was feeling negative, that worried me. But Sagmir was working on the case and I knew he was good. No problem. July 17 was Independence Day.

The air grew fresh and clear as summer approached. I was ready for freedom. I was thinking clearly. It had been nearly eight months since I last smoked hashish.

On May 24 I rose early as usual and took care of the day's first task. With a big black felt-tipped pen I crossed through number 54 on my calendar. Then I slipped downstairs for yoga and meditation. A brief walk in the yard, breakfast, then a mild surprise. A visitor's slip. Whoever it was waited in the lawyer's room, not the visiting booths. Sagmir? Yesil? My *tastik?* Had it finally arrived? Today, would I finally know for sure that July 17 was the day?

I entered the visitors' room to see Willard Johnson, his face not the usual pink but grim and grey. What's wrong?

'Sit down for a moment,' he said. 'I have some bad news for you.'

Had something happened at home? Did someone die?

Willard swallowed hard. He didn't want to say whatever he had to say.

'We have been notified that Ankara has rejected the Istanbul court sentence. They've made a decision. You will have to have a new court in Istanbul. They'll have to go along with Ankara's request . . . Ankara's demand.'

158

'Well, what do they want?'

A slow, hesitant voice. 'They're demanding . . . they're demanding . . . life. . . .'

'Give me a cigarette.'

He gave me one of his Camels. I took a long, choking drag on it.

'The lawyers will be coming out this week,' Willard said.

'When's court?'

'Early July. But nothing will happen there.'

'Why?'

'We're delaying it. The lawyers are. They won't show up. There will be a summer judge. He doesn't know the case. He'll have to delay the trial until September. The regular judge will be back then. We've already spoken to him. He'll do the only thing he can do under the law. He'll reduce the sentence to thirty years.'

Thirty years.

Willard was silent. There was nothing to say. We smoked our cigarettes.

'Do you want anything from the canteen?'

'No.'

'Do you need anything?'

'No.'

Silence.

'We've notified your family.'

'Yes. Thanks. Can we appeal?'

'Yes. The lawyers will. But it won't make any difference. There are thirty-five judges on the court. Twenty-eight of them voted for the life sentence.'

Numb, dazed, in a trance I walked back to the *kogus*. I sat down on my bed. Popeye came over.

'Who was the visitor?' he asked.

'Willard Johnson.'

'What did he want?'

'Well, he had some personal news for me.'

'Are you OK? What happened?

'Remember the *tastik* that never came? Well, we just heard from Ankara today that they disapproved the four years. Now I'm going to get a new court. I'm definitely, one hundred per cent, getting life.'

'What! Are you kidding me? They can't be giving you life.'

'Johnson has already talked to the judge. He's going to lower it to thirty years. It's all he can do.'

'Holy God!'

Give me some cigarettes.'

'Sure.'

A silence.

'Willie, what can I say? *Getchmis olsun*, brother. May it pass quickly.'

'Yeah. Thanks, man.'

Popeye left me alone. His pessimism had certainly been justified. Thirty years!

I lay on my bunk, trying to swallow the hard, painful lump stuck in my throat. Suddenly my eyes caught the one hundred-day freedom calendar. I ripped it off the locker and threw it on to the floor.

I needed air. All day I walked furiously up and down the yard, chain-smoking cigarettes and speaking to no one. Everyone gave me plenty of room.

I thought of Lillian. I thought of Mom and Dad and Rob and Peg. I thought of my wasted life, rotting in this stinking hole while the world spun on without me. I saw the collection of people I was forced to live with and the effect they had on me.

And then, in my mind, I saw the file, the prison plans, the rope in the locker. Now it was settled. Better to be dead than to remain in this prison.

CHAPTER SIXTEEN

30 May 1973
Dear Senator Buckley:

My name is William Hayes and I am the father of a boy who has been imprisoned for the past three years (approximately) in Istanbul, Turkey. An article on this situation was scheduled to be published in Newsday *on either May 30th or May 31st. Possibly by now you have seen it.*

I am writing to you in the hope that you will be sympathetic to my plea for help to gain the release of my son from this Turkish prison. I do not condone what my son did. I despise drugs as much as any decent citizen. But, to my way of thinking, a thirty-year sentence, or any harsher sentence that might be imposed by the Ankara court which would prevent his release after three years' confinement, is completely unjust and illogical. We are not talking here of hard drugs like heroin, cocaine, etc. But of hashish which, like marijuana, will possibly be declared legal in this and other countries in the near future.

His original sentence we have lived with but, frankly, any additional imprisonment imposed by Ankara will just about kill my wife and ruin the life of a young man who has much to offer the world. His major crime was stupidity and I feel that three years of his young life should be penalty enough for his actions.

Newsday *has been kind enough to help me in my pleas for assistance. All I can do is ask you to consider the facts of the case, the severity of the 'crime' involved, and the punishment that looms over our heads. I am sure that pressure from your office, applied at the right level, could help us tremendously. You have potential influence to intervene in our behalf.*

I realize how crowded a Senator's schedule must be but I implore you please to heed my plea for help. Any man who is a father surely will understand my feelings.

Thank you.
William B. Hayes

The publicity was amazing. My old friend Mark Derish wrote *Newsday*, the Long Island newspaper, a letter about me. Then a reporter called our home. Dad, who had so often lied to people about me, telling them I was ill in a European hospital, wasn't sure whether publicity would help. But how could it hurt any more? The people at *Newsday* were sympathetic. They printed a feature article about my 'lonely ordeal' and the horrible news of my thirty-year (or life) sentence. The reporter even went back to Seton Hall in Patchogue and interviewed my high school principal, Sister Mary Louise. She remembered me as a boy 'most likely to succeed'.

Some of the things they printed worried me. They quoted from one of my letters home where I said that if Ankara didn't approve my four-year sentence Mom and Dad could 'expect something very rash'.

'He won't sit there,' Dad told the reporter. 'He'll try to get out. And they'll kill him.'

What effect would all this have on the Turkish judges, I worried? I still had to go to court for the smuggling trial. Maybe the publicity would anger them into giving me life, rather than thirty years. I sure hoped Dad knew what he was doing.

Over the next few weeks the barrage continued. *Newsday* reporter Annabelle Kerins learned that Ankara's decision seemed based partly on political pressures. The Nixon administration had made its foreign aid dependent on a ban on opium poppy growing. Turkish farmers were mad. They wanted pressure applied to the U.S. The Ankara court said that it had stiffened the penalties for drug offenders 'for the benefit of the international social order'. The decision in my case was in accordance with 'international agreements'. The court ignored the fact that the maximum penalty for opium smuggling was only ten years in Turkey.

Newsday called me 'a pawn in the poppy game'. The paper sent reporter Bob Greene over for a visit. They ran story after story. They even asked me to write my impressions of prison life for them. Me! After all the dreaming I had done about being a writer and all the rejection slips I'd collected back in Milwaukee, *Newsday* was requesting that I write for them. Maybe the publicity wouldn't be such a bad thing after all.

In a Sunday edition *Newsday* ran a photo of me as a three-year-old, riding a pony at the Bronx Zoo. It was printed right under a headline that said 'Dean Charging President Talked About Cover-up 35 Times, Sources Say.'

What a crazy world.

Dad wrote to New York's senators, James Buckley and Jacob Javits, and several congressmen, trying to get help. They all promised to do what they could. Senator Buckley even mentioned my name on the floor of the United States Senate in a plea for government help.

Letters poured in from all over the United States, from old friends, acquaintances, and strangers. Everyone tried to cheer me up. They all assured me that the government would work hard to get me out soon.

Responding to the publicity, criminal lawyer John Sutter offered his services for free. Though he was busy defending some of the Watergate personalities, he found time to talk with State Department officials about me. He, in turn, was contacted by another lawyer who wanted to help. His name was Michael J. Griffith. His office was in Mineola, Long Island, just west of home. He talked with my father and also offered to work for nothing. He wrote to me and said he was about to leave for a vacation in Greece and asked if he could stop in and visit me. I wrote back my thanks; I didn't mention that if he didn't hurry I might not be here.

Sagmir may have helped Jean-Claude escape, but he hadn't helped me any. His explanation was that the Turkish courts didn't want to lose face. But he could still work for me behind the scenes. For the proper amount of money Sagmir claimed that he could persuade the prison officials to lose track of my papers. There would be no record of me as a prisoner after July 17. He could have me in Greece by the time the Turkish courts discovered the error. Since it would be a simple clerical foul-up no one would be in any trouble.

The cost would be 30,000 lira, about $2000. But Sagmir warned me that we had to act before the official sentence was changed to thirty years. For my part, I warned Sagmir that he would not receive one *kurus* until I was completely safe outside Turkey. He agreed with a broad smile.

I wrote to Dad and explained the situation as best I could Dad replied that Mr Franklin was taking a second mortgage on the house in North Babylon. He would come visit me as soon as possible.

I was walking in the yard a few days later when a visit card arrived for me. I went out to meet a young American just about the same age as my own twenty-six years. He was Michael Griffith, the lawyer from Mineola. He was a tall, friendly guy, eager and energetic. I liked him immediately.

He spoke to me about John Sutter and the response to the newspaper publicity. The State Department was investigating the possibility of arranging to transfer me to an American prison. I told Mike about Arne's transfer. He was optimistic. But he said it might take time Turkish-American relations were strained at this point.

Since the proceedings had just begun, there wasn't really much to discuss about the transfer. So we just talked. Mike and I had both grown up on Long Island, and we shared a lot of memories. We'd both been life-guards too. We even knew some of the same people.

I told him how I longed to swim in the ocean. He grinned and said, 'Hold on, you'll be there soon.'

'Right.'

'And I hear you play softball.'

'A bit. I might be a little out of practice now.'

'No problem. I play for the Broadway Show League in Central Park. You'll have to play with us when you get back.'

'Yeah. I'd sure like to play this summer.'

Mike laughed. 'Maybe. Who knows? But for sure you'll be at next year's spring training.'

Now I laughed. 'Sure. OK. Keep in touch. Say hello to everyone back home for me. And soak up some Greek sun for me, too.'

'Right, I will. Keep your chin up. Good things are happening.'

It was good to see Dad again. The strain of the past few years had put wrinkles into his face. But his body was still trim and fit from handball. Dad had the money for Sagmir. But he wanted to talk to me first. 'There's a new train running,' he said.

'The Transfer Special?'

'Yep. Mike Griffith and I have been on radio and TV shows back home. We're trying to get the State Department working harder. Mike thinks we can arrange it.'

Dad wanted to postpone the deal with Sagmir until we found out more about the Transfer Special. But I reminded him that Sagmir said the deal had to be completed before I was retried. So we decided to see what the Turkish lawyer could do.

We worked out a careful plan for the deal. Dad kept the 30,000 lira on deposit at the American consulate. He would show Sagmir the receipt to assure him that the money was there. Sagmir would hold Dad's passport. When I was on a plane flying out of Turkey, Dad would buy back his passport for 30,000 lira.

Nervously I awaited Dad's return from his meeting with Sagmir.

He looked worried when he came out to see me the following day. 'He's changed his tune,' Dad said. 'He claims that he needs 15,000 lira up front. Says he can't arrange it until he can pay off certain people in Ankara.'

I wanted to believe. I wanted to be free so bad. But I couldn't allow Dad to be burned. The deal smelled very bad. 'What's he trying to pull?'

'I don't know,' Dad said. 'Do you think he's telling the truth?'

'No. He's trying to cheat you. He's rich. He can come up with 15,000 in an hour. Why don't you go back and tell him no deal. He can get the 30,000 lira C.O.D. But not one *kurus* up front.'

Dad returned the next day. He looked tired, depressed. I read Sagmir's answer in his eyes. 'I'll keep the money in the bank,' he said as he left for home. 'If you need it, it'll be waiting.'

CHAPTER SEVENTEEN

So it had come to this. After three years of hassling and haggling and paying lawyers and hoping and talking and worrying and praying, the end result was still thirty years. On Monday, 10 September 1973, soldiers chained my hands and drove me from Sagmalcilar prison to the basement room where I had juggled my way out of a beating several lifetimes ago. It was hot that day and the soldiers in their wool uniforms smelled strongly of the Istanbul heat. We waited there all morning. Noon came and went. Finally, late in the afternoon, they marched me through the long dark back corridors and stairways up towards the tiny waiting room. I found my name still scratched on the wall there among those of all the other lost souls.

The empty courthouse corridors were quiet and still. Dust floated through long slanting shafts of yellow sunshine. Most of the day's business was finished. There weren't many people around.

Outside the closed door of Courtroom No. 6, three old cleaning women, swathed in black, turned from their sweeping to look at me as I passed.

As in Macbeth? The Fates? I laughed.

The door opened and we entered.

The same kindly old judge, Rasih Cerikcioglu, was presiding. But the prosecutor was different, a younger man. When I entered the crowded courtroom the judge turned to the prosecutor and spoke in Turkish. By now I could understand some of the phrases. The judge said. 'This is the case I was telling you about.'

A reporter from *Newsday* was there, and a couple of people from the wire services. Law students who had followed my case all along were there as well as my special unknown girlfriend in the miniskirt. But I felt a strange detachment. This wasn't really happening, yet it was. So I let it happen.

The judge opened the proceedings by explaining that he had no choice. The Supreme Court in Ankara had made its decision binding. He cited the provision of the Turkish law that called for a mandatory life sentence.

Before pronouncing the sentence, the judge asked if I had anything to say.

I had. I'd thought a lot about it.

I stood, trying to keep my backbone rigid. I spoke slowly, in English, allowing the interpreter to translate for the whole court.

'It is time for me to speak,' I began. 'But what is there to say? When I finish, you people will sentence me for my crime So let me ask now . . . what is a crime? And what is the proper punishment for a crime? These are difficult questions to answer. The answers vary from one place to another, from one man to another. Justice is affected by geography, politics, religion. What was legal twenty years ago may be illegal today. And what is illegal today may be legal tomorrow. I'm not saying this is right or wrong. It's just the way things are. . . .

'I stand here today before you, my life in your hands . . but you actually don't know the first thing about who I really am. It doesn't matter. I have spent the past three years of my life in your prison. If your decision today must sentence me to more prison, I cannot agree with you. All I can do . . . is forgive you . . .'

The judge recessed the court for about ten minutes. All was silent around me. Then he came back, flanked by his two black-robed assistants. He stood up behind the bench and held his hands out towards me, crossed at the wrists. 'The Supreme Court has tied our hands,' he said.

Slowly, clearly, he pronounced the sentence in Turkish. I heard the word *Muebbed*, life Then I heard *Otuz Sena*, thirty years.

The translator turned to repeat the words in English, but the judge interrupted. 'I'm calling off the session,' he said. 'Please translate the verdict outside the courtroom. I cannot stand it. I wish I had retired before I rendered this verdict.'

The soldiers took me away. The translator followed and officially informed me of my sentence. Life, reduced to thirty years. My release was set for the year 2000. With time off for good behaviour I would be free on 7 October 1990. In seventeen years I would be forty-three years old. Lillian would be forty-two. George Orwell's 1984 would have come and gone. Halley's comet would have returned and left again. I would miss four more Presidential elections and four Olympics. Dad would be retired, Mom would be grey. My brother and sister would probably both be married and have teenage kids to greet their ageing uncle when he returned from Turkey. The prime of my life would evaporate in a Turkish prison.

'*Getchmis olsun,*' said one of the soldiers as he led me away. 'May it pass quickly.'

CHAPTER EIGHTEEN

Joey and Popeye came to me one morning. It seemed that Popeye woke up in the middle of the night to go to the bathroom. But before he moved he heard a slight noise. Peering across the *kogus* he saw Ziat hovering behind his huge radio. Carefully Ziat removed screws from the back and pulled off the cover. He looked around suspiciously. Then he slipped money into the back of the radio. He tightened the cover and replaced the radio on top of his locker.

That was where Ziat kept his money! Everyone thought he used the obvious place – his double padlocked locker. But no, the crafty Jordanian threw everyone off the track. He kept the money unlocked in the back of his radio. And, as everyone knew, Ziat had a lot of money. He'd been the main source of drugs in the *kogus* for as long as any of us could remember. And he ran the *chi* shop with a careful eye towards maximum profits.

Joey rubbed his hands together with glee. Since the day of Ziat's fight with the children, the Jordanian had been his worst enemy. 'I'm gonna rip him off,' he whispered. 'It's gonna be so much fun.'

'Count me out,' I said. 'That man is a bad one to have for an enemy.'

'Hoo, boy!' Popeye said. 'He's going free next month. This is your last chance to burn his ass.'

'No thanks. But good luck.'

Popeye threw both his hands in the air and whistled.

I forgot about the incident until a few nights later. It was about 2 a.m. I was having one of my frequent dreams about Lillian. I could almost feel her next to me. She reached over with her soft hand and caressed my face . . .

But the hand was hard and rough. And it clamped down over my nose and mouth. It cut off my air. I started to struggle, but a voice said, 'Shhhh!'

I opened my eyes to see an upside-down view of Joey's handlebar moustache. 'Hide this,' he whispered. 'One-third is yours.' He pressed something into my hand and disappeared. I looked down. To my amazement I was holding a huge wad of bills with a fat rubber band wrapped around it.

It was a dream. No, the dream was fading. Lillian was gone. She was back in Alaska. And there I was, lying naked in bed with a thick wad of money in my hand.

I unbound the money and studied it. There were blue bills and pink ones and green ones and yellow and black and red ones. There were one hundred dollar bills and one thousand mark notes and ten pound certificates. There was Syrian money and Spanish money and Italian money and Australian money. Fare for the Midnight Express? Maybe. But where would I hide it until the train came along?

Quickly I peered around. The *kogus* was snoring and grunting in what passed for peace and contentment there. I saw Joey across the *kogus*, huddled under the covers. I couldn't see Popeye's bunk, but I figured he was doing the same. I dove under my covers too.

For maybe a half hour I huddled with the money under the covers, discussing hiding places with myself. Finally inspiration struck. I worked all night. I dozed off to sleep just after Ziat woke up and went down to heat the water for his *chi* shop.

It was the middle of the morning. I woke, exhausted. But my brain was clicking. I couldn't sleep. The *kogus* was quiet. I went downstairs, bought a glass of tea from Ziat, and walked out into the yard. Popeye raced over immediately. He was tense.

'Where is it?' he asked. 'What did you do with it?'

'Calm down,' I said. 'I'm not telling you.'

'What! You cheating . . .'

'Shhh. You want to send a telegram to Ziat? I'm not telling you.'

Popeye stormed away. In a few moments Joey appeared. 'What happened? Why won't you tell Popeye where the money is?'

'No. It's hidden. There's gonna be a control, you know that. I'm the only guy who knows where it is. So if they find it I'm the only guy who gets into trouble. I'm also the only one who can tell them where it is. And I'm not talking. So be cool.'

Joey realized the sense of my argument. 'OK. Take care of it.' Joey would be the first one to fall under suspicion. I especially didn't want him to know where the money was hidden. If he didn't know, the guards couldn't beat it out of him.

Later in the day, I heard Ziat's excited voice chattering to Necdet, the trusty. Within minutes came the cry, '*Sayim, Sayim.*' Popeye, Joey, and I lined up as far apart from each other as possible.

Mamur walked in, followed by Hamid, Arief, and a dozen other guards. Mamur had fire in his eyes. He paced up and down the line, glaring at the prisoners one by one. He yelled and screamed in Turkish. Necdet followed behind him, translating in English.

'Some money has been lost in the *kogus*,' Mamur said 'Twenty-five thousand lira. I want everybody to take a little time to think about it. We have moved all of the children to another *kogus*. We are going to lock you all in their *kogus* while we search yours. We will bring you out one by one. If anyone has anything to say, he can say it. No one will know who spoke.'

His voice rose to a high pitch. 'Whoever has it better give it up now. If you do, there won't be any problems,' he lied. 'No beating. No court. All we want is the money back.'

They searched us one by one as they sent us over to the children's *kogus*. No problem. I didn't have the money on me.

Locked inside the children's *kogus* we all paced back and forth in the lower room. No one wanted to be upstairs near the kids' filthy beds or any place near the toilet.

Joey stopped me. 'What's Mamur's game?' he asked 'Think Ziat promised him some of the money?'

I shrugged and walked on. Popeye eyed me nervously.

After about an hour, Arief came into the children's *kogus* and gave a speech too. 'We're going to keep you people here all day,' he promised. 'And all night. And all day tomorrow. And all the next day.' He began to shout. 'We'll keep you here a week. We'll keep you until we find that money! We'll take everything out of that *kogus* that can be taken out. We'll take all the lockers, all the beds, every piece of clothing. We'll bring it all out into the yard and break it so that it's no bigger than a match until we find that money.' He crouched low, leaning forward. 'And when we find it, we'll destroy the prisoner who has it.' He straightened up. 'But if he tells us now, we'll just take the money. No beating.'

Silence.

'Bastards!'

Hours went by. No one had been prepared to leave the *kogus*. Men were walking in their pyjamas, barefoot, on the cold stone floor.

Popeye grew worse. He drew me aside and said, 'Let's give it back, man.'

'You're crazy. They'll really give us trouble. We're in it now. Ride out the storm.'

Popeye paced the hallway. Each time he passed me I started to whistle an old song by the rock group known as The Doors. It was called 'Riders on the Storm'.

I was as nervous as Popeye. I didn't know whether my hiding place would hold up. I could see the soldiers through the windows. They were pulling everything apart, shaking the stuffing out of the mattresses. I tried not to think about where the money was, lest someone pick up a stray vibration.

After several hours of tension, help finally came from an unlikely source. Nadir, a new Iranian prisoner who slept on a mattress on the first floor, ran over to a guard at the door. He demanded to see Mamur. The Weasel came over. Nadir spoke excellent Turkish. He yelled that he could see Ziat poking around on the first floor of our *kogus*. He said he had personal possessions there that he wanted to protect. He had, he said, 3000 lira hidden in his pillow. He became enraged. We all could see Ziat, indeed, searching on the first floor of the *kogus*.

Mamur took him over to the *kogus*. We heard Nadir rant and rave on the way. 'Where does this Ziat' – he spit the name – 'get 25,000 lira anyway? How does he get this money in prison? Why do you believe him? Has anybody seen the money? He goes free soon. Maybe he just wants to get even with everybody?'

Nadir's pillow was empty. He yelled and screamed that

he'd been robbed. He accused Ziat. All hell broke loose. Guards screamed. Ziat screamed. Nadir screamed. Who knew the truth? Nadir could have had money – or maybe just brains. Mamur yelled for silence. He barked an order. As quickly as they had come, the guards left the *kogus*.

We went back. Everything from everywhere was piled into a heap on the floor, crushed, broken, torn, and mixed together. My mattress was pulled from its bunk and flung across the floor. Everything had been grabbed from my locker and thrown to the ground – even the few things I had sitting on the top. I picked my diary up from the floor and checked to make sure the prison plans were still in place. I felt for the file. I could barely feel it still hidden in the binding. I picked up my towel, writing pads, pens, candles, cigarettes, and my photo of Lillian, and placed them all back on top of my locker.

Joey and Popeye walked by, not daring to come over and talk. I looked up and whistled, 'Riders on the Storm'.

A week passed. Ziat eyed Joey constantly. He seemed to have lost all his ambition. He gave up his *chi* shop concession. Nadir moved himself into that job. All the money Ziat had worked for – lying and cheating and stealing and selling dope and slaving all day over a hot *chi* stove – was gone. Now his term was almost up. He would go back out on the streets of Istanbul with thousands of enemies and no money. Everyone in the *kogus* felt so sorry for him that we all toasted him with Nadir's strong, refreshing tea.

But we forgot that Ziat had friends among the guards. One afternoon I walked downstairs. I was startled to see Ziat sitting at a table neatly dressed in a suit and tie. Ziat?

Suddenly the *kogus* door was unlocked. In strolled Mamur and Arief. '*Sayim. Sayim,*' they yelled.

Normally the prisoners jostled for position near the end of the line so they could be inconspicuous. I saw Ziat stroll casually to the second spot in line. He stood next to Necdet.

Arief began to search the line. In a moment he had reached into Ziat's pocket and pulled out a match-box. '*Nebu?*' he growled. He opened it to find a tiny piece of hashish. Arief pulled Ziat out of the line and slapped him around a bit without much vigour. 'Where did you get this hash?' he growled.

'From Joey,' Ziat said.

Joey standing next to me, stiffened.

Guards took Ziat away. Mamur called for Joey. My friend walked down to the end of the line. 'What's happening with this hash?' Mamur asked.

'I know nothing about it. I don't sell it to him. I don't have anything to do with it.'

Mamur looked at him closely. 'I know your face,' he said. 'I . . .'

. . don't say anything,' Mamur snapped. 'I know you. Where did you get the hash?'

He grabbed one end of Joey's handlebar moustache. He lifted Joey to his tiptoes. 'Where did you get the hash?' he repeated.

'I tell you I don't know anything about it.'

'Take him to the cellar!'

They dragged Joey off. Mamur looked at the rest of us. 'Anyone fooling around with hash is going to get his ass broken,' he promised. Then he turned quickly and left.

The search was over in less than a minute. They weren't after Joey for hash. They wanted the money. They wanted an excuse to get him into the cellar and under the *falaka* stick.

I ran up to Necdet. 'Can't you go downstairs?' I pleaded 'You know what happened.'

'Sure I know,' Necdet said. 'But what can I do?'

'They're going to break him to pieces downstairs. You know what a set-up that was. You know Ziat's been selling hash for years in here.'

Necdet, as trusty, didn't *want* to know such things.

'Ziat's been selling hash in here?'

'Well, maybe you don't know,' I said, trying to be diplomatic. 'But they're going to break Joey apart down there. They're after the money. You know that.'

Necdet went to speak to the guard at the door. The guard had his orders. We could do nothing for Joey except hope. I was glad that he didn't know where the money was hidden. They couldn't beat that out of him. But he knew *who* had the money.

174

I hurt for him all afternoon. I imagined what the guards were doing with their fists and feet and *falaka* sticks. And all the while a great glowing fire of hate for Ziat grew into an inferno.

It was my bath night. Popeye and I and a few others put on bathing trunks to wash in the hot water. One of our regular companions was conspicuously missing. We didn't talk about it. Our feelings were beyond words. The sloshing sound of water was the only noise.

I had soap all over my body. I was just lifting up the pitcher to pour a rinse over my head when the *kogus* door opened. I heard the sound of laughter. Ziat came in, joking with the guards. His suit was clean and unruffled. Ziat walked past the bath area and down the corridor. Soapy and wet I raced after him.

'Ziat!'

He turned and caught my fist in the side of his face. He crashed into the barred window. I lost my balance on the wet, slippery concrete floor. Ziat jumped up and raced off into the *chi* room. I followed, cursing him and the soap suds. Several men grabbed me. I stood there dripping water and yelling at Ziat.

Then Nadir pulled out a knife. He moved towards Ziat. The Jordanian screamed and ran upstairs.

In a moment Necdet came down to calm everyone. 'It's finished,' he said. He walked to the door of the *kogus* and called the guard. 'Take Ziat away,' he commanded. 'It is necessary to keep him out of the *kogus*.'

Ziat quickly packed his belongings. He stayed in the *revere* for the last few weeks of his sentence.

Joey returned to the *kogus* the next morning. He limped, but only slightly. After the first few blows of the *falaka* stick he had cried out that he was going to report Mamur to the American consul. The Weasel had thought it over. Sometimes the prison authorities seemed willing to resist diplomatic pressures, sometimes not. Mamur walked out. The guards had left Joey alone in the dark basement room all night. Then they had simply brought him back upstairs.

CHAPTER NINETEEN

The whole *kogus* received an early Christmas present in 1973. Ziat left. And although I would have preferred leaving my self, being separated from him was a good feeling. His pres ence always unsettled me.

His departure also meant money for Popeye, Joey, and me. They bugged me for it the morning after Ziat finished his term.

'Joey,' I replied, 'why don't you go get us some tea and come up to my bunk? We've got to have us a little talk.'

Joey bought especially strong tea from Nadir. We sipped it slowly. Joey and Popeye puffed excitedly on their cigarettes.

'Where is it? Where is it?'

'You've been staring at it for weeks. It's been right in front of your eyes.'

'Huh?'

I reached over to the top of my locker and grabbed a thick yellow candle. Their mouths dropped open. I put the candle between me and the wall. Joey and Popeye sealed off the view. I slowly scraped the wax off with a nail file. When I finished, there was wax all over my bed and about $1500 worth of multicoloured currency in my hand.

'How the hell did you get it in there?' Popeye wanted to know.'

'Took me all night. Under the sheet. I just kept burning candles and letting the wax drip onto the money I thought for sure I'd set the *kogus* on fire.'

We divided it into thirds. About $500 apiece.

'If anybody's busted with this, they make up their own story,' I said. 'You don't know me and I don't know you.'

'Yeah, yeah,' Joey said. 'Come on. I'm gonna bribe some guard to get us some *food!*' We ate well for the next few days. I noticed Popeye wearing an expensive Seiko watch that had belonged to Muhto, a Malaysian prisoner. And Muhto or- dered Rothman cigarettes from a little Turk who came around hustling foreign brands.

176

I bought bunches of fresh fruit that I kept on the window sill near my bunk. It was cold outside and they stayed fresh for a while.

But I hid most of the money in my diary, slitting open the cardboard facing as I had seen Max do. Working casually, blocking anyone's view with my body, I pretended to read or write on my bunk. In reality I was making a deposit in the Freedom Savings Bank.

One cold winter morning Popeye came running over to me, whistling with alarm and shouting, 'Circle up the beds. We're under attack!'

'What are you babbling about?' I asked.

'The 'Afghanis are here. Invading. Quick, before they bring in their camels.'

Popeye was exaggerating, of course. But not much. The Afghanis were a whirlwind of flapping robes and gaudy, baggy pants. There were fifteen of them. They'd been travelling in a bus loaded with scarves, bolts of cloth, cheap men's suits, and other small handcrafted items. When stopped by the police, they said they were pilgrims returning from Mecca and the items were gifts for friends at home. The problem was that Istanbul wasn't anywhere near the route between Mecca and Afghanistan. They were charged with smuggling.

All the bunks upstairs were full. So the Afghanis slept on the floor downstairs. They were given old mattresses and blankets. If they stayed only one night the bedding would still be a total loss. No one would want any of it.

The Afghanis pitched camp at the far end of the lower room. They made it their own. The line for *Sayim* was especially crowded now. Everyone was bunched up uncomfortably in half the room, jockeying for position away from the new prisoners. When they weren't praying the Afghanis were pushing to get ahead in the soup line. They grabbed any scrap of paper or thread or bit of garbage and stuffed it into their bulging calico bags.

And they were loud. They played and shouted like children. They argued like old ladies. But they carried scars that made us wary.

The old man who was their chief had one milky blue eye

and one black eye that glared like a hawk's. One man had only three fingers on one hand. Another had a huge chunk of an ear missing.

All of us hardened hashish smugglers in the foreigners' *koguş* were shocked by the latest verdict handed down against Americans. While most of the civilized world seemed to be reducing penalties for marijuana and hashish offences, Turkey was taking a harder line. Robert Hubbard, Jo Ann McDaniel, and Kathy Zenz went to court on 28 December expecting another boring continuation of their case that had dragged on for more than a year. But the judge cited them for conspiracy to smuggle one hundred kilos of hashish from Syria into Turkey and sentenced them to death . . . commuted to life in prison. Suddenly I no longer held the record for the longest sentence of any American prisoner in Turkey. I felt a deep pain for them. I prayed that we might all find some sort of common solution. Maybe diplomacy was our best bet.

Willard Johnson came out from the American consulate with a report from Ambassador Macomber. In the ambassador's judgment, an amnesty would be declared shortly after the Turks managed to form a new government Everyone believed there would be a general amnesty in 1973, to celebrate the fiftieth anniversary of the glorious Turkish republic. But even when it came it would probably leave me with many years yet to serve. Macomber thought there was a 'slim chance' that the amnesty would deport foreign prisoners The possibility of a transfer to the U.S. was being discussed by Ankara and Washington, but also seemed slim There was even the chance the Turkish Parliament would consider a private bill to deal with my own case. But this had been done only once in history for a foreigner . . . all of which left me staring at sixteen and a half blank years – thirty minus time off for good behaviour.

I was in this state of mind when I learned that Dad was coming to visit for a fourth time.

He had changed. The gleam in his Irish eyes had dimmed. He looked tired.

'A present for you,' he said softly. Something in his voice

178

warned me. Switch to code. Make sure Willard doesn't understand what we're really talking about – the consul played the game straight.

I looked at the present. It was a family photo album, a new one. Dad had had copies made of many of the pictures in our album back home. 'When I put together the photos for *Newsday* I got the idea that you might like some to look at here.' He grinned. The warning tone again.

I paged through the album. A lump grew in my throat as I saw Mom standing in front of the house, holding the hand of a small blond-haired kid. There was Rob on his bicycle. The two of us in a snowball fight. Mom showing off a tiny pink bundle. Peg in her cheer-leading outfit . . . I could distract the attention of a lot of guards with that one. There was Nana and Aunt Mickey and Uncle Jimmy.

'And there's a lot of pictures of your old friend Mr Franklin from the bank,' Dad said.

'Right. I remember him well.'

'Sure you do. He's the one who always wanted to be a railroad engineer. He had all those trains running around his house.'

My eyes shot down toward the photo album. Dad ran his finger slowly across the edge of the back cover. The old silver fox! I wondered where he picked up that trick.

'Dad. All this is costing you so much money. The lawyers. The travel.' I touched the photo album. 'I'll pay you back some day.'

'I know you will, Billy. But don't worry about it.' He sighed. 'You know, one thing I've learned from all this – don't let the little things in life upset you.'

'Right. Don't sweat the small stuff,' I said.

'It's actually a lot easier for me at work now,' he said. 'The petty things don't bother me any more. I can see that some things aren't as important as I used to believe.'

'I'm glad we can talk about it now, Dad.'

'Yeah. We should've talked more. There's room for different opinions. They don't have to close people off from one another.'

'Dad. If I . . . when I get out of this mess, we'll talk a lot more.'

He smiled.

We visited for a long time. Dad still had a lot of hope for a transfer or an amnesty. But it was clear that escape might be the only way out.

'Be careful, son. Take care of yourself.'

I left to go back to the *kogus*. The guard stopped me to examine the photo album.

'My sister,' I said proudly in Turkish.

The guard stared at Peg. Then he happily waved me back inside the *kogus*. Other prisoners gathered around to hear news of my visit, grab bits of chocolate bars, bum cigarettes. I tossed the photo album casually to Joey. Several men gathered around to peer at the snapshots. Peg was a hit in Istanbul.

Dad only stayed for a few days this time. He tried to hide it, but I knew the financial pressure on him was rough. I kept bringing the discussion back to the Midnight Express. I could see that he was worried. For three years he had opposed any thought of escape. Now he had mortgaged his home to finance my attempt. If I should fail, I knew it would kill him. During his last visit before returning to America he rose to say goodbye. He grabbed my arm. He opened his mouth to say something, but words wouldn't come. He hugged me.

Then he turned and walked out of the room.

Curiosity drove me nuts. But I let the photo album circulate freely around the *kogus* for several days. Then I set it on top of my locker and ignored it. Only after a week or so did I search for the money. Late at night, holding my work under the sheet as I lay in bed, I carefully sliced open the back cover of the album. There, underneath the cardboard backing, were crisp new $100 bills, stacked neatly in groups of three. Twenty-seven pictures of Benjamin Franklin.

Too many people were interested in the photo album. I had to move the money to a safer place. For several nights I worked secretly. I slit open the back lining of my diary. I arranged the money inside, next to Ziat's money, and covered it with several sheets of soft, onion-skin drawing paper. Then I glued the cover back together. It was good. The diary

180

was crammed thick with drawings, letters, and my own notes. Now the money, the file, and the plans were all in one location. I even had a bit of LSD to slip to a guard if necessary. All I had to do was grab my diary and I had an escape kit.

I wasn't sure exactly how I would use the money. I had to play a waiting game. I had to see what would happen with the amnesty and transfer trains. I didn't want to try to escape, get caught, and then find out I *would have* gone free.

Prison time went on. Moments turned into hours and days and weeks and months. When would it end? When would it end? When would my life begin again?

I saw no reason for this particular chilly morning to be different from the others. I sat in the yard, early A couple of German prisoners goose-stepped the thirty-two paces back and forth. It looked like rain, but the cold air felt fresh.

Nadir ran out into the yard. 'It's Hamid. Hamid,' he shouted, grinning.

The very name made my spine shiver.

'What?'

'Good news. Hamid is dead.'

'Hamid? The Bear? Dead? What?'

'Yeah. He gets shot.'

'Wow!'

Nadir ran back inside the *kogus*. In moments I heard the cell block begin to buzz excitedly. Chabran ran up to me from the kids' *kogus*. '*Allah buyuk*' (God is great), he called out.

Such fine news. Prisoners ran out into the yard, jumping and shouting. Joey raced over and patted me on the back. Popeye ran into the yard whistling, doing a dance of joy. Across the yards we could hear the laughing and cheering from the other *kogus*. The roar of happiness grew to a crescendo. Out in the hallways the guards looked nervous and scared.

Suddenly I realized what we were celebrating. A man had died. A human being. And we were happy. This shouldn't be. How could people be so happy about the destruction of another person? But I *was* happy. I gave in to the feeling of

181

relief: that the Bear's cruel fists would never again smash into my face.

No one knew the details. But Hamid was dead, for sure. He had been shot by someone outside the prison. In a restaurant. That was all we knew.

Later that morning I used a pack of Marlboros to persuade a guard at the cell block door to let me go to the *revere*. If anyone knew the story, it would be Max. He sat on his bed, glassy-eyed but grinning, as he talked with a couple of Turks. He greeted me warmly.

'He was eating breakfast,' Max told me. 'Across the street from the prison entrance there's a restaurant. He eats breakfast every day there. There was this guy . . . Hamid busted him for hash maybe a couple of years ago . . . a prisoner . . one of the Turks. Hamid took him down to the basement and did a number on him with the *falaka* stick. But the guy wouldn't squeal. For a couple of days they let him lay there and came back to beat him . . . you know Hamid . . . while he's beating the guy he's screaming, "I fuck your mother, I fuck your sister, I fuck your father, I fuck your brother, I fuck your grandmother . . ." all that kind of thing.

'The guy never forgot it. How could he?

'So anyway, a couple of days ago the Turk finished his sentence. And this morning he just walked into the restaurant while Hamid ate his breakfast. He pointed a gun at him. He pulled the trigger and he said, "You remember me? Well, here's something for my mother." Blam! "And my sister." Blam! Blam, blam, blam, eight shots. Hamid was on the floor. The gun clicked a few times and the guy set it down on the table. He sat down and waited for the police. Incredible!'

A few weeks later the killer arrived back at his old *kogus*, a celebrated hero. He was a brand-new *kapidiye*. He became known as *Aslan*, 'The Lion'.

For weeks the prisoners kept the guards on edge. If you thought you could pull it off, as you passed them, you'd mutter, '*Hamid onutma*.' (Don't forget Hamid.)

The guards didn't forget.

Arief suddenly disappeared. Rumour had it that the Bone-breaker had to go into the hospital for an operation. Mamur requested a transfer of duty to İzmir.

182

CHAPTER TWENTY

7 March 1974
Lillian,

 Your letter and the stillness of the night and so many things so wrong. I feel like I'm dying here at times. It's so hard here without anyone to help, to be a companion along this strange road. My friend Arne brought me to realize how little I know about most everything; and stranger still, how much I unknowingly know about other things, important things like laughing and feeling people and loving life. I miss Arne, but his presence remains, just as crazy Patrick remains with me even with his body two years in the earth.

 It's been hard these past months. So many plans and possibilities seem to have fallen apart. It's getting hard for me to breathe.

 Spring is here and I'm trying not to be hasty but I so need some softness. Your softness. I have your letters. They charge me, give me strength. News about amnesty and getting out – tangled, complicated. I am patient only for those people, my parents and friends, who are trying so hard. I don't know how much longer I can wait.

 Don't let go, Lil. Hold us.

                Billy

On my very first night at Sagmalcilar, three and a half years earlier, the prisoners were talking amnesty. Finally, on 16 May 1974, the Turkish Parliament managed to vote an amnesty bill. It was to be effective the next day. Everyone in the entire *kogus* gathered around the few who could read the Turkish newspapers. Here is what we learned:

Every prisoner in Turkey was to receive a twelve-year amnesty on each of his sentences. Killers, rapists, armed robbers, kidnappers – all received twelve years off. Time off for good behaviour was tacked onto that. So a prisoner with a thirty-year sentence would get ten years off for good behaviour and twelve more off with the amnesty. He would have eight years to serve.

Except that smugglers only received a five-year amnesty.

Better than nothing, I supposed. But it still left me with a release date of 7 October 1985. I turned and walked back to my bunk, ignoring the party atmosphere all around me. Twelve years would free just about everybody. Even most of the smugglers had less than five years left. Joey would go. Timmy would be freed from Izmir. I was happy for them, of course, but miserable anyway. Of my old group of friends only Max and Popeye would still be here. And Max was in the *revere* most of the time.

Joey stopped at my bunk to wish me luck. He reminded me of the transfer possibility. He assured me that I would be free soon myself.

'Look, did you hear about the extra seven years for smugglers?'

'What?'

'The paper says some civil liberties groups are protesting that the smugglers only got five years off. They want Parliament to give them another seven. So, who knows? Maybe you'll get the whole twelve-year amnesty.'

'Joey, I've got a thirty-year sentence. Even a twelve-year amnesty wouldn't do me much good.'

'Yeah. But you're better off than Necdet.'

'What do you mean?'

'Didn't you hear? In all of Turkey there's only one prisoner who wasn't included in the amnesty. A Syrian spy. The Parliament even named him and said he couldn't get amnesty. Necdet.'

Across the *kogus* Necdet visited with the happy prisoners, congratulating them and wishing them luck. In all my time in prison I never met anyone who deserved amnesty more. He was fair. He was clean. He was a good man. Turkish justice.

That evening the loudspeakers began to blare out the names of those who would go free the next morning. Cheers rose after each name. Then a quick hush followed so that the next man could hear. The names were read alphabetically. Joey's last name began with 'M'. I sat on his bed with him waiting for the happy moment. But near midnight, when they were just finishing the 'L's, the voice on the loudspeaker said that it was getting too late. They would continue calling names in the morning.

184

A loud groan of protest rose. Joey went absolutely insane. He leaped off his bed with a shriek.

'They're not gonna let me go,' he screamed. 'The Turk bastards want to keep me here. I can't stand it. Guard!' he screamed. 'Let me out. I've got to talk to the director Guard!'

I pulled him down on his bed and tried to reason with him. 'Are you completely crazy? Think! You're going free tomor row. You are. They'll call your name in the morning. Don't blow it now.'

'I know they're gonna pull some crap on me, just to keep me here. I know it.'

After five years of prison Joey couldn't handle even one more night. He hunted up Nadir to buy some hashish. Nadir wouldn't even take his money.

'Here,' he said. 'For you, my friend. You need them. *Getchmis olsun.*' He dumped five 'yellow bombers', Nembutol, into Joey's hand. Joey gobbled them all. He washed them down with a cup of *chi*.

'I can't take this any more,' he screamed. 'My nerves are like ping-pong balls in a washing machine. If I don't ever wake up, great! And if they call my name tomorrow, the hell with 'em. Let them wait for me. I've been waiting five goddamn years for them.'

He burrowed down beneath his pillows. He pulled the blankets up over his head.

Meanwhile I tried to plan quickly. I had money. Maybe now was the time to use it. It might be easy to slip out the gate tomorrow with all the others. There was bound to be confusion.

I walked over to talk to François, a new young French kid who'd just gotten twenty months for possession of a single hashish cigarette. He was trying to stuff his raggedy possessions into an old burlap sack. He was kind of loony. Everyone called him 'Ding-Dong'. I knew he didn't have much money and that he wanted to go straight to India when he got out.

'Hey, Ding-Dong. Want to make 5000 lira?' I asked.

He grinned. Then a suspicious mask dropped over his silly-putty features. 'How?'

'Easy. Just let me tie you up tomorrow in the bathroom.

I'll use your ID to go out when they call your name. When they find you later, you tell them I tied you up and gagged you. They'll have to let you go. What do you think? You want the money?'

He might have been a Ding-Dong but he was no fool.

'Buzz off,' he said.

By 6 a.m. the voice on the loudspeaker was calling more names. The lucky men lined up for their day of freedom. Popeye and I rolled Joey out of his bed and he groggily walked out to the open world. Fifty-two of the seventy-five prisoners from our *kogus* left that day. Nearly 2500 of the 3000 men at Sagmalcilar were freed. Except for those first few horrible days in prison, this was the loneliest time I could remember. Arne, Charles, Joey, nearly all my best prison friends were gone. Even my enemies had disappeared. Slowly, I paced the yard all day long. Summer was coming. There was life to live, Lil to love, happiness and sadness to experience. My old friends back home were getting married, having children, making money. And the Turks said I must stay in prison until I was thirty-eight years old.

It was a quiet May morning. I sat against the yard wall in the soft sunshine. Shouts and laughter from the few children remaining accentuated the stillness of the day. And my loneliness.

'Vilyum Hi-yes.'

What?

'Vilyum Hi-yes.'

I went inside to the door of the *kogus*. I reached through the hole and took a visit card from the smiling guard. He pocketed the five lira piece I placed on the window ledge. A visitor. But it wasn't the consul or lawyer. When they came out the visits were in a long open room. The card said *kabin*. Whoever it was had come alone. I would have to see him through the glass window of one of the visiting booths.

Who could it be?

I was dressed in blue jeans. Not proper attire for an unexpected visitor. I raced upstairs and changed into my suit

I walked down the corridor to the checkpoint. The guard there took my paper and told me to wait. The cabins were lined up to my left like a string of narrow wooden phone booths. All grey. One after another, fifty-four in a row.

The guard said, '*Kabin on-yedi.*'

I walked toward cabin no. 17 and closed the door behind me. I peered through the dirty plate glass. There was no one on the other side. I waited.

The little booth was hot and grimy. It smelled strongly of sweat and stale cigarette smoke. There were two glass panes separating the visitor's cabin from the prisoner's cabin. And a set of bars between the windows. A *Turk-mali* microphone and speaker system provided the only means of talking. It would be difficult to hold a conversation.

I was wet from the heat. The damned suit. I was wiping my face with a handkerchief when the door on the other side of the bars opened.

Lillian stood before me.

She smiled shyly and pressed her palms up against the glass. I pressed mine against the other side of the window. My heart filled my chest. Her name floated off my lips. 'Lil? . . .'

The smile burst across her face. Her eyes shone.

'Oh, Billy . . .'

We stood there in silence. Smiling. Breathing slowly. Enjoying the sight of each other

Then I burst out laughing.

'Lillian! Lillian! What are you doing here? Is this real?'

'It's real, Billy. How are you?'

'Fantastic! Except for being in prison. Lily, you look great. Look at your hair! It's so long!'

She laughed. 'Yes, it's been growing since Alaska. I knew you'd like it.'

'I love it. You're beautiful.'

'And don't you look dapper in your sharp blue suit. Is this the normal prison wear?'

'Hell no! I just put this on to impress you. Actually, I won it in a poker game.'

'I'm glad to see that you haven't lost any of your old vices.'

187

'Ooh. Don't ever say that word. I might have to bust through this glass to get at you. You look so luscious.'

Her face went serious.

'Billy? You OK? Really?'

'Yeah, Lil. I'm OK'

'I've been so worried about you doing something stupid and . . .' She stopped speaking. She glanced around the booth. She looked at me questioningly.

'No,' I said. 'Don't worry. It's not bugged. They can't even get the loudspeakers to work in the cell block. Or keep the electricity running.'

'I knew what the amnesty terms would mean to you, Billy. Please be careful, babe. Don't make a mistake now.'

'It's all right, Lily. I won't.'

'Your last letter scared me.'

'Yeah. I'm sorry about that. You always seem to get the overflow when I can't hold it any more.'

'Oh, Billy, that's all right. That's what I'm made for. I'll share the weight. But I know you're getting ready again. It scares me.'

'Hey! Come on, now. I wouldn't do anything foolish. You know me.'

She was still serious. 'I know you, all right. That's why I'm scared'

I hadn't seen Lillian in six years. But our letters seemed to rekindle feelings we had for each other long ago. Time hadn't changed her outwardly. She still looked soft and beautiful. But there was a strength within her softness. The healthy outdoor life she led had given her skin a glow. Her body looked firm beneath the tight jeans and tucked-in shirt. Gone was the self-conscious, perfectly groomed girl of yesterday. A woman stood before me now. She was searching. I could see the force of it in her eyes. A sorrow behind the sparkle. Her breasts strained beneath the cloth of her top. 'Unbutton your blouse,' I said suddenly.

She made a face. 'Oh, Billy, I can't do that. You might get in trouble. The guards might come.' She looked around at the empty booths beside us.

'*I* might come. God! I can see your nipples standing already'

188

'Stop that now. You'll just make yourself crazy,' she said, as the top button came loose. 'What about all this emotional control you've been writing about?' Her long thin fingers undid another button. 'And with all this glass in the way, it couldn't be very exciting anyway.' She leaned up close to the window. With both hands on the front of her blouse, she slowly drew it apart. Ripe breasts. Deep cleavage. Her hard dark nipples caught on the white material and held for an instant. Then they sprung free, quivering, as her full breasts hung loose from her shirt. I moaned.

'Oh, Billy,' she whispered, pressing herself up against the window. 'If only I could make it better for you.'

I moaned again. 'You do, Lil. You do.'

There was some noise outside. She drew the blouse around herself. I almost screamed at the interruption. Guards stolled past our cabin. One banged on the door to indicate time was finished. Then they were gone.

'Open it again!' I said quickly.

She laughed and buttoned up. 'You're still crazy. I'm glad to see that, at least. I'd have been worried if you weren't.'

'Can you stay long in Istanbul?'

'Sorry, Billy. I don't have much money. I really had to scrimp to get here. But I just *had* to see you.'

'And look how glad I *still* am to see you,' I said, indicating the bulge in my pants. She opened her mouth wide, then laughed.

'There's a ride back to Switzerland tomorrow that I just have to catch. And I couldn't stay until visiting day next week anyway.'

I was a little disappointed, but not much. Seeing her this once, hearing her voice and gazing into her eyes, was enough. It would hold me through a lot of lonely time.

'Well, you just keep yodelling around those mountains,' I said. 'One of these days you're going to hear some strange echoes come bouncing back down the valleys towards you. And I'll be right behind them.'

'Billy, please be careful. You mean so much to me. Don't get yourself killed.'

'Hey! I mean a lot to me, too. I've survived this long. I don't plan on getting killed.'

She wasn't smiling. 'The transfer is coming. Just give them some time back home. A lot of people are working hard to get you free. give them a chance.'

I will, Lily.'

A lot of people are praying for you.'

'I can feel it. I know.'

'I love you, Billy.'

'I love you, Lily.'

We stood staring through the glass. A guard came and opened her cabin door. He called her out. I watched her moving backward out of the cabin, our eyes fixed on a line that held us long after she was gone. . . .

'New guy,' Necdet announced. 'American. American.'

'Oh, no.' I rolled over on my bunk and blocked out Necdet's voice. A new prisoner meant another babbling idiot like I had been. New prisoners were a hassle.

Popeye ran downstairs to greet him.

But he was no beginner. His name was Harvey Bell and he had transferred here from Elazig so he could have an operation. He had a hernia as the result of a severe beating the guards had given him after an unsuccessful escape attempt. Popeye helped him upstairs to our *kogus*. Somehow he had managed to get himself drunk during the trip from Elazig.

'Oh, man, it's clean here,' he said in amazement.

I looked around at the dirt and scum. I sniffed at the putrid smell coming from the bathroom. I made a mental note never to transfer to Elazig prison.

'Ah'm from Alabama,' he told Popeye. 'And it's *so* nice to be away from those damn Turks.'

They walked past my bed and Popeye whistled to me. What could I do? I was the only other American in the *kogus*. I had to go over and say hello.

'How long do you have?' he asked.

'Thirty years.'

'Oh, wow!' He pumped my hand. 'So do I.'

Suddenly I liked him.

He gulped a cup of tea that Popeye offered. He glanced quickly around the room. 'How do we bust outta this hole?' he asked loudly.

'Shhhh,' I warned. 'Careful. These aren't Turks. A lot of people here know English. They all understand what you say.'

'Oh, yeah.' He grinned and lowered his voice. 'So, how do we bust outta this hole?'

I laughed. Harvey brushed back a lock of white – a widow's peak – that streaked his dark brown hair.

He wanted to escape as badly as I did. Over the next few weeks I developed trust in him. I told him about my file, rope, and prison plans – even about Johann in Istanbul. The one thing I didn't tell him about was my money.

In the bathroom we studied the barred window. I explained my plan to file through the bars, climb out and up to the roof, tie the rope to the antenna, and drop over the wall.

'Why don't you do it?' he asked.

'It's suicide. The bullet percentage is too high.'

'Well, then, give me the stuff. I'll do it.'

'No, not yet. That's my ace in the hole. If this transfer thing doesn't work, then maybe . . .'

A surprise visit by Michael Griffith. A beaming, smiling face. Warm handshake. He just came from Ankara, the capital, where he met with Ambassador Macomber and a lawyer named Farouk Eherem, president of the Turkish Bar Association. Eherem was the author of Section 18, Statute No. 647, of the Turkish Criminal Code, the one which states that foreign nationals imprisoned in Turkey can be transferred to jails in their home countries. Eherem had promised Mike that he would put in a good word for me with Premier Ecevit. Mike thought something would happen soon, and told me that a couple of detectives from Nassau County had volunteered to escort me back to a U.S. prison. Then I could get parole or work release.

'So everything's set,' Mike said. 'All we're waiting for is the final paperwork to be completed. Then we're going home.'

Home. Where did I hear the definition? 'Home is the place where, when you have to go there, they have to take you in.' Robert Frost. I sure had to go there . . . so bad I could taste it.

And it tasted like roast beef and mashed potatoes and gravy and corn on the cob and watermelon.

My hopes were high, my expectations low. After the shock of getting a life sentence when I had only fifty-three days left, I had resolved never again to believe in freedom until it had actually arrived. But it was difficult not to believe this time. Mike was so hopeful. Finally, after nearly four long horrible years, was I at the end of my punishment? I had paid my debt.

It was 10 July 1974.

Three days later the buzz began while I was doing my yoga. It grew louder. Excited voices roared across the walls of the other courtyards. A newspaper boy came running. Prisoners gathered around to read the news. War! Ecevit had ordered Turkish troops into Cyprus to protect the rights of the Turkish Cypriot citizens, who were being oppressed by the Greeks. At least that was the 'truth' as seen by the Turkish journalists.

Each prisoner, as always, tried to figure out what good could come from the news. All the Turks yelled for an amnesty so they could join the army and go smash the Greeks. All of us foreigners were willing to join the Turkish army, too. Just long enough to fight our way to the border. Harvey Bell and I discussed the possibility of the Greeks invading, and maybe liberating, Istanbul. Greek tanks smashing down the prison walls. Now *that* would be a sight to see.

It was over quickly. The Turkish troops overcame the Greek resistance. Ecevit picked up the nickname 'Lion'. He was a national hero. After nearly two weeks I heard from Mike, who had returned to the U.S. Now that the brief war was grinding to an uneasy peace, he felt sure Ecevit would once more consider the transfer request. Surely this would be a time of good will.

Ecevit thought so too. Riding the crest of popularity, he resigned and called for new elections. He figured that he would win a working majority within the Parliament.

He lost. The country sputtered along trying to function without a government.

The American government was equally powerless to help me. I followed the increasing reports of America's Watergate troubles closely. Over the years my interest in outside politics had dropped off. But now I wanted to follow this tremendous moment of American history.

My non-American friends cornered me for talks. To them, Nixon, Agnew, Mitchell, and the others were like comic book characters. It hurt. I realized as never before that I loved the United States. Not the politicians. The people. Not the government. The form of government. The fascism in Turkey made me long once more for a place where I could speak my mind.

Then one day in August I heard some news. Nadir came running to me. 'Nixon!' He spat. '*Ipnay pesavek* (queer pimp). *Asina covacim* (I stick it in his mouth).'

'What's the matter?'

'You didn't hear. Nixon quit.'

I sat down on my bunk and started to write a letter to the ex-President: 'Dear fellow prisoner . . .'

CHAPTER TWENTY-ONE

'Hi, Willie.'

'Max, what are you doing back from the *revere*? They run out of *Gastro*?'

Max grinned. 'No. I came to see you. There's this one guard at the *revere* who'll let me go anywhere in the prison for a pack of Marlboros.' A pause.

'Still want to get out of here?'

I sat up. 'You know I do.'

'Man I gotta get out.' Suddenly tears poured out of Max's eyes and he rubbed at them with his bony fingers. 'Goddamn *Gastro* is killing me. Making me blind, too.'

'Do you have a plan?'

'Well, I think I can bribe the doctor to send me across the street to the hospital. And there's a *kapidiye* in the *revere*. I think he can get me some acid. Can you get to . . . uh . . the hospital?'

'Yeah, I guess so. I could fake something. But how do we get out of the hospital?'

'Well, we . . . what?'

'The hospital, Max. How do we get out?'

'Oh. Well, I figure we drop some acid onto the guards. In their coffee or something.'

'So, we're out in Istanbul?'

'Yeah, I got it all worked out. When we get to the hospital we drop some acid onto the guards.'

'Yeah, yeah. Then we're outside. Then what?'

'What?'

'After we're out of the hospital, Max.'

'Yeah, with acid.'

'No. How do we get out of Turkey?'

'Oh. Out of Turkey . . .'

Silence. Max seemed to be asleep.

'Max?'

'Yeah? What?'

'How do we get out of Turkey?'

'Is . uh . . . Johann . . is he still in the city?'

'Yeah. He'd help us.'

'So we . . . uh . . . go see . . . uh . . '

'Johann?'

'Johann.'

'Gee, Max, I'm glad you've got this all worked out. You seem to have it planned down to the finest detail. What if we can't drop anything into the guards' coffee?'

'Uh . . . gun.'

'You have a gun?'

'No. Do you?'

'Max, I thought you had this all planned!'

'Willie, don't you trust me?'

'Max, I trust your heart completely.' He blinked at me through his thick glasses. 'But I don't trust your head.'

Max just stared. Slowly, his head nodded down towards his lap. His cigarette ash dropped onto his shirt and began to burn.

'Max! Your shirt!'

'Oh Christ!' Max brushed the ashes off his shirt. Again his eyes clouded with tears. 'Willie, there comes a time when you know you're never going to get it on.'

He shuffled back to the *revere*.

I lay on my bunk staring at the ceiling. If I was ever going to get out of here, I realized, it would take all the energy I could muster. And I had to direct all that energy out on one straight beam. Like the headlight of a speeding train cutting through the darkness. I knew it meant clicking all my switches to GO.

Then a letter from home arrived.

15 November 1974
Billy,
. . here I am remembering about long ago. They say that's a sign of growing old. I'm fine. Still the same. Life goes on, even with a little heartache every day for my oldest child so far away.

Love,
Mom

The letter dropped me into one of the lowest moods in four

long years. I ached inside. Loneliness and hollow longing. My mother! The pain she had to bear.

I picked up Arne's guitar.

By now I'd begun to play it a little and knew a few chords. Harvey came over. Softly he began to sing some old Alabama blues. We picked up a simple beat and improvised a few lines together. The song just sort of wrote itself.

> Mmmm . . . got the blues, babe,
> Got those old Istanbul blues.
> Said, yeah, I got the blues, babe,
> Got those old Istanbul blues .
> Thirty years in Turkey, babe,
> Ain't got nothin' left to lose.
>
> Busted at the border,
> Two keys in my shoes.
> Said I was busted at the border,
> With two keys in my shoes . . .
> An' they gave me thirty years, babe,
> To learn the old Istanbul blues.
>
> I said now Lord save me, save me,
> Please save me from this pain,
> I said Lord come and save me,
> Come save me from this pain.
> And set me free Sweet Jesus,
> I won't never sin again.

We played on awhile. The song wore down to a stop.
'How long you been here, Willie?'
He knew the answer. 'Four years.'
'How many summers?'
'Four.'

'Four summers. Those Turks are stealing your summers. They're stealing your sunshine. You could be lying on a beach somewhere with your woman by your side and a free blue sky stretched for ever above your head. Instead you're four summers in here. And now here comes another winter. I mean, can you ever get back a lost summer? Can you?'

196

I thought about it. Harvey was silent, plucking some strings.

'OK,' I said suddenly. 'Let's go.'

'The window?'

'The window.'

The window. So it had come down to that, bullet percentage and all. The file, the bars, the window, the roof, the wall, the guards, the machine guns, the searchlights, the rope in the darkness, Johann, the border, the Midnight Express to Greece. I felt a weight lift off my head. Maybe the window plan would kill me. But I was already half dead. It might work. Like the song said: '. . . thirty years in Turkey, babe, ain't got nothin' left to lose . . .'

Except my life.

'When?' I asked Harvey.

'Tonight,' he said quickly. 'My horoscope is right for it. Scorpio rising.'

We spent the afternoon getting our things together. I read my diary carefully. I removed all the money and stuffed it into my jock. The file and rope remained ready in their hiding places. I stained my white sneakers with black ink.

I dusted off my lucky hat.

At two o'clock in the morning I looked around the sleeping barracks. I let my eyes rest on each snoring man. Quietly I slipped down off my bunk, carrying my sneakers. I walked over to Harvey's bed. He was waiting for me. We moved into the bathroom, around a corner out of sight from the rest of the *kogus*.

'OK, let's do it.'

I slipped the file out of my sleeve and tiptoed back to the window. Slowly, carefully, I pulled it across the edge of one of the iron bars. It screeched like a fingernail on a blackboard. We froze.

Harvey checked the *kogus*. No one seemed to have heard. Carefully I worked, trying to move the file slowly with heavy pressure. The noise wasn't very loud; it just seemed that way. Harvey kept watch.

I worked at it nervously. I was certain the guards would show up to haul us away at any moment.

'I thought you said this would take five minutes,' Harvey whispered.

'I thought so. Something's wrong with this file.'

'Here, let me try.'

Harvey worked at it for a while. The bar had only a slight scratch mark on it. This would take for ever.

We worked in shifts, one man filing while the other stood guard. By 5 a.m. we had barely dented the tough metal. Harvey mixed some window putty with cigarette ashes and covered up the markings. We went back to bed.

Later that morning we tried to figure out what was wrong. Then we compared the metal on the bunk beds to the heavy iron on the windows. I realized my mistake. I had seen the file cut easily through the paint coating on the bed and calculated it was eating easily through the iron. I was wrong. The process could take weeks. And it was such a dangerously exposed spot.

But Harvey was determined. The bars were spaced widely. If we could just cut through one we thought we could squeeze out. Then the hard part would begin.

We worked for two more nights. We sliced through about a third of the bar.

'It's no good,' I told him during the day. 'The bar will take weeks and the putty doesn't cover it worth a damn. We're gonna get caught for sure.'

'Look, I'll tell you what,' said Harvey. 'All you gotta do is wake me up. Stand guard for me a little bit. I'll cut. When it's cut through we'll both go out together.'

I thought about it again.

'All right. I don't like it, Harv. But all right.'

Harvey worked silently but viciously for three, four, five more nights. The stubborn bar wouldn't give way. The noise of the filing made it impossible to work with abandon. He kept at it.

At five o'clock one morning he predicted that one more night's work would do it. 'Day after tomorrow,' he promised, 'I'll buy you *souvlaki*.'

Arief! The Bonebreaker was back again. We thought he'd never return after he'd seen what had happened to Hamid.

The *kogus* fell silent as he walked in. Several big guards followed him. Necdet came over and greeted him but Arief just scowled.

'The prisoner with the white in his hair,' he growled. 'Where is he?'

There could only be one man to fit that description. He was snoring in his bunk after a long night's work.

Guards dragged him out of bed. He complained and shook their arms off him. Arief smashed him across the face.

'We want the file!' he shouted.

'What?' said Harvey.

Another smash. Harvey fell back into the arms of the guards.

Arief dragged Harvey to the bathroom. He rubbed away at a few bars until he dislodged the putty off one on the end. 'The children saw you,' he said. 'We know it's you. We want the file.'

Harvey shrugged. What could he do? He went to his locker and dug the file out from under the metal moulding in the back.

Arief grunted satisfaction and the guards dragged Harvey downstairs. The *kogus* was alive with speculation about the window.

I spent a nervous day jumping at every noise. I tried to concentrate on a book . . . couldn't. Popeye came over and started joking around to cheer me up. But I ignored him and he left. I stared at the ceiling much of the night.

The next morning I slipped the door guard a couple of packets of cigarettes. He got me some information. Harvey was in the *revere*. A couple more packs and I was on my way over there to get something for my 'headache'.

I entered and walked down past a row of small cells. Where was Harvey? Had the guard been wrong? He wasn't there. I turned to leave.

I saw a prisoner lying in bed with a puffy blackened face Who was this poor man?

'Harvey! Oh, my God! I didn't recognize you.'

Yeah. They really did a number on me,' he mumbled through swollen lips. Several teeth were loose and crooked His ears stuck out raw and bruised. 'I'm afraid for my hernia

They kicked me in the balls a few times. I think that opened it. Willie, you've got to get hold of the consul. I'm in big trouble. I need a doctor. And these bastards are going to take away my good behaviour time and bring me to court for the escape. I need the consul to press charges for the beating. Maybe we can make a deal or something. I don't know. But if they're going to screw me, well, I'm going to screw them.'

'They wanted my name, didn't they?'

'Yeah, how did you know?'

'I heard Necdet talking with the guard. They said the kids saw someone else at the window. Thanks, Harv.'

'Yeah, well, what could I do, give them your name?' He managed a grin through his swollen lips. He grimaced. 'But at least I busted that pimp Arief in the mouth before the lights went out. Have you seen him?'

'No, but I've heard he's got a shiner and a mouse under the eye.'

'That's something, anyway. Listen, Willie, get in touch with the consul. I think the Turks are going to hustle me away to some little prison out in the sticks. I'm afraid what might happen.'

'I'll contact him, Harvey.'

'And why don't you do yourself a favour and get the hell out of this prison while you still can? This place is bad news.'

'That's the truth.'

Two days later Harvey was quietly shipped out to Antakya, the same prison in southeast Turkey that held Robert Hubbard, Jo Ann McDaniel, and Kathy Zenz.

Slowly, slowly, I put together the lessons of four years. I thought a lot about Weber and Jean-Claude, the two foreigners who had escaped from Sagmalcilar. Both of them had approached the problem directly, with full energy. Both of them had been careful not to confide in any other prisoners. They had planned well. As far as the prison administration was concerned, neither man had been interested in escape. Weber had built a prison career for himself. Jean-Claude had had 'tuberculosis'. Now both were free.

It was obvious to me that I had to get out of Sagmalcilar to another prison if I was going to escape. Too many guards, too many prisoners, knew that I hadn't adjusted to prison routine, even after this long. They watched me. I had to move into a new situation where I could plan quietly by myself. But where? How?

Then help came from the Turkish government itself. Suleiman Demirel managed to put together a coalition government. He was sympathetic to the cry of the smugglers. They had been cheated out of seven years in the previous amnesty. He promised to work in Parliament to grant smugglers those extra seven years. By May the Turkish Parliament gathered enough votes together to approve the additional seven-year amnesty. Popeye left us, grinning and whistling in anticipation of a night on the town. Whatever came after that night, he said, didn't matter. Once again the departure of a friend left me with mixed emotions. I was happy for Popeye, miserable for myself.

The amnesty reduced my time to three and a half more years. My release date was 7 October 1978. That was good. I had no intention of refusing it. But I also had no intention of sticking around for it. What the amnesty really meant for me was new life for the island transfer. Willard came out from the consulate and helped me fill out the forms. I requested Imros, the half-open prison of my dreams. There was a slim chance. As second choice I put down Imrali, where Charles had worked off his sentence.

CHAPTER TWENTY-TWO

14 July 1975
Folks,

So here I am on Imrali island, writing you a letter in the clear blue open air. I'm so amazed at the nature about me. Tall trees in the wind. White-capped water. A horseshoe-shaped bay, and a lavender mist at the far horizon where the deep blue of the Marmara meets the Asian hills.

This prison is just a handful of old buildings that might have been a village, time past. Dormitory-style rooms with creaky wooden floors and metal bunk beds. A bit dirty but that doesn't bother me anymore. I'm in a room with about thirty other guys. The atmosphere here is much different from Sagmalcilar. All the prisoners have small time remaining and fairly good records . . . not much of the fighting and stabbing that was routine in the other place.

The first day I arrived here was Friday, our free day. Do you believe it? I'm swimming in the sea! I mean, after five years of washing from a sink, I'm swimming in the sea. It's just amazing.

I'm working in the factory, which is just an old building fitted out to process the many varieties of fruit grown here and elsewhere. First workday we picked the stems off of forty million strawberries. I couldn't believe it. Five years without and then all the strawberries I could eat. After three hours of cleaning them and wolfing them down I had to run to the toilet. But it was fantastic. Now I work at a machine, doing monkey-work, making the metal covers for the cans we use for the conserve. It's all right.

I'm sunburned, not much but just enough to make me feel good. Laid on the beach yesterday and today from twelve until two. I don't eat the lunch offered. We're allowed to walk around the island, and so I go far off down the beach, up one leg of the bay where I'm alone. Just me and the sea. It's so fine to be alone, to be away from people for the first time in five years, to lie so still in the sunshine and listen to the gulls.

They say the winters here are really cold. But I can stand anything now. It will be a small price to pay for the freedom of movement, not to mention opportunity . . . more about this in coming letters when I've become better acquainted with the place.

I still can't get over that picture of the whole clan together. Nana looks like she's getting younger all the time. And Dad, it struck me as so strange to hear that you had to prune the trees in the backyard to let the sun in. I thought, 'What trees?' and then remembered that trees grow a lot in five years. Like people.

Lillian should be back in North Babylon on 24 July. I've asked her to stop in for a visit. She should be able to tell you a lot from the letters I've written her. I really don't know what's to become of my life in days to come. But Lillian's gotten me through some of the hardest times. I wonder what could be if we could be together in the good times. Seems as if I've learned something about loving and giving while in here . . . too late for Kathleen but Lillian, yes, Lillian, who knows? Anyway, I'm still here for three more years. Maybe. I'll write next week when things have developed a bit more. Don't worry.

> *Love to you all,*
> *Billy*

At first it seemed like paradise. And compared to Sagmalcilar it was. But guard towers at the mouth of the harbour reminded me it was still prison. At night searchlights played along the beach. Sentries patrolled. Despite the blue sky over my head, the grey mood of despair settled back down on me before long. If I had to be in prison, I wanted to be here. But did I have to be in prison?

Max said I could never escape from Imrali. Charles in his letters had said maybe. *Sula bula.*

As I gazed out over the calm waters of the Sea of Marmara, I knew I could. Marmara is an inland sea, cutting across the north-western tip of the country between the Black Sea and the Aegean. The north shore is Europe. The south shore is Asia. Imrali is an arc of land about twenty miles off the south-eastern coast. A swift current sweeps around the island, moving down towards the Dardanelles.

The water was so calm those first few days that I thought maybe I could swim the twenty miles to shore. But what then? I'd still be in Turkey, further than ever from Greece. I studied my Turkish map carefully. Bursa was the largest city near by. I could get a bus from there back north to Istanbul. Could I still depend on Johann to get me out of the country?

Every Friday a ferry boat came out to Imrali from the mainland, carrying a few new prisoners or visitors. The week after I arrived on the island the boat brought two unexpected, very welcome, guests. One was Michael Griffith, my Long Island lawyer. The other was Joey, grinning from under his moustache.

Friday was our day off. No one worked. Prisoners with guests sat together in the shade of a small garden area. 'I've never seen so many flies,' Mike complained, swatting at them with both hands.

I laughed. 'I guess I didn't notice. You forget about things like that after living with them for five years.'

Joey offered me a carton of Winstons. He had forgotton that I'd quit. 'How you doin'?' he asked.

'I'm fine. I go swimming every day.'

'No kidding?'

'Yeah.'

'What the hell is prison coming to?' he asked, looking around. Joey had a job now as a deckhand on a tourist boat that sailed the Bosporus.

Mike opened his briefcase and showed me a pile of legal papers. 'Your Dad and I have been talking, Billy. We both know what train you're waiting for. And we don't want to see you get hurt.'

I shrugged 'I'll be careful.'

'Billy, this is the last stop for fuel before we get on the tracks. The transfer is all set. If you'll let us use those medical records – the psychiatric reports – we think that will be enough to persuade the Turkish government to allow the transfer. We just don't want you to blow it by trying something stupid here.'

'Sure. Why not? Use the records. I'm for anything that will get me home.'

Mike relaxed. 'So you'll stick around and wait?'

'I'm not promising anything, Mike.'

The morning passed too quickly. I was filled with the joy of just sitting in the shade and making small talk with friends. But when Mike excused himself to use the toilet, Joey and I got down to business quickly.

'What do you need?' he asked.

'A boat. Joey, with a boat it would be so easy. I can roam the island all I want until ten o'clock at night.'

'I'll see what I can do. Might take me a little time to put it together.'

'Hurry, Joey. It's July. I've got to get out before the weather turns cold. Charles said the sea gets really bad in the winter.'

'OK. I'll write to you.'

Mike came back. 'Phew, what a stinking toilet. How do you put up with it?'

I threw back my head and laughed. Mike looked puzzled.

'Mike, the Minister of Justice is coming here tomorrow for a special visit. They just cleaned that toilet yesterday. It's real clean today.'

'Phew. I'm glad I didn't see it when it was dirty. And there wasn't any paper, either.'

'They don't use paper.'

'What the hell do they use?'

'Their fingers. They use water and . . .'

'Stop. That's enough. I just won't go again till I'm back at the Hilton.'

The ferry boat returned. It was time for my friends to leave. Mike turned to me before he boarded. 'Look, Bill,' he said, 'I'll beg you, if I have to. Don't leave this island. Just give me a chance. You'll mess up the transfer. They'll give you ten more years. They could shoot you.'

'Mike, why do you keep talking escape? Do you think I'm really going to blow this beautiful deal?'

'Billy, it's written all over your face.'

I lowered my voice. 'Mike, you've done a great job for me. If it wasn't for some stupid luck you would've had me home long ago. So please, keep working hard for me. Do what you have to do. But I'm going to do what I have to do.'

And so I waited. Whoever came through first, Mike or Joey, was all right with me. But after five years of disappointments with the Turkish government I held little faith in the transfer. Escape had come to seem the best way out.

The other prisoners assumed that I was merely waiting for the U.S. and Turkish governments to sign an arms accord that would clear the way for better diplomatic relations and, finally, my transfer would come. With that possibility so close, there was no reason for anyone to suspect me of planning an escape. That's the way I wanted to keep it. I remembered Weber and Jean-Claude.

I volunteered for harder work. All day long I hauled fifty-kilo (about 110-pound) sacks of beans from the processing plant to shipping carts. It drained me of energy. But I could feel strength growing in muscles that had been too little used for five years. During the two-hour lunch break I forced myself to swim constantly, building stamina. In the evenings I ran long miles around back-island trails.

And every Friday I waited anxiously for the mail boat, for word from Mike and Joey.

Weeks passed. Nothing but silence from the outside world. Then a letter from home. I could read the tears between the lines. Dad pleaded with me to wait for the transfer. And even if the transfer didn't come, he said, I should keep patient. I had only three years left, he said, soon only two. Then I'd be counting down from the last year and be free. Better than ten more, he said. Better than getting shot.

But these were arguments I'd had with myself long ago. I decided no one could really understand unless he, too, had spent five years locked up. I wrote back and assured Dad that I wouldn't move until I was sure the track was clear all the way to home.

More weeks passed. Finally there was a postcard from Joey. He was coming to visit me the next Friday. There was also a note from Mike Griffith. He felt the transfer would come through any day now. SIT STILL, he wrote in capital letters.

Joey showed up on visiting day.

'I can get a boat,' he said. 'But the engine needs work. I need some money.'

'How much?'

I went back to my barracks and brought my diary out to show Joey. We read it carefully during the next few hours. Joey left with about $2000 tucked into his sleeve. He said he'd come out and visit again next week. We'd discuss the final plans then.

That evening a sudden storm blew up. I climbed to the top

of a one hundred-foot cliff to watch the sea pound against the old wooden docks below me. Suddenly the harbour began to fill with boats! Fishermen from the mainland, caught out in the open sea, were bringing their boats into the harbour to escape the storm. The fishing boats were too big and bulky for me to handle alone. But each one trailed a dinghy behind it. Could I row twenty miles to the mainland? In a storm?

Those dinghies obsessed me the following night. Next Friday came. Joey was not on the visitors' boat. Where could he be? There was no mail for me on the boat, either. That meant a week of waiting before the next possible news.

A strange silence descended upon Imrali. For weeks I heard nothing from Joey. No further word from Mike. Nothing. Had Joey run out on me? Was Mike finding out that the transfer was just another train to nowhere?

I woke early one morning to do my yoga. There was something different, a cool crispness to the sea air. I noticed it immediately. The first hint of autumn. Winter storms would follow soon. If I delayed any longer I'd be trapped for another six months. I couldn't stand another winter.

Five years ago I'd gotten myself into this mess. For five years I'd been waiting for my family, my friends, my lawyers, to get me out. I was twenty-eight years old now. Maybe it was time I took matters into my own hands.

'It's time,' I said to the morning air. 'It's time.'

CHAPTER TWENTY-THREE

28 September 1975
Dad,

 Don't know whether this may be the last letter I'll be writing to you. I'm waiting daily for the aligning of certain weather factors which will finalize the plan I've decided to act upon. I'll explain a little better. There are, as we've discussed before, advantages to keeping as many trains running at the same time as we possibly can. Coming down the middle track, at an indeterminable speed, is that two-year running transfer-train. Circumstances always throw this train off the track. I mean, for two years it's been chugging. And maybe, maybe it's going to get home one of these fine days.

 But now there's that train that I've been watching here on the far outside track which just can't be kept running very much longer before it gets bogged down by the cold winter weather. And spring is just too far away after five years. I know you'll find it difficult to appreciate and will surely disagree with the logic of a sure three versus a possible thirteen. And do not think I haven't considered the anguish of loved ones hurt in the derailment. I have. But I've just got to move . . . just got to move to get on this train. Please don't fret or write any entreating letters. I'm at the station waiting, like you.

 Love to you, Mom and Dad, and everyone.

                Billy

 In the evening after work I raced back to the barracks to make my preparations while the other men went to dinner. I changed into dark clothing – my blue jeans and the sneakers I had inked for my window escape with Harvey Bell. I took my precious map of Turkey, now tattered from much handling, from its hiding place and wrapped it in wax paper, then put it in my leather carrying pouch, along with my address book. I counted my meagre supply of money and cursed Joey; he had taken most of it. I now had only about forty dollars in Turkish lira. I put the money into my wallet and the wallet into the pouch too. I strapped the pouch tightly to my side, and pulled on a navy blue turtleneck sweater.

I went to the window and double-checked to see that no one was coming. Then I went to my bed and drew a knife from under the mattress. I was scared to death to be caught with that knife; to possess a weapon was an extremely serious offence. I had stolen the knife from the conserve factory. It was short and pointed, the kind used for paring fruit, and its wooden handle was splintered and just barely held on by worn screws. I had hidden it under a rock in the orchard and the day before had transferred it to my bed. All night long, even when I was asleep, I was conscious of that forbidden knife under the mattress. Now I wrapped paper around it to sheathe it and slipped it into the pocket of my jeans. And then I put on my lucky hat.

I couldn't just sit out on the dock waiting for a boat to appear. So the plan was this: Up a slight hill from the harbour was the tomato paste processing area. Five large concrete bins were used to store the paste. I knew from working around them that the one on the end was empty. I could hide inside each night, whenever the weather looked right, watching the harbour while avoiding the guards on patrol. Sooner or later the Marmara would churn up another storm, and the boats would appear.

I waited till dusk. Then I took a walk along one of the trails. That was normal enough. Just another prisoner out enjoying nature. My path took me near the tomato paste bins. I checked around me. I looked into the empty bin. Then I jumped inside.

It was cool and dark. I huddled in the bottom. The sky slowly turned black above me. At times I checked the harbour, not really expecting to see any boats there in good weather, but hoping.

I heard footsteps, the measured pace of a guard. I sat motionless. If he looked inside, what could I say? I thought of the knife. I prayed he wouldn't stop. He passed by.

I waited quietly until nine forty-five. Not tonight. I jumped out of the bin and dashed back to the barracks before the curfew. No one really counted us until morning, but I didn't want to take chances.

I watched and waited for a full week. Lazy Indian summer days were followed by calm quiet evenings.

And then on Thursday, 2 October, I awoke to the sound of wind and rain beating against the window pane of the barracks. I looked out at the grey sky and my heart began to pump. I knew it was the day. The storm grew worse during the evening. I worked furiously at my job until lunchtime, then raced to the harbour. A half-dozen fishing boats had already dropped anchor. More were heading my way! If only the storm would keep on until after dark.

I worked more easily that afternoon, trying to save my strength for what I hoped was a full night of rowing. At five-thirty the guards released us from work. The rain had stopped but the sky was dark and low and the wind was strong. I ran to the harbour. The sea was rough and choppy. Boats were strung out all over. I headed back to the barracks to prepare.

When darkness closed in on Imrali island I climbed into the tomato bin. A prison spotlight routinely swept the area. By now I knew its pattern. Crazy shadows rose on the wall of the bin whenever it passed over. There were lights on the boats in the dark harbour.

I wanted to wait until after the curfew. Then I could be sure that other prisoners were not around. So I crouched and planned. I would swim out to the farthest fishing boat and untie its dinghy. And then row for the Asian shore.

Time passed slowly. I realized that I had to relieve myself. I crawled to a far corner of the bin and peed. The urine mingled with the rain puddles, then trickled back across the floor of the bin and settled in the corner where I'd been hiding. If I changed my position I might be more exposed to a patrolling guard. So I had to squat in the liquid. The smell hardly bothered me any more.

Time crawled now. I felt as if I'd been waiting for days. My watch only showed eight o'clock. I tried to relax. My thoughts flew to all the things I would do when I got out. I thought of Lillian. I thought of Mom and Dad. I imagined myself walking down a street in a city. Any city. A free man. I was so close. I *had* to make it.

A noise! Footsteps. I didn't dare breathe. A guard moved up the pathway towards the bins. I could hear him stop next to my hiding place. A bright orange glow flared up, flickered ın the wind and went out. The guard coughed Then he moved on.

The rain began again. It soaked me to the skin. The wind was icy. I huddled in the bottom of the bin and waited.

Finally my watch showed ten-thirty. I eased my head up over the top of the bin and listened. The sounds of the storm filled the night. I took a couple of deep breaths and raised one leg over the edge of the bin.

What was that?

Quickly 1 dropped back down inside. I huddled against the wall. Off in the distance a dog barked. I thought of the guard tower and its machine guns.

I waited another ten minutes, listening. Again I poked my head over the edge of the bin and looked through the driving rain. Then lifted one leg up. Again I thought I heard a noise and dropped back down. I shivered in fear.

I decided it must have been my imagination. My hands shook. I wondered if I really had the nerve to go through with this.

For a third time I gathered my courage. I took several deep breaths. 'All right,' I said to myself. 'All right. Let's just go.'

The bank down to the harbour was covered with a mixture of broken stones and rotting tomato pulp. The earth was muddy and puddled. Slime covered me as I crawled carefully down the bank on my belly. I was in the open, exposed to the searchlight. Each time it passed over I dug deep into the slime. I lay motionless. I prayed.

Slowly I worked my way down the bank. Now for the hard part. The first fifty yards of water lay directly in front of the guard tower. I could see one soldier in it operating the searchlight. Another paced quietly with a machine gun. I was thankful for the noise of the wind and waves. Even so, I would have to be careful.

I slipped into the cold water. Above me the searchlight moved across the harbour. I pushed off from the shore, my heart pounding with the knowledge that my escape, so long dreamed of, had begun, and that there was no going back now. I had committed myself.

I swam slowly, afraid to splash. The heavy clothes weighed me down. A wave caught me in the face, driving salt

211

water down my throat. I fought back a cough. I tensed for the bullets to rip into my back.

I swam breast-stroke so that only my head would break water.

When I could swim no farther without a rest, I stopped and looked back. The dim lights of the harbour had fallen behind. Ahead I could see bobbing lanterns, each one indicating a fishing boat. I would swim to the farthest one.

I fought against the storm. Several times I stopped, treading water, checking my position, gulping air. Then I started again, heading for the last fishing boat.

There it was, a tiny dinghy tied to the rear. Would it hold up in this sea? It had to.

I hoisted myself over the side of the dinghy. It took every bit of strength I had left. Exhausted, I sank onto the wet floorboards. I lay there for several minutes, shivering in the cold, trying to catch my breath. Then I raised my head slowly until I could see over the side of the boat. I studied the shore, expecting to see a patrol boat bearing down on me. But there were no lights following me out.

The front of the dinghy was covered over, offering maybe three feet of shelter. The rest of the boat was totally exposed. I felt in the dark for the oars. I found them. They were thick and heavy.

Bang! A window crashed open right over my head. I froze. Above me a Turkish fisherman gargled the poisons out of his throat and spat across my head into the water.

My heart had stopped beating.

The window creaked on its hinges and banged shut.

Slowly I slid up under the covering in front of the boat. I shivered in a puddle of cold water. I curled up as tightly as possible, but my legs still lay exposed. I wanted to get out of there before the fisherman opened his window again.

I glanced up at the underside of the covering. Over my head I could dimly see a large knot, the end of the rope that tethered the dinghy to the fishing boat. The knot was thick and tight – impossible to untie. I reached into my blue jeans for the knife. My pants were soaked. They clung to my legs. Finally I reached the knife. The rope was wet and sinewy. The knife cut through it at an agonizingly slow pace. I hacked away until my muscles ached and my arms and back were bruised from rubbing against the ribs of the boat. I desperately had to cough, and the effort of holding back the spasms wracked my chest. A damp chill settled in my lungs.

I drew numb fingers back and forth, back and forth. And then only a few strands of rope were left. I stopped. Once more I looked around me. I listened. I held my breath and slit through the final strands.

The knot fell. The severed end of the rope trembled and moved an inch up through the hole in the covering. And then it rasped out through the hole and disappeared. The boat was free!

I was adrift. As quietly as I could I crawled to the centre of the dinghy and got up on the seat. I looked out. I was drifting toward the prison shore! I grabbed for the oars, and then discovered there were no oar-locks, none that I could see. There was no light now. My hand touched a twist of rope at the centre of one oar-shaft. It was shaped like a figure eight. I realized that the loop of the pretzel must fit over something. I felt the gunwale. Ah, yes. There were pegs on the sides of the boat. The rope-twists slipped over the pegs.

Hurrying now, I was scared to death because the dinghy was drifting not just toward shore but toward the hulk of another fishing boat. I jammed the oars into position. I pulled. One oar failed to catch the water, and the boat lurched, and I pitched around in the darkness. The second fishing boat loomed larger. I centred myself on the seat again and adjusted the oars until I could tell both blades were at the right angle. And then I pulled, and again. And the drift slowed, then stopped. The dinghy began to move in the other direction.

It was hard rowing. The tossing sea kept me bobbing at different angles. The oars often failed to bite into the water. I had to shift my balance quickly to keep from being thrown off the wet bench. I braced my feet against the bottom and gradually after several minutes, a rhythm developed.

Now I had to steer a careful course down the inside of the horseshoe-shaped island. There were huge rocks in the breakerline. And there were many more fishing boats anchored further south, I discovered. I had to weave a path for

213

the dinghy between the two sets of hazards. The rain lashed down in sheets, driven by the wind. Its ferocity scared me. But the rain also gave me cover.

My muscles were hardened from yoga and from hefting sacks of beans. I pulled and heaved on the oars. Slowly, the edge of the island slid past.

I watched the lights of the harbour. They receded to a small cluster, pinpoints of brightness in the dark night. I knew I wanted to steer a course in line with the lights and the edge of the island. If I lost sight of the lights I'd be too far over to one side. I strained against the wind to keep the boat in line.

The current was much stronger in the open sea. It pushed the dinghy to the west. Waves slammed the boat broadside, and the wind threw salt spray into my eyes. Quickly I grew exhausted. The island lights had focused down to a single point when I stopped rowing and checked my position. Behind me, somewhere through the storm, was the Turkish mainland. Twenty miles south.

I rowed till I thought I'd collapse. Then I checked again. Did I see lights in the direction of the mainland? I looked again and there were none. More rowing, back breaking. Another look, lights! Three pale lights. But they were off to one side. I was being pulled far off course.

A wave of self-pity swept over me. I loosened my grip. One of the oars caught the current. It lifted from its peg and nearly pulled from my hand. I jerked it into the boat. I threw both oars to the bottom of the dinghy. The tiny craft veered off down the waves.

This would never work! It might take me days to row to the shore. If I didn't drown first. My breathing came in heavy sobs. I held onto the seat and sat still for a moment. The dinghy rode up the face of a long swell. It hung suspended for an instant, then rushed down the other side. Another long swell rolled under me. Again the boat rose and then plunged. I was terrified.

But it was a strange sort of fear. I could die out here in the open sea, but at least I'd die free. Just the word filled me with new strength. Free! I was free! The lights of Imrali had faded behind me. For the first time in five long years I was beyond the bounds. My heart leapt up. I was free! All that remained was to stay alive. To finish this boat ride and set my feet on solid ground.

I grabbed the oars and set back to work. I pulled on them angrily, wrenching the boat around, back on course. Then I worked to resume my rhythm. I chanted aloud to myself as I struggled.

> 'If they catch me . . .
> They'll beat me . . .
> Shoot me . . .
> If I make it . . .
> I'm free . . .
> I'm free . . .
> I'm free . . .'

I had waited five years for this ride. I wouldn't give up now. *I would not!*

Still the current pulled me to the west. I rowed twice as hard with my right arm, trying to get back on course for the three pale lights.

I sang to myself. I yelled at myself. I cursed myself in Turkish and English.

Hours passed in dark wet agony. My right hand ached where, long ago, Hamid had smashed it with his *falaka* stick. Then it cramped. The skin of both hands was raw, and salt water stung in broken blisters.

I stopped rowing. Carefully I pulled the oars into the boat. The fingers of my right hand didn't work. I had to pry them off the oar with my left. I grabbed my soggy handkerchief and tied it around the throbbing hand. I pulled the knot tight with my teeth.

Then back to work. I rowed. I rowed with fixed determination. All that mattered was to keep pulling, keep going, keep the rhythm. My body stopped complaining. I was beyond pain. I exulted in the movement. I was free.

The lights were closer now. They were! I could do it. Even the sea began to co-operate. The storm seemed to calm. The first hint of light blue glow tinted the sky to the east. Another hour.

Thud. The oar scraped something. Then the bottom of

the dinghy scratched across sand. A small wave lifted the boat and sent it forward a few more feet, then set it down again. I rolled over the side and found myself in one foot of water. I rushed up the beach and sank down on my knees.

But I was still in Turkey.

My next goal was the city of Bursa. I knew from the map that it lay somewhere along the coast to the north-east. It had about 250,000 people. I could lose myself there. And from Bursa I could get transportation to Istanbul. Then, Johann. He would hide me for a couple of weeks until the search died down.

The search! The rising sun in front of me reminded me that fishermen would soon be stirring. One of them, when he opened his window for his morning gargle, would certainly miss his dinghy. It would take the prison guards little time to make a head count. I had to move fast.

My watch still worked. It was after five a.m. I got up and sucked salt air deep into my lungs. Then I set off trotting towards the sun. The warm orange light gave me new strength. Ahead of me stretched the deserted north coast of Asia Minor. This was the finest morning of my life.

I ran on. I should have been tired. I should have been hungry. But my legs pumped without stopping. Each step took me farther from prison. How much time did I have? When would they find the dinghy?

I ran on and on. Still the shore was wild and deserted. The sun dried my clothes. My face and arms were caked with salt. My mouth burned.

Then I came to a huge outcropping of rocks that jutted into the sea, blocking the beach. I waded into the water up to my waist and worked my way around the rocks. As I moved past the point my eyes caught sight of what looked like a modern village in the hills up ahead – a strange cluster of buildings here in the middle of nowhere. I saw three towers. Were they the three glowing lights I'd sighted on during the night?

Oh, no! An army camp!

I melted back behind the rocks. I waded back around to

the beach and walked inland to the cover of the woods. In a long circle I moved past the army base.

Another hour of walking. I knew I must be very careful. Surely the alarm was out by now. Why hadn't I shaved my blond moustache before I left? I should've brought shoe polish or something to dump onto my hair.

I came to tilled fields. In the distance I could see a few peasants working. Around a bend, a small village.

Careful. Don't blow it.

I followed a dirt road until it entered the town and became a cobblestone street. An old man with a stringy grey beard leaned back on his heels against a wall. He sucked on a pipe.

'I must get to Bursa,' I said.

The old man looked at me. *Turist*, obviously. Dirty, wet, crusty, muddy, bandaged right hand. Floppy hat pulled low. 'How do you know Turkish?' he asked.

I answered hesitantly. 'Twenty months in Istanbul prison. Hash.'

He grinned. 'What are you doing here?' he asked.

'I was on the beach with some friends. We had a jeep. I drank a lot of *raki* last night and got lost. Now I need to get to Bursa.' With the tip of his pipe he pointed up the narrow road to an old Volkswagen bus.

'Bursa,' he said.

The roof was piled high with burlap bags filled with onions, olives, other produce. The inside was packed with peasants. I found someone who looked like the driver.

'Bursa?'

'Six lira.'

I paid. Then I squeezed into a back seat against the window. I pulled my hat even lower and tried to keep a hand over my moustache.

The bus bounced along the muddy coast, up mountain roads winding towards Bursa. The old driver whipped around turns at high speed. I hadn't ridden in an open vehicle for years, and it was frightening. On the outside turns gravity pushed me out over the edge of the cliffs. *How ridiculous it would be to die here, I thought. Now. When I'm finally free.* But there was nothing I could do. And the driver had to know the roads.

217

We stopped at markets along the side of the highway. Peasants tumbled out to sell their wares. Gradually the load lightened. The bus driver increased his speed.

Finally Bursa came into view. It was the only city of its size along this coast. Its streets were hot and dry and dusty, lined with crumbling buildings of the old Turkish architecture, with an occasional Western-style office building that was also falling apart. I checked my watch. Nine-thirty. I knew they had missed me now. I hadn't showed up for work.

A battered cab sat at the curb. I approached the driver carefully.

'Istanbul?'

'Seven hundred lira.'

'Four hundred fifty.' It was all I had.

'*Yok*. Seven hundred.'

I shrugged. The cabbie pointed to the bus station 'Twenty-five lira,' he said.

Yes, but I didn't want to go near the bus station. They'd be looking for me there. For sure. As I peered down the street I could see two policemen standing out in front of the bus station. I wondered whether they had a description of me and were watching for me in particular.

But I had no choice. I had to get to Istanbul. To Johann. The longer I waited, the greater the risk.

I walked towards the station. As I passed the entrance one of the policemen yawned.

I bought a ticket to Istanbul. The bus would leave in a half hour. I sat down to wait and was suddenly exhausted. Hungry, too. I found a snack counter and bought a chocolate bar and a big bag of pretzels.

The bus arrived. Again I had to walk past the policemen. They seemed to ignore me. I climbed in and took an aisle seat. My heart raced. Please, please let me get to Istanbul.

I waited for the bus to leave. I thought it never would. But at last it began to move. It left the station and headed for the open road that swings around the eastern edge of the Sea of Marmara to Uskudar. I began to breathe again.

The trip was bumpy. The bus buzzed with Turkish chatter. Flies fought for my pretzels.

We came to Uskudar. Across the Golden Horn, rising

218

steeply from its shores, I saw Istanbul, with the spires of minarets crowning its hills. There was where it had all begun. The bus crossed the Yeni Kopru bridge, and once again I was in Europe.

It was nearly noon. I was frantic. No doubt at all, the Turkish police were after me now. I could only hope to blend with the other *turists* who crowded the Istanbul bus depot.

I stepped off the bus and kept my eyes low to the ground. I moved into the middle of a group of people and walked with them out onto the streets. Only from a distance did I stop to look back at the station. Two policemen stood outside the front entrance. There was no sign of alarm.

Now, Johann's hotel. It was almost over. I found a cab driver and gave him the name of the hotel. We wound through back streets until we arrived at the door. Not the Hilton, that was for sure.

I wondered about my lucky hat. It covered my blond hair, but the hat was conspicuous, too. Maybe it was more obvious than the hair. Before I stepped into the hotel, I pulled off the hat and shoved it under my arm.

I walked into the lobby. Behind the desk was a baldheaded Turk. He looked up.

'Johann?' I asked. 'I'm looking for Johann.'

'Johann?' He eyed my clothes. 'Johann left yesterday for Afghanistan.'

CHAPTER TWENTY-FOUR

Bewildered, numb, tired, dazed, I stumbled out onto the street. Johann in Afghanistan? Why? And why now, when I needed him most?

I walked the streets for about a half hour before I remembered I had to hide. I entered a drugstore and bought a tube of cheap black hair dye. I was in the red-light district. Across the street was a run-down hotel. I walked inside.

'I need a room,' I said in Turkish to a pimply-faced clerk.

He looked me up and down.

'Where's your luggage?'

'It was stolen.'

'Where's your passport?'

'Stolen. In my luggage.'

The eyes narrowed. 'You speak Turkish?'

'Yeah. I was in prison for a while. *Tamam?*'

'*Tamam*. Fifty lira for the room.'

I started to protest. Ten lira would be too much for this hole. But I paid.

The clerk grinned and gave me the key.

The room was up a couple of flights of rickety stairs. It was roach heaven. I pulled the tube of hair dye out of my pocket. It was a gooey paste. The instructions said to mix it with four white pellets that smelled like ammonia, then dab a small amount on the inside of your wrist. I was supposed to wait twenty-four hours to see if there was an allergic reaction. I didn't really have time for that.

With a cotton ball I rubbed the pasty mess into my hair and moustache. My hands trembled from weakness. By accident I kept splotching the black colouring onto my face. I stepped back and studied myself in the mirror. The hair looked strange, but believable for Istanbul. My moustache, however, was a big black licorice stick pasted above my lip. The moustache had to go.

Nervously, I slipped out of the hotel and back into the

crowded street. I found a shop and bought a razor and a blade.

The moustache came off in a glob. Now my face was really naked. The skin of my upper lip was outlined in black where the moustache had been. It looked worse than ever.

I fell onto the bed and gulped for air. Sleep overcame me, but not for long. Every footstep on the stairs, every suspicious sound from the street, woke me in fear. I looked out the back window. Rickety stairs led down to a narrow alleyway. Dangerous but possible. I lay back down on the bed. After a long time I dozed off again.

Morning. I studied my maps carefully. I reached back into memory for the countless prison conversations about escape. The main road west out of Istanbul led to Edirne. No good. It was the major border crossing. Too heavily guarded. I had no passport. For sure the customs men had my description now.

To the south of Edirne lay Uzun Kopru. A possibility. Max had always talked about the country down there. In places it was empty and primitive. The Maritas River ran down out of the mountains of Bulgaria and formed the border between Turkey and Greece. It was guarded but not so heavily as up near Edirne.

Another possibility was the train between Edirne and Uzun Kopru. The one that crossed the river and actually ran through a section of Greece for a while. But I probably didn't have enough money left for the fare. And the train station sounded too risky. And how could I know where to jump off?

I decided to take a bus to Uzun Kopru. From there I would find some way across the border.

My hotel was set into a steep hill just above the harbour. Across the Galata Bridge, on the other side of the Golden Horn, was a tram station. From there I figured I could get to the bus station on the outskirts of Istanbul.

It was a bright clear morning, about seven a.m. The streets were surprisingly crowded for that hour. I bought a newspaper and filtered into a crowd of people scurrying across the bridge. My clothes were rumpled, my eyes bloodshot. My hair was black. The naked skin above my mouth was red and irritated where I'd tried to rub off the black dye. I knew I smelled of sweat and seaweed. For the first time in five years, I really must have seemed like a Turk. I sure hoped so.

I found the tram. Policemen patrolled in a leisurely way. If they were looking for me, they were looking for a blond with a moustache. I knew this but my skin crawled to think how close I was to capture. I told myself to be *very* careful. I took a seat on the tram and raised the newspaper up in front of my face. I scanned through the pages looking for any story about me. Thank God, there was no news. The last thing I needed was to have the whole country warned that a dangerous escaped convict was in their midst.

The bus terminal was mobbed.

What was going on? People thronged about the huge dusty parking lot and scrambled to get on the noisy buses. But it was so early!

I bought an apple from a vendor and sat under a tree across from the station. I had to figure this out. Again I checked the paper. Then I realized. This was the first day of *Sugar Bayram*, a four-day feast that followed thirty days of Moslem fasting. It was the biggest holiday of the year. Everyone was visiting. It was like travelling on Christmas Eve.

Pushing my way through the crowds, I crossed to the station. I found myself at the end of a long line of people waiting to buy tickets. When I finally reached the window, the ticket seller said the bus to Uzun Kopru was full.

'I'll pay extra,' I said. 'Just get me on the bus.'

He looked up sharply. 'It is full!' he snapped.

Careful. Don't draw attention. 'All right. A ticket to Edirne, please.'

I paid. He stamped the ticket and pointed. The bus was ready to leave. I stepped inside and found a seat next to a fat peasant woman who reeked of garlic.

What was I going to do now? I couldn't risk a crossing at Edirne. As the bus pulled out of the station I checked my map. Edirne was forty miles north of Uzun Kopru. The country looked rugged. Maybe I could cross somewhere in between. I spotted the railroad line, where it ran back and forth from Turkey to Greece. It was tricky terrain. Countless wars between the two nations had moved the border back and forth. The small map was bad. In most places the Maritas River seemed to form the border, but in other areas, it looked as if Turkey extended far beyond the water.

Though the October morning was cold, the bus soon became hot and smelly. It bounced along the country roads like a rattling stagecoach. I tried to relax. It was useless. My nerves were too tight. Each time the bus slowed I was afraid we were being stopped by soldiers. I'd have to wait until I got to Greece to relax. I closed my eyes and thought of a hot bath. It would be so nice to soak off five years of dirt in a tubful of clean steaming water.

I woke suddenly. Something was wrong. The bus had pulled up to a quick halt. I leaned forward to see. Oh, God! A policeman was standing in the road, his arm outstretched, forcing the driver to stop. I looked around quickly. There was only one door. I was trapped. Think! Think!

The door slammed open and the policeman jumped on. He took a quick glance at the passengers. I read my newspaper and watched carefully from the corner of my eye. His big body completely blocked the doorway. There was no way out except through him.

The policeman asked the driver for his papers. He read them carefully. Another glance at the passengers. He was gone.

I let out a quiet sigh. They must have been looking for me, I figured. They're on my trail. But they haven't told the newspapers. Maybe the police don't want to be embarrassed.

Huge white thunderclouds loomed at the edge of the horizon. I wished them on. I didn't know what to expect at the border, but I figured the cover of a rainstorm would help It had worked once.

The bus arrived in Edirne about noon. It was an over-grown village, crowded, dirty. I decided to wait until after-noon to move south. I'd try the border at night. Meanwhile I would lose myself amid the jostling holiday crowds.

I walked streets jammed with chattering, bustling people. I drank tea and bought fruit in the covered bazaar. Under different circumstances I would have enjoyed myself. Max had told me a lot about Edirne. It used to be called Adriano-polis. That was back when it belonged to the Greeks. How I wished it still belonged to them. From places in the city I could look out to some distant hills that were surely in Greece. I could *see* freedom. I just had to get there.

Soldiers and police were everywhere. I could only keep moving, hoping that my black hair and blind luck would protect me.

By late afternoon I was ready. I walked carefully through the bazaar, looking for a cab driver who seemed trustworthy. I found a young one with long hair.

'My friends are camping,' I said. 'They're south of town. I was supposed to meet them here this morning but must have missed them in the crowd. Can you take me there?'

'Forty lira,' he said.

It was a lot of money for the ride. But I had a hundred lira left and this was no time to bargain. 'Sure.'

We drove out of town on a dusty dirt road.

'Where'd you learn to speak Turkish?' he asked.

So my disguise hadn't fooled him.

'I spent twenty months in prison in Istanbul.'

'Hash?'

'Yeah.'

'You want to score some? Cheap?'

Oh, no! This was where I came in. If there was one thing I didn't need it was hashish.

We drove to a small village about ten miles south of Edirne. On my map it was the last village until the outskirts of Uzun Kopru. South of this village lay a great expanse of wild, open land on both sides of the river. Border land.

The cab driver slowed down when he saw some people by the side of the road.

'Where's the camp-ground?' he asked.

They looked at him in bewilderment.

'The camp-ground?'

They shrugged.

We drove on to a small tavern. The driver stopped and yelled to some men sitting on the porch. 'Anybody seen any *turists* in a camper-bus?'

To my shock three policemen came sauntering down toward the car. Their collars were open. They had glasses of beer in their hands. One of them leaned into the open window right next to my head. I could smell the beer on his breath.

I didn't breathe.

'*Noldu?*' the policeman said to the cab driver.

'Seen any *turists* in a camper-bus?'

The policeman pulled his head back out the window and looked down the road. He took a sip of beer and looked in the other direction. Finally he shook his head.

I nudged the driver to move on.

'*Turists*,' he shouted out the window. '*Kamper. Volkswagen.*'

The policeman shrugged.

Again I poked the driver, urging him on.

Finally the cops got disgusted and walked back up onto the porch. I let out my breath.

We drove on.

At the southern edge of town, even the dirt road disappeared.

'I can't go any further,' the driver said.

'I think my friends may be just a little way ahead.'

'It'll destroy my car.'

'Just beyond the village a little way. Just a little way. I'll pay you extra.'

He muttered under his breath, but jammed the cab into gear. We followed rutted tracks into low hills. Soon we found ourselves in the middle of a field. The driver stopped.

'I can't go any further. We must go back.'

'Let me take a look.' I climbed out of the cab and scrambled up on the battered hood. I looked west into the setting sun. I needed to take my bearings. The horizon was covered with rolling hills and forests. Somewhere down there was the river.

I jumped down. 'Listen, you go back. I'll find my friends.'

'I can't leave you here. What's the matter with you? It's getting dark. You'll never find them.'

'It's OK. I'll find them. I know they're here.'

'What are you, crazy, man? You'll get lost out here. You'll be alone and it's not . . .' He stopped. A hundred lira note waved in his face.

He shrugged. He grabbed the money and turned his cab around.

225

'Good luck.'

And he was gone.

Quickly I crossed a ploughed field and hid in a patch of dry corn. I waited for the coming of night.

West of me I had seen one hill larger than the others. That would be my first goal. In fields stretching far off to my right I could see sheep, and a couple of shepherds, making their way back towards the village. The bells clinked a soft, lazy rhythm. The sound travelled far in the clear autumn twilight. I would have to be very quiet.

Mosquitoes attacked. I swatted but there were too many of them. They even bit through my clothing. Finally I closed my eyes and ignored them. It was the last chance, I hoped, for Turkish mosquitoes to feed off my blood. I tried to think of Lillian.

Darkness closed in. On the ridge of the large hill I could see a few flashlights moving slowly back and forth. Border guards! Careful.

I moved from my hiding place. The ground was rocky and eroded. It was difficult to move quickly. I catstepped, pausing after each step to listen.

After about half an hour I stopped. This was too slow. I had covered . . . I didn't know how far . . . but it wasn't much. I thought it would be quieter if I went barefoot. I sat at the base of a gnarled tree and peeled off my sneakers and socks. I dug a shallow hole and buried them. If the border guards used dogs I didn't want to leave any clues.

I moved slowly up the slope of the big hill in a sideways crawl. Like a mountain climber I carefully tested my balance before putting my weight down. Though slow, it was exhausting. My body was soon drenched in sweat. I shivered as the night air grew cold. Every other step I paused to listen.

I could see the flashlights closer now on the crest of the hill. I studied them but could find no pattern to the movement. Sometimes the guards shut them off and walked in darkness, then suddenly turned them on. I wondered if this wa all normal, or were they being especially careful?

When I'd almost reached the crest of the hill I came to a concrete drainage ditch. Slowly I eased into it. My feet stuck into the thick mud. It was soothing. I rested. Snuggled down into the mud. In a few moments the air around me burst into happy chirping. Frogs!

I waited for several minutes in the darkness, happy to be off the exposed hill. Slowly, silently, I started to pull my way up out of the ditch.

A noise! Footsteps! I slithered back down into the mud. I curled up my body. My head pressed into my knees. I tried to cover the whiteness of my face. I blanked my mind. I was inanimate. A stone upon the ground.

The footsteps came closer. Voices. Singing? Two guards walked slowly past the edge of the ditch, singing the words of a Turkish song very softly to each other.

Their voices were thick and slow. They were in the mood of *Sugar Bayram*. They moved away down the crest of the hill. I waited until the frogs were chirping again.

Quickly I pulled myself up to the ground. In a low crouch I ran over the crest and down the hill. No time now to catstep. No time now to stop and listen. I ran maybe two hundred yards, then dropped to my belly. I listened for sounds of pursuit. There was nothing. Nothing but the sound of my own heartbeat, racing in fear.

The air was still. My body calmed, then tensed. More voices? Off to the left? I couldn't be sure.

Flitting from clumps of scraggly bushes to small erosion gulleys, I moved quickly down the hill. My bare feet were bruised but it didn't seem important now. I went off to the right, away from the voices. I found a clump of trees. Where's that river! It had to be somewhere near by.

Then through the darkness of the tree branches my eyes caught a glimmer of light reflecting off metal. What was that? Quietly I parted the branches. Oh, my God! There was the huge, long muzzle of a tank. It looked like a hungry animal, crouched and waiting.

Then I spotted other tanks. But they were all still and silent – unmanned. They were camouflaged with netting, sitting in the forest, pointed toward Greece. This wasn't where I wanted to be.

Where there are tanks there must be soldiers. Catstepping once again, I moved carefully through the woods. Now I

227

turned left, away from the tanks. The woods grew thicker. Even the starlight was gone. A branch gouged me in the face. I kept a hand straight out in front of me for protection.

I went down the slope of the hill. Finally the woods thinned. The ground became moist, then muddy. I stopped after each step, listening behind me. Voices? Movement? I couldn't be sure. But I had to make it now. I was so close.

Then I heard . . . could it be . . . Yes! The soft gurgling sound of water. Straight ahead. I moved into marshland. Then suddenly the bushes parted and the waters of what I was sure was the Maritas River rushed past in front of me. I sat on the bank to rest for a moment before the swim. The current looked strong. My feet ached. I reached down and pulled out thorns as best I could in the darkness.

Then I slipped into the freezing water. The muddy bottom sucked at my feet. The water rushed around me, almost knocking me off balance. The cold was numbing. I moved very slowly, concentrating hard on not splashing. There could be soldiers on the other side, too. Turkish or Greek. The nationality of the bullet wouldn't make any difference.

The water swirled up past my waist, then suddenly got lower. Quickly the bottom rose to another bank. I was over. I was in Greece. Or was I?

High trees shut out the sky. Still moving carefully I walked another ten yards through the trees and came to more water. What was this? In the faint light I could see that the water stretched out for several hundred yards. Then I realized I must have merely crossed to a little island. I wasn't in Greece yet.

Freedom was too close to rest. I waded right in. The river here was far deeper, the current far stronger. I lashed into it with a fierce breast-stroke. The current swept me downstream. I fought it frantically, angling across the dark river.

My body forgot its exhaustion. My arms pulled against the current. My feet kicked furiously at the icy water. No time to worry about noise now. This is survival. The hell with splashing – I kicked as hard as I could.

Again and again I thrust with my arms, then thrust with

my legs, forcing myself through the current, with no sense of the progress I might be making. I wondered if I was actually not moving at all but hopelessly caught by the river. Suddenly my knee struck a rock – the bottom. I stood up, bracing myself against the pull of the water. I looked back upstream. The island had disappeared. The river had pulled me far to the south. I had no idea where the border was.

I waded to the river bank. I threw my body down on the gooey mud. I was freezing and terribly afraid. But I had crossed that river.

I lay on the bank for several minutes. I don't know how long. Maybe I passed out. Suddenly I sat up with the realization that I wasn't free yet. Maybe I was in Greece. Maybe not. But this border was tense. I didn't want to be caught by any soldier. I had to keep moving. West.

More woods. I was sleepwalking now. I'd gone three full days with only one fitful night of sleep in the Istanbul hotel. I was hungry, tired, cold, wet, confused. The woods grew thick. Stickers dug into my bare feet. Then the woods turned to overgrown fields. My sore right hand throbbed. My heart pounded at hundreds of sounds – real or imagined, I didn't know.

Still I moved west.

Behind me, the eastern sky showed faint signs of sunrise. I stumbled onto a dirt road. Dimly I could see a farmhouse, black against the blackness of trees behind it. Dogs suddenly rushed out at me, barking. Quickly I went down the road until the dogs stopped following.

I had to get off the road, I told myself. It was dangerous. But the smooth dirt felt so good on my battered feet. Just a little while. Then I'd move back to the open country.

My head throbbed. I was only moving because I had to. I couldn't stop now. Somehow I forced my feet to keep shuffling down the road. My filthy clothes clung to me. I shivered and coughed.

Ahead of me was a line of dark trees on either side of the road. My feet moved towards them. What was that in the shadows? It looked like an outhouse. Was I so exhausted that I was hallucinating?

I padded into the tunnel of trees.

Suddenly a bayonet whizzed down in front of my face, stopping inches from my nose.

A sharp voice growled, 'Huhhh!'

CHAPTER TWENTY-FIVE

16 October 1975
Michael J. Griffith, Esquire
1501 Franklin Avenue
Mineola, N.Y. 11501
Dear Mike,

It was a sad irony that your good letter about the progress in your effort to get Bill transferred to an American jail reached me almost simultaneously with the news that Bill had escaped. You can imagine our feelings – when we had finally begun to see a glimmer of light at the end of the tunnel.

Now all we can do is hope and pray that he is all right. If we hear anything, we will be in touch with you and the Hayes family immediately, as I know you will do vice versa.

> *Warmest regards,*
> *William B. Macomber*
> *United States Ambassador to Turkey*

The cell measured four steps by four.

It was high-ceilinged and ringed by nothing but the oh-so-familiar concrete walls. There were really only two differences. It was clean, And it was Greek. It had to be. I couldn't understand a word the soldiers said, so they couldn't be Turkish.

After several hours a guard came, blindfolded me and walked me somewhere to another building. The blindfold was removed. I was in a small room. There was a table, two chairs, and a man in a business suit.

The man spoke very good English. He introduced himself as an officer in the Greek intelligence service.

He listened briefly to my story and took notes.

'Do you have to keep me in a cell?' I said. 'I'll go crazy in there.'

He sat back in the chair. He studied my eyes. Then he said calmly, 'We could do several things with you. We could give you back to the Turks. We could take you back to the border and throw you across. We could prosecute you for illegal entry. We could even take you out into the woods and *shoot* you. No one would ever know.'

I shuffled my feet.

'Or . . . if you just relax and wait quietly for a while . . . we could arrange to deport you. To the United States.'

'I'll relax and wait quietly.'

'Good. We need time to check your story. If you're telling the truth, everything should be OK. And we also want to talk to you. We want to learn what you know about Turkey.'

Days went by. In the evenings I paced the cell. My interrogator supplied me with books in English. I read Herodotus. Several books by Nikos Kazantzakis, who was the interrogator's favourite author. I read *Catch-22* again. And *Papillon*, again.

Each day the interrogator spent long hours with me. He wanted to know about Sagmalcilar and Imrali. What about the soldier bases? What was the colour of the uniforms? What did the insignia look like? And the tanks at the border. I described them over and over and over. He recorded each minute detail. He probed my mind to recreate the glimpse I'd had in the dark woods. He pulled out huge, detailed maps of the Turkish side of the border. I showed him where I'd made the crossing.

'You're a very lucky man, William.'

'I know.'

'No, you don't. You're luckier than you think. This entire area here' – he indicated where I had crossed – 'is very heavily mined. You could have been blown up. Easily.'

God looks out for saints and fools.

Two full weeks passed. I knew my family was going crazy with worry. I wanted to phone them, and Lillian. Still the officer wouldn't let me contact anyone.

I had escaped Imrali on the night of October 2–3. On the night of the fourth and fifth I had crossed the border. Finally, on Friday, October 17, my interrogator gave me the news.

'You are being deported.' He grinned. 'On the grounds that you are a bad influence upon the youth of Greece.' Then he shook my hand and wished me luck.

On Saturday, October 18, I was driven to Thessaloniki. The two young policemen with me didn't even bother to chain my hands. They knew how content a prisoner I was.

I gazed out the window of the bus at the rugged Greek countryside sliding by me.

Free.

I'm free.

I thanked the ancient gods of the hills and the gods of the infinite blue sky. Sweet Jesus, I'll be your friend.

Late in the afternoon they dropped me off at the Thessaloniki police station. I was allowed to call the American consulate. A fine young man named Jim Murray came right out to see me.

Jim had his arms full. There was a bucket of fried chicken and some apples and oatmeal cookies and several cans of butterscotch pudding. There were also copies of the *International Herald-Tribune*, some *Time* magazines, and a copy of *Hurriyet*, one of the Turkish newspapers. There on the front page was a ridiculous full-colour drawing of me. The artist portrayed me as a fierce heavy-muscled barechested man viciously sawing at the rope of a fisherman's dinghy with a long knife. It was typical Turkish journalism.

Jim also gave me a warm sweatshirt, socks, and a pair of old sneakers. They were his own clothes. He said that he'd already contacted the State Department. They would inform my folks. Thank God! I knew how hard these past five years had been for them. The last two weeks must have been the worst of all.

The Greeks said I could leave as soon as my passport was ready. Jim figured that would be Monday. I asked him to call my folks himself. 'Tell them I love them,' I said.

'Sure. You'll need money, should I ask them to send it?'

'Yes, please.'

'How much?'

'Enough to get me home.'

I was escorted downstairs by two policemen and led to a cell. It was about fifteen feet square with a small sink and toilet section in the corner. It wasn't very clean, I suppose. Unless it was compared to a Turkish cell. Two narrow

233

wooden platforms stood against the wall. The jailers gave me three thin blankets and locked the door.

I was ecstatic. Soon I'd be free. Soon my folks would know I'm free. In two days I'd be on an airplane. I ripped into the fried chicken.

Two days flew by. I was alone in the cell. There didn't seem to be any other prisoners around. Some of the Greek police spoke Turkish and we began to talk. After they heard my full story I became friends with all of them. Anyone who was an enemy of the Turks was a friend of the Greeks.

On Monday, October 20, I went to the American consulate with my police escort. Dad had sent $2000.

My passport was ready.

Jim called the travel agency just across the street. 'When do you want to leave?' he asked.

'What's the first flight west?'

'Frankfurt. Six p.m.'

'I'll take it.'

I counted out the fare. An aide went for the ticket while Jim readied a call for me to faraway Long Island and a little home with two mortgages.

'Dad?'

'Will? Will! How you doing, boy?'

'Great, Dad. I did it! I did IT!'

'You sure did.' He choked with joy. 'Here's your mother.'

I heard Mom's voice for the first time in five years. My heart was bursting.

'Mom!'

'Oh, Billy, it's so good to hear your voice. We were so worried about you.'

'Well, you can stop worrying now, Mom. It's all over.'

'Oh, Billy, I'm so happy I can't speak.'

I laughed. 'No need to speak, Mom. I can feel you right through the wire. I missed you so much.'

'When will you be home?'

'As soon as I can. I have to clean up first. And sleep. I'm really filthy and tired.'

'Well, just be careful. Come home safe.'

'It's all downhill from here, Mom. Give my love to everyone, and would you call Lily and tell her I'm all right? I'll see you soon.'

'All right. Here's your father back again. I love you.'

'Will?'

'Right, Dad.'

'What's the plan from there? Reporters and TV newsmen are calling me. They want to know when you'll arrive.'

A sudden fear hit me. I didn't know if I was ready for all that. What would New York be like after five years? I was different now. I knew I had to catch my breath. 'Dad, I just bought a ticket to Frankfurt. I need a couple of days to get back into life, to get ready to see Mom . . . and everyone.'

'Sure, Will. When do you think you'll be home?'

'Not long. Probably Friday.'

'OK. Let us know when. And be careful, Buddy. You're not home yet.'

'I will, Dad. And I'll call you about the flight.'

We paused.

'Dad?'

'What, Will?'

'Thanks . . .'

The police wouldn't let go of me until I actually got onto the plane. We drove back to the prison to await the flight. Then out to the airport. It was five-thirty. The customs man was ready to stamp my passport.

'William Hayes,' a soft voice said over the loudspeaker. 'Telephone call. William Hayes. Telephone call.'

A call? For me?

Jim Murray was on the line. 'Billy, the State Department has just informed me that West Germany has an extradition treaty with Turkey. Police may be waiting for you at the Frankfurt airport.'

'My God! . . . What do you think I should do?'

'Billy, stay over one more night. We'll get you on a direct flight tomorrow Athens and then New York.'

But one more night was one more in jail. No. I couldn't. Not after five years. I had momentum now. I didn't want to lose it.

'Do I have to stay?' I asked.

235

'Well, I suppose if you don't go through customs at Frankfurt, you'll be OK.'

'Good. I'll be careful.'

The plane rose into the air. I never looked back.

After we landed in Frankfurt, I stayed in the transit lounge area, avoiding customs. There was a ticket counter there. I asked about the next flight west. Amsterdam. Perfect! I had fond memories of Amsterdam. The plane left in forty minutes.

At a newsstand I bought a copy of *Playboy*. Of course, I immediately opened it to the centrefold. I slammed it shut quickly, wondering if anyone had seen. Then I looked again. There had been a lot of changes in five years. It would take time to get used to them.

In Amsterdam a customs officer with long stringy hair stamped my passport and waved me on. I caught a bus to the centre of the city. Just like any other free man.

I found a hotel. A small one, near a canal. I checked in. Then I called home. I told Mom that I'd be arriving in New York on Friday. Dad told me there would be a news conference at the airport.

I found the bar. People sat around laughing, drinking beer. Funky saxophone music blared from the jukebox – music had changed a lot too. A beautiful waitress brought me a beer. Ah life! So sweet. I went to the hotel restaurant and drank two strawberry ice cream sodas.

Back upstairs I took a long hot shower. Five years of dirt slid off and swirled down the drain. I eased my exhausted body in between the clean crisp sheets of the bed. I lay there and thought about it all. It seemed like a strange dream. I was beyond it now. I felt so full. And so thankful. Life lay before me. I knew it stretched for ever .   .

I drifted into luxurious sleep.

About three a.m. I suddenly woke myself. I was laughing out loud.

AFTERWORD

My plane arrived at New York's Kennedy International Airport on Friday, October 24, 1975. Dad was there to meet me, along with my brother Rob and my lawyer Mike Griffith. Mom and Peg stayed home. They wanted to greet me in private.

The four of us went downstairs to the lobby of the Pan Am terminal to face the press. I kept my arm around Dad while I answered questions. It was easy to smile for the cameras.

I spent the next several weeks just enjoying freedom with my family and friends. I ate pizza, cheeseburgers, vanilla shakes, and lobster. I walked the streets of New York with wide eyes. I rode Dad's bicycle around the tree-lined roads of home. And I went to see my first movie in five years – *Jaws*.

Then I met with several of the literary agents, editors, and Hollywood producers who had called. This book is a result of those meetings. With the advance money I was able to pay off the second mortgage on the home in North Babylon. I sent Mom and Dad on a vacation to California. Now I'm paying off the rest of my old student loan at Marquette and in time I will repay all the money Dad had paid to Turkish lawyers and for travel and for my escape fund. Now that the book is finished I'm making plans to enter business.

Lillian was in the mountains of British Columbia when I escaped. She didn't hear the news until two weeks after I got home. She flew to New York. We had happy times together, but we soon realized that the images we had formed during five years didn't match reality. Lillian went to Europe. She is travelling in Asia now.

Johann returned from his visit to Afghanistan and is still living in Istanbul.

Arne has formed a band. The musicians outfitted an old London double-decker bus and are on their way to India.

Charles is back in Chicago, writing poetry, trying to get his book published.

Popeye is living in Israel.

Max finished his sentence a few months after I escaped.

I never heard from Joey again.

Harvey Bell, Robert Hubbard, Kathy Zenz, and Jo Ann McDaniel are still in prison in Antakya, Turkey. *Getchmis olsun* – may it pass quickly.

Billy Hayes
5 August 1976

The Mighty All-Action Superseller from Sphere:

Raise the Titanic!

Mightiest of ocean liners, the *Titanic* lies two-and-a-half
miles down in the North Atlantic. And in her hold –
perhaps the only amount anywhere of an incredibly rare
substance that could make the free world invulnerable to
foreign attack forever!

The Americans want it. So do the Russians. And the sea
never gives up its secrets without a struggle. Which makes
the task facing ace maritime troubleshooter Dirk Pitt one
of the most stupendous tests of human courage and
ingenuity ever . . .

RAISE THE TITANIC is the ultimate sea-adventure
thriller, a spellbinding, breathtaking blockbuster of action
and suspense that will grip the reader until the last page
has been turned.
Soon to be a major film!

0 7221 2744 8   £1.25p

Also by Clive Cussler in Sphere Books:

MAYDAY!
ICEBERG
VIXEN 03

A selection of bestsellers from SPHERE

Fiction

SHARKY'S MACHINE	William Diehl	£1.50	☐
THE GLENDOWER LEGACY	Thomas Gifford	£1.25	☐
WOMAN OF FURY	Constance Gluyas	£1.40	☐
BAAL	Robert McCammon	95p	☐
SEASON OF PASSION	Danielle Steel	£1.25	☐

Film and Television tie-ins

THE PROFESSIONALS 5: BLIND RUN	Ken Blake	85p	☐
THE PROFESSIONALS 6: FALL GIRL	Ken Blake	85p	☐
THE PROFESSIONALS 7: HIDING TO NOTHING	Ken Blake	85p	☐
THE PROFESSIONALS 8: DEAD RECKONING	Ken Blake	85p	☐
THE PROMISE	Danielle Steel	95p	☐

Non-Fiction

SECRETS OF OUR SPACESHIP MOON	Don Wilson	£1.10	☐
ARISTOTLE ONASSIS	Nicholas Fraser, Philip Jacobson, Mark Ottaway & Lewis Chester	£1.60	☐
SECRETS OF LOST ATLAND	Robert Scrutton	£1.50	☐

All Sphere books are available at your local bookshop or newsagent, or can be ordered direct from the publisher. Just tick the titles you want and fill in the form below.

Name ....

Address ....

....

Write to Sphere Books, Cash Sales Department, P.O. Box 11, Falmouth, Cornwall TR10 9EN

Please enclose cheque or postal order to the value of the cover price plus:

UK: 25p for the first book plus 12p per copy for each additional book ordered to a maximum charge of £1.05.

OVERSEAS: 40p for the first book and 12p for each additional book.

BFPO & EIRE: 25p for the first book plus 10p per copy for the next 8 books, thereafter 5p per book.

Sphere Books reserve the right to show new retail prices on covers which may differ from those previously advertised in the text or elsewhere, and to increase postal rates in accordance with the GPO.